THE
HEALTH & SAFETY HANDBOOK

a practical guide to health and safety law, management policies and procedures

JEREMY STRANKS

RECOMMENDED BY
INSTITUTE OF DIRECTORS

KOGAN
PAGE

This book has been endorsed by the Institute of Directors.

The endorsement is given to selected Kogan Page books which the IoD recognizes as being of specific interest to its members and providing them with up-to-date, informative and practical resources for creating business success. Kogan Page books endorsed by the IoD represent the most authoritative guidance available on a wide range of subjects including management, finance, marketing, training and HR.

The views expressed in this book are those of the author and are not necessarily the same as those of the Institute of Directors.

Publisher's note
Every possible effort has been made to ensure that the information contained in this book is accurate at the time of going to press, and the publishers and author cannot accept responsibility for any errors or omissions, however caused. No responsibility for loss or damage occasioned to any person acting, or refraining from action, as a result of the material in this publication can be accepted by the editor, the publisher or the author.

First published in Great Britain in 2006

Kogan Page Limited
120 Pentonville Road
London N1 9JN
United Kingdom
www.kogan-page.co.uk

British Library Cataloguing in Publication Data

A CIP record for this book is available from the British Library.

ISBN 0 7494 4392 8

Typeset by JS Typesetting Ltd, Porthcawl, Mid Glamorgan
Printed and bound in Great Britain by Cambridge University Press

Contents

4   Engineering safety   80

Introduction 80; Machinery hazards 80; Hand tools 83; Provision and Use of Work Equipment Regulations 1998 83; Work equipment risk assessment 93; Machinery guarding 93; Safety devices 96; Safety mechanisms 98; Second-hand, hired and leased work equipment 98; Mobile handling equipment 99; Mechanical handling equipment 100; Lifting Operations and Lifting Equipment Regulations (LOLER) 1998 102; Schedule 1: Information to be contained in a report of a thorough examination 105; Safe lifting operations 106; Pressure vessels 107; Simple Pressure Vessels (Safety) Regulations 1991 108; Pressure systems 111; Internal transport 112

5   Fire prevention and protection   114

Introduction 114; Principles of combustion 115; Heat transmission 115; Sources of ignition 115; Fire spread control 116; Classification of fires 117; Fire extinction 118; Fire alarm systems 120; Fire instructions 121; Fire drills and sounding of alarms 121; Flammable substances 121; Fire safety law 122; Fire risk assessment 129

6   Electrical safety   132

Introduction 132; The principal hazards 132; Electric shock 132; First aid 133; Legal requirements 134; The risk of fire 138; Precautions against electric shock 138; Portable electrical appliances 140; Electric storage batteries 142

7   Health and safety in construction operations   144

Introduction 144; Construction activities – the principal hazards 144; Clients and contractors – civil and criminal liability 148; Construction safety law 150; Construction activities – the principal precautions 158

8   Occupational health   165

Introduction 165; What is occupational health? 165; Occupational health practitioners 166; Classification of occupational health risks 168; Reportable diseases 169; Prescribed diseases 169; The principal occupational diseases and conditions 170; Occupational health practice 173; First aid 175; Manual handling operations 176; Noise 176; Display screen equipment 177; Stress at work 178; A healthy lifestyle 180; Occupational health-related legislation 180

9   Personal protective equipment   188

Introduction 188; Classification of personal protective equipment 188; Personal Protective Equipment at Work Regulations 1992 189

10   Human factors   **192**

Introduction 192; People at work 192; The perceptual, physical and mental
capabilities of people 193; Human error 195; The influence of equipment and
system design on human performance 197; Organizational characteristics
which influence safety-related behaviour 198; Communication 199; Health
and safety training 200; Ergonomics 201; The total working system 202;
Anthropometric studies 204; The right safety culture 204; The role of the
supervisor 206; Atypical workers 206; Lone working 208; Vulnerable groups
at work 209

11   Hazardous substances   **212**

Introduction 212; Classification of hazardous substances 212; Safety data for
hazardous substances 213; The physical state of hazardous substances 213;
Principles of toxicology 216; Occupational exposure limits 218; Control of
Substances Hazardous to Health (COSHH) Regulations 2002 220; Health risk
assessments 222

Abbreviations

ACOP   approved code of practice
AER   *All England Reports*
BEBOH   British Examination Board in Occupational Hygiene
BS   British Standard
CBI   Confederation of British Industry
CDMR   Construction (Design and Management) Regulations
CHIP   Chemicals (Hazard Information and Packaging for Supply) Regulations
CHSWR   Construction (Health, Safety and Welfare) Regulations
CORGI   Council for the Registration of Gas Installers
COSHH   Control of Substances Hazardous to Health Regulations
dB(A)   decibels measured on the 'A' network of a sound pressure level meter
DC   direct current
DSE   display screen equipment
DSS   Department of Social Security
ECJ   European Court of Justice
ELCB   earth leakage circuit breaker
EMAS   Employment Medical Advisory Service
FPWR   Fire Precautions (Workplace) Regulations
GN   guidance note (HSE)
HGV   heavy goods vehicle
HSC   Health and Safety Commission
HSE   Health and Safety Executive
HSWA   Health and Safety at Work etc Act

ID	internal diameter
IEE	The Institution of Electrical Engineers
ISO	International Standards Organization
kV	kilovolt
LOLER	Lifting Operations and Lifting Equipment Regulations
LPG	liquid petroleum gas
LTEL	long-term exposure limit
MEL	maximum exposure limit
mg/m^3	milligrams per cubic metre
MHSWR	Management of Health and Safety at Work Regulations
OEL	occupational exposure limit
OES	occupational exposure standard
PAT	portable appliance tester
PPE	personal protective equipment
ppm	parts per million
PS	maximum working pressure
PUWER	Provision and Use of Work Equipment Regulations
RCD	residual current device
RGN	registered general nurse
RIDDOR	Reporting of Injuries, Diseases and Dangerous Occurrences Regulations
ROES	representatives of employee safety
RoSPA	Royal Society for the Prevention of Accidents
RSI	repetitive strain injury
Sk	'Skin' annotation
STEL	short-term exposure limit
SWG	standard wire gauge
SWL	safe working load
TLV	threshold limit value
WATCH	Working Group on the Assessment of Toxic Chemicals
WHSWR	Workplace (Health, Safety and Welfare) Regulations

To Val, Fiona, Simon, Marg, Hannah and Joshua

1

Principles of health and safety law

INTRODUCTION

Health and safety law is concerned with both the criminal and civil liabilities of employers towards their employees and to other persons who may be affected by their activities, such as the employees of contractors, visitors and members of the public. It takes the form of both common law and statute law.

Common law

Common law is the unwritten law in that it is not specified in statutes or regulations. It is based on the decisions of the civil courts over many years and bound by the doctrine of precedent. It is essentially law made by judges, which has been formed into a body of principles and rules. As such, it is synonymous with case law and is the principal area of law concerned with civil liability. Its various rules and principles are to be found in the law reports, such as the *All England Reports* (AER).

Statute law

Statutes, or Acts of Parliament, are the written law, such as the Health and Safety at Work etc Act (HSWA) 1974, the principal statute dealing with health and safety at work. The HSWA is an enabling Act entitling the Secretary of State for Employment to make regulations, such as the Control of Substances Hazardous to Health (COSHH) Regulations.

Statutes and regulations generally give rise to criminal liability. Employers who breach, for instance, the HSWA, or regulations made under the HSWA, may be subject to prosecution by one of the enforcement authorities, such as the Health and Safety Executive (HSE) or the local authority, in the criminal courts.

Most prosecutions commence in the Magistrates' Court. This court handles the bulk of the less serious health and safety offences where an offender, if found guilty of the charges levied, can be fined or imprisoned, or both. More serious cases are dealt with, on indictment, in the Crown Court, where trial is before a judge and jury.

CIVIL LAW

The duty to take reasonable care

A breach of the common law gives rise to civil liability. Under the common law, employers owe their employees a duty to take reasonable care in order to avoid death, injuries and disease arising from work. These duties of employers at common law were established in *Wilson's & Clyde Coal Co Ltd* v *English* [1938] 2 AER 68. In particular, employers must:

- provide a safe place of work with safe means of access to and egress from same;
- provide and maintain safe appliances and equipment and plant for doing the work;
- provide and maintain a safe system of work; and
- provide competent co-employees to undertake the work.

The tort of negligence

A tort is a civil wrong. Negligence is commonly defined as 'careless conduct injuring another'. The duties of employers at common law outlined above are part of the general law of negligence. Under the common law, 'negligence' is defined in *Lochgelly Iron & Coal Co Ltd* v *McMullan* [1934] AC 1 as:

1. the existence of a duty of care owed by a defendant to a claimant;
2. breach of that duty; and
3. injury, damage or loss resulting from or caused by that breach.

These three elements of negligence must be established by an injured employee, the claimant, before he can bring a civil claim for damages against his employer, the defendant.

Negligence is a very broad area of the law and does not, however, apply only to employer–employee situations. For instance, a person who tripped and fell as a result of an uneven pavement may be entitled to sue the local authority for negligence.

Vicarious liability

This doctrine is based on the fact that a 'master', the employer, is vicariously or indirectly responsible for the actions of his servants, ie his employees. Thus, if an employee, while acting in the course of his employment, negligently injures another employee, a contractor's employee or even a member of the public, the employer, rather than the employee, will be liable for that injury.

Vicarious liability rests with the employer purely on the basis that he is the employer and, as such, is deemed to have total and ultimate control over the actions of his employees. This 'master and servant' relationship goes back to the 18th century and forms part of the law of negligence. The Employers' Liability (Compulsory Insurance) Act 1969, together with the Employers' Liability (Compulsory Insurance) Regulations 1999, lays down requirements whereby employers must carry insurance to cover any claims that may arise in this way.

CRIMINAL LAW

The hierarchy of duties under health and safety law

The criminal law covering health and safety at work is written down in statutes, such as the HSWA, and regulations made under the Act. The extent of these duties varies, however, according to the nature of the duty. For instance, certain duties are of an absolute or strict nature. Other duties may be qualified by the terms 'so far as is practicable' or 'so far as is reasonably practicable'.

Absolute or strict duties

Where there is a high degree of risk of death or serious major injury if safety precautions are not taken or where the duty is considered very important, duties on an employer may be absolute or strict. In this case, the duty is qualified by the term 'shall' or 'must'. For example, the Management of Health and Safety at Work Regulations place an absolute duty on every employer thus: 'Every employer shall make and give effect to such arrangements as are appropriate, having regard to the nature of his activities and the size of his undertaking, for the effective planning, organisation, control, monitoring and review of the preventive and protective measures.'

'So far as is practicable'

'Practicable' means more than physically possible. Precautionary measures must be able to be carried out 'in the light of current knowledge or invention' or 'in the light of the current state of the art'. This means that, if there is the technology available to comply with the requirement, irrespective of cost, then the appropriate action must be taken to comply (*Schwalb* v *Fass (H) & Son* [1946] 175 LT 345).

A duty qualified by 'so far as is practicable' implies a higher level of duty than one qualified by 'so far as is reasonably practicable'.

'So far as is reasonably practicable'

This level of duty is to be found in the HSWA and many regulations. For example, under the HSWA: 'It shall be the duty of every employer to ensure, so far as is reasonably practicable, the health, safety and welfare at work of all his employees' (HSWA, s 2 (1)).

A duty qualified by the term 'so far as is reasonably practicable' implies that a person charged with an offence is entitled to balance the cost or sacrifice involved, in terms of money, time and effort, in complying with the requirement, against the risk to people involved. Here, the burden of proof lies with the defendant to prove that the requirement was not 'reasonably practicable'. Thus, if it can be proved that there is disparity between the degree of risk and the sacrifice involved, ie the risk is very low compared with the cost of compliance, then a defendant may be said to have discharged his duty under the statute or regulations.

COURTS AND TRIBUNALS

The court system operating in the UK comprises the civil courts and criminal courts. While these two organizations tend to operate separately, some courts have both criminal and civil jurisdiction.

The civil courts

These are the County Courts and the High Court.

Table 1.1 *Civil and criminal law – the distinction*

Civil Law	Criminal Law
Remedy:	
Action for damages.	Prosecution by the State.
Purpose:	
To compensate.	To punish.
Parties:	
Claimant and respondent.	Prosecutor and defendant.
Withdrawal:	
At any time.	Only by leave from the court.
Criteria:	
No presumption or favour: case decided on the balance of probabilities.	Innocent until proved guilty beyond reasonable doubt.
Trial:	
Normally heard before a judge alone.	Indictable cases tried before a judge and jury.
Limitations Act:	
Does apply.	Does not apply.

County Courts

Operating on an area basis, County Courts deal in the first instance with a wide range of civil matters, such as civil claims for negligence. Cases are generally heard by a circuit judge or registrar, the latter having limited jurisdiction.

The High Court

The High Court of Justice deals with the more important civil matters, largely because of the financial sums involved or the legal complexities. Cases are heard before a High Court judge. There are three divisions of the High Court:

- Queen's Bench – deals with contracts and torts;
- Chancery – deals with matters involving land, wills, bankruptcies, partnerships and companies;
- Family – deals with matters involving, for instance, adoption issues, marital property and disputes.

This court hears appeals on matters of law:

- from the Magistrates' Courts and from the Crown Court on a procedure known as 'case stated'; and
- from some tribunals, for example the finding of a tribunal relating to an enforcement notice served under the HSWA.

The High Court also has a certain degree of supervision over the lower courts and tribunals where those courts may have exceeded their jurisdiction, have failed to exercise their responsibilities properly or have neglected to undertake any of their duties.

The High Court, Crown Court and Court of Appeal are known as the Supreme Court of Judicature.

The criminal courts

These comprise the Magistrates' Courts and Crown Courts.

Magistrates' Court

This is the lowest of the courts dealing with criminal matters and has limited jurisdiction. Lay magistrates, appointed by the Lord Chancellor, hear cases and determine sentences within certain parameters for the less serious criminal cases.

Magistrates' courts also hold preliminary examinations into other offences to ascertain whether the prosecution can show a prima facie case on which the accused may be committed for trial at a higher court.

Crown Court

Serious criminal charges are heard before a judge and jury on indictment in this court. The Crown Court also hears appeals from Magistrates' Courts.

The Court of Appeal

This court has two divisions:

- the Civil Division, which hears appeals from the County Courts and the High Court; and
- the Criminal Division, which hears appeals from the Crown Court.

The House of Lords

Law Lords deal with important matters of law only, in many cases following an appeal to the House from the Court of Appeal and, in restricted circumstances, from the High Court.

The European Court of Justice (ECJ)

This is the supreme law court, whose decisions on the interpretation of European Union law are sacrosanct. Such decisions are enforceable throughout the network of courts and tribunals in member states. Cases can be brought before the ECJ by organizations only or by people representing organizations.

EMPLOYMENT TRIBUNALS

Employment tribunals deal with a range of matters, such as cases involving unfair dismissal, sex discrimination and equal pay. They are also empowered to deal with a number of health and safety-related issues, namely:

- appeals against improvement and prohibition notices served by enforcement officers (HSWA);

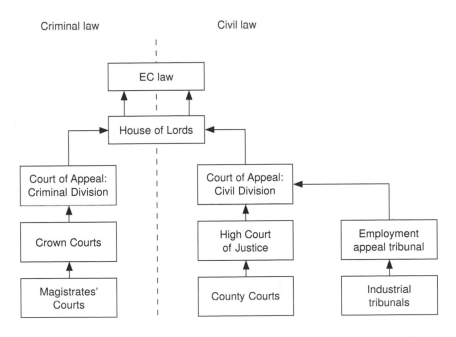

Figure 1.1   _The court structure and hierarchy in England and Wales_

- time off for the training of safety representatives (Safety Representatives and Safety Committees Regulations 1977);
- failure by an employer to pay a safety representative for time off to undertake his functions and when receiving training (Safety Representatives and Safety Committees Regulations 1977);
- dismissal, actual or constructive, following a breach of health and safety law and/or term of employment contract; and
- failure by an employer to make a medical suspension payment (Employment Protection (Consolidation) Act 1978).

STATUTES, REGULATIONS, APPROVED CODES OF PRACTICE AND HSE GUIDANCE NOTES

A distinction must be drawn between the various forms of law, and guidance on same, and their relative significance.

Statutes

Statutes, or Acts of Parliament, such as the HSWA, are the principal form of law, overriding all other forms of law, such as regulations. In the case of the HSWA, the Secretary of State for Employment has the power to make regulations on a wide range of issues.

Regulations

Known as 'subordinate' or 'delegated legislation', regulations are generally drafted by the Health and Safety Executive (HSE) and submitted through the Health and Safety Commission (HSC) to the Secretary of State for his agreement.

Approved codes of practice (ACOPs)

Under the HSWA, the HSC is empowered to prepare and approve codes of practice on matters contained not only in regulations but in sections 2 to 7 of the HSWA. Before approving a code of practice, the HSE, acting for the HSC, must consult with any interested body.

An ACOP has a special legal status comparable with that of the Highway Code. Broadly, an individual cannot be prosecuted for breach of an ACOP. However, if prosecuted for a breach of the HSWA and/or regulations to which an ACOP applies, the requirements of the ACOP are admissible as evidence of failure to do all that was reasonably practicable. In this case, the defendant would need to prove categorically that he had complied with the legal requirements in some other way, for instance that he had undertaken 'works of an equivalent nature' to those required in the ACOP.

HSE guidance notes

The HSE issues guidance notes on a wide range of health and safety-related topics, in some cases to supplement and provide advice on the requirements of both regulations and ACOPs. As such, a guidance note has no legal status.

HEALTH AND SAFETY AT WORK ETC ACT 1974

The HSWA lays down a range of general duties on employers, the self-employed, controllers of premises, manufacturers, etc of articles and substances for use at work, and employees.

Section 2 – General duties of employers to their employees

1. It shall be the duty of every employer to ensure, so far as is reasonably practicable, the health, safety and welfare at work of all his employees.
2. Without prejudice to the generality of an employer's duty under the preceding subsection, the matters to which that duty extends include in particular:
    (a) the provision and maintenance of plant and systems of work that are, so far as is reasonably practicable, safe and without risks to health;
    (b) arrangements for ensuring, so far as is reasonably practicable, safety and the absence of risks to health in connection with the use, handling, storage and transport of articles and substances;
    (c) provision of such information, instruction, training and supervision as is necessary to ensure, so far as is reasonably practicable, the health and safety at work of his employees;
    (d) so far as is reasonably practicable as regards any place of work under the employer's control, the maintenance of it in a condition that is safe and without risks to health and the provision and maintenance of means of access to and egress from it that are safe and without such risks;
    (e) the provision and maintenance of a working environment for his employees that is, so far as is reasonably practicable, safe, without risks to health, and adequate as regards facilities and arrangements for their welfare at work.
3. Except in such cases as may be prescribed, it shall be the duty of every employer to prepare and as often as may be appropriate revise a written statement of his general policy with respect to the health and safety at work of his employees and the organization and arrangements for the time being in force for the carrying

out of that policy, and to bring the statement and any revision of it to the notice of all his employees.

Section 3 – Duties of employers to persons other than their employees

1. It shall be the duty of every employer to conduct his undertaking in such a way as to ensure, so far as is reasonably practicable, that persons not in his employment who may be affected thereby are not thereby exposed to risks to their health or safety.

Section 4 – Duties of controllers of premises to persons other than their employees

1. This section has effect for imposing on persons duties in relation to those who:
   (a) are not their employees; but
   (b) use non-domestic premises made available to them as a place of work or as a place where they may use plant or substances provided for their use there, and applies to premises so made available and other non-domestic premises used in connection with them.
2. It shall be the duty of each person who has, to any extent, control of premises to which this section applies or the means of access thereto or egress therefrom or of any plant or substances in such premises to take such measures as it is reasonable for a person in his position to take to ensure, so far as is reasonably practicable, that the premises, all means of access thereto or egress therefrom available for use by persons using the premises, and any plant or substance in the premises or, as the case may be, provided for use there, is or are safe and without risks to health.

Section 6 – General duties of manufacturers etc as regards articles and substances for use at work

1. It shall be the duty of any person who designs, manufactures, imports or supplies any *article* for use at work:
   (a) to ensure, so far as is reasonably practicable, that the article is so designed and constructed as to be safe and without risks to health when properly used;
   (b) to carry out or arrange for the carrying out of such testing and examination as may be necessary for the performance of the duty imposed on him by the preceding paragraph;

(c) to take such steps as are necessary to secure that there will be available in connection with the use of the article at work adequate information about the use for which it is designed and has been tested, and about any conditions necessary to ensure that, when put to that use, it will be safe and without risks to health.

2. It shall be the duty of any person who undertakes the design or manufacture of any article for use at work to carry out or arrange for the carrying out of any necessary research with a view to the discovery and, so far as is reasonably practicable, the elimination or minimization of any risks to health or safety to which the design or article may give rise.

3. It shall be the duty of anyone who erects or installs any article for use at work in any premises where that article is to be used by persons at work to ensure, so far as is reasonably practicable, that nothing about the way in which it is erected or installed makes it unsafe or a risk to health when properly used.

4. It shall be the duty of any person who manufactures, imports or supplies any *substance* for use at work:
   (a) to ensure, so far as is reasonably practicable, that the substance is safe and without risks to health when properly used;
   (b) to carry out or arrange for the carrying out of such testing and examination as may be necessary for the performance of the duty imposed on him by the preceding paragraph;
   (c) to take such steps as are necessary to ensure that there will be available in connection with the use of the substance at work adequate information about the results of any relevant tests which have been carried out on or in connection with the substance and about any conditions necessary to ensure that it will be safe and without risks to health when properly used.

Section 7 – General duties of employees at work

It shall be the duty of every employee while at work:

(a) to take reasonable care for the health and safety of himself and of other persons who may be affected by his acts or omissions at work; and
(b) as regards any duty or requirement imposed on his employer or any other person by or under any of the *relevant statutory provisions*, to cooperate with him so far as is necessary to enable that duty or requirement to be performed or complied with.

The 'relevant statutory provisions'

This term is commonly encountered in health and safety legislation and implies:

(a) all the provisions of the HSWA, Part I (ss 1–54);
(b) health and safety regulations passed pursuant to the HSWA, eg Noise at Work Regulations 1989;
(c) existing statutory provisions, ie all enactments specified in HSWA Schedule 1, including any regulations made under them in so far as they continue in force.

Section 8 – Duty not to interfere with or misuse things pursuant to certain provisions

No person shall intentionally or recklessly interfere with or misuse anything provided in the interests of health, safety or welfare in pursuance of any of the relevant statutory provisions.

Section 9 – Duty not to charge employees for things done or provided pursuant to certain specific requirements

No employer shall levy or permit to be levied on any employee of his any charge in respect of anything done or provided in pursuance of any specific requirement of the relevant statutory provisions.

ENFORCEMENT PROCEDURES

The HSWA established the Health and Safety Commission (HSC) and the Health and Safety Executive (HSE).

Health and Safety Commission

The HSC comprises a chairman and members, representing employers' organizations, trade unions, and other organizations, such as professional institutions and local authorities.

The principal function of the HSC is to carry out the general purpose of Part I of the HSWA. In particular, the HSC has a number of duties:

• to assist and encourage people concerned with matters within Part I of the HSWA to further those purposes;

- to make appropriate arrangements for research, publication of the results of the research and provision of training and information in connection with these purposes, including encouraging research and training by others;
- to advise and keep informed, as it considers appropriate, government departments, employers, employees, and organizations representing employers and employees, on matters relevant to these purposes;
- to submit proposals for regulations to the relevant authority.

The Health and Safety Executive

The main function of the HSE is to make adequate arrangements for the enforcement of the general duties of the HSWA and of any other relevant statutory provisions, eg regulations. Certain responsibilities for enforcement are undertaken by local authorities.

Powers of inspectors

Inspectors appointed under the HSWA are:

- inspectors of the HSE;
- environmental health officers of local authorities; and
- for certain functions, fire officers.

Under section 20 of the HSWA, inspectors have the following powers:

- at any reasonable time (or, in a situation which in his opinion is or may be dangerous, at any time) to enter any premises which he has reason to believe it is necessary for him to enter;
- to take with him a constable if he has reasonable cause to apprehend any serious obstruction in the execution of his duty;
- on entering any premises to take with him:
  - any other person duly authorized by the enforcing authority;
  - any equipment or materials required for any purpose for which the power of entry is being exercised;
- to make such examination and investigation as may in any circumstances be necessary;
- to direct that premises or any part of them, or anything therein, shall be left undisturbed for the purpose of any examination or investigation;
- to take such measurements and photographs and make such recordings as he considers necessary for the purpose of any examination or investigation;

- to take samples of any articles or substances found in any premises, and of the atmosphere in or in the vicinity of such premises;
- in the case of any article or substance found in any premises, being an article or substance which appears to him to have caused or to be likely to cause danger to health or safety, to cause it to be dismantled or subjected to any process or test;
- in the case of any article or substance mentioned above, to take possession of it and detain it for so long as is necessary for all or any of the following purposes, namely:
  - to examine it;
  - to ensure that it is not tampered with before his examination of it is completed;
  - to ensure that it is available for use as evidence in any proceedings for an offence under any of the relevant statutory provisions or proceedings relating to a notice served;
- to require any person whom he has reasonable cause to believe to be able to give any information relevant to any examination or investigation to answer (in the absence of persons other than a person nominated by him to be present and any persons whom the inspector may allow to be present) such questions as the inspector thinks fit to ask and to sign a declaration of truth of his answers;
- to require the production of, inspect and take copies of or any entry in:
  - any books or documents which by virtue of any of the relevant statutory provisions are required to be kept; and
  - any other books or documents which it is necessary for him to see for the purposes of any examination or investigation;
- to require any person to afford him such facilities and assistance with respect to any matters or things within that person's control or in relation to which that person has responsibilities as are necessary to enable the inspector to exercise any of the powers conferred on him by this section;
- any other power which is necessary for the purpose of carrying into effect the relevant statutory provisions.

Notices

An inspector appointed under the HSWA may serve two types of notice.

Improvement notices

Where an inspector is of the opinion that a person (a) is contravening one or more of the relevant statutory provisions or (b) has contravened one or more of these provisions in circumstances that make it likely that the contravention will continue or be repeated, he may serve an improvement notice on that person requiring that

HEALTH AND SAFETY EXECUTIVE   Serial No. I

Health and Safety at Work etc. Act 1974, Sections 21, 23 and 24

IMPROVEMENT NOTICE

Name and
address (See
Section 46)
(a) Delete as
    necessary
(b) Inspector's
    full name
(c) Inspector's
    official
    designation
(d) Official
    address
(e) Location
    of premises
    or place and
    activity
(f) Other
    specified
    capacity
(g) Provisions
    contravened

To ....
....
(a) Trading as ....
(b) ....
one of (c) ....
of (d) ....
.... tel no. ....
hereby give you notice that I am of the opinion that at ....
(e) ....
you, as (a) an employer/a self-employed person/a person wholly or
partly in control of the premises
(f) ....
(a) are contravening/have contravened in circumstances that make
it likely that the contravention will continue to be repeated.

....
....
(g) ....
....
The reasons for my said opinion are: ....
....
....
and I hereby require you to remedy the said contra-
ventions or, as the case may be, the matters
occasioning them by
(h) ....

(h) Date

(a) In the manner stated in the attached schedule
which forms part of the notice.
Signature .... Date ....
Being an Inspector appointed by an Instrument in
writing made pursuant to Section 19 of the said Act
and entitled to issue this notice.
(a) An Improvement notice is also being served on

....
of ....

LP1

related to the matters contained in this notice.

Figure 1.2   *Improvement notice*

he remedy the contraventions or, as the case may be, the matters occasioning it within such period (ending not earlier than the period within which an appeal may be brought) as may be specified in the notice (HSWA, s 21) (see Figure 1.2).

Prohibition notices

If an inspector is of the opinion that a work activity involves or, as the case may be, will involve a risk of serious personal injury, he may serve on that person a prohibition notice. The notice may be served on an employer, an occupier of premises or the person having control of the activity. The notice will direct that the specified activity in the notice will not be carried on by or under the control of the person on whom the notice is served unless certain specific remedial measures have been complied with.

It should be appreciated that it is not necessary that an inspector believes that there has been a breach of one or more of the relevant statutory provisions. A prohibition notice is served where there is an immediate threat to life and in anticipation of danger.

Such a notice may have immediate effect after its service by the inspector. Conversely, the coming into operation of the notice may be deferred for, say, 48 hours, thereby allowing the person to remedy the situation quickly. The duration of a deferred prohibition notice will be specified in the notice (see Figure 1.3).

Appeals against notices

In both cases, a person may appeal to a tribunal against the enforcement of the notice. In the case of an improvement notice, the operation of that notice is automatically suspended on giving notice of intention to appeal. However, in the case of a prohibition notice, the requirements of the notice continue in force, unless the tribunal directs otherwise.

Failure to comply with a notice

Failure to comply with both forms of notice can result in the person being prosecuted. On conviction for the offence(s) stated in either type of notice, and where the contraventions are continued after the conviction, he may be found guilty of a further offence and be liable on summary conviction, ie in a Magistrates' Court, to a fine not exceeding £200 for each day on which the contravention is continued, in addition to the original maximum fine of £20,000 for each of the contraventions specified.

Prosecution

A person who fails to comply with a notice can be prosecuted. However, it is not necessary for an inspector to serve a notice prior to prosecution. An inspector can

HEALTH AND SAFETY EXECUTIVE   Serial No. P

Health and Safety at Work etc. Act 1974, Sections 21, 22–24

PROHIBITION NOTICE

Name and
address (See
Section 46)
(a) Delete as
    necessary
(b) Inspector's
    full name
(c) Inspector's
    official
    designation
(d) Official
    address

To ....
....
(a) Trading as ....
(b) ....
one of (c) ....
of (d) ....
.... tel no. ....
hereby give you notice that I am of the opinion that the following
activities,
namely:- ....
....
....
which are (a) being carried on by you/about to be carried on by you/
under your control

(e) Location
    of activity

at (e) ....

Involve, or will involve (a) a risk/an imminent risk, of serious personal
injury. I am further of the opinion that the said matters involve contraventions of the following statutory provisions:- ....
....
....
....
because ....
....
....
and I hereby direct that the said activities shall not be carried on by
you or under your control (a) Immediately/after

(f) Date

(f) ....
unless the said contraventions and matters included in the schedule,
which forms part of this notice, have been remedied.
Signature .... Date ....

LP2

Being an inspector appointed by an instrument in writing made
pursuant to Section 19 of the said Act and entitled to issue this
notice.

Figure 1.3 *Prohibition notice*

simply institute proceedings without service of a notice. These cases are heard in the Magistrates' Court but there is provision for the more serious cases to be heard on indictment in the Crown Court before a judge and jury.

STATEMENTS OF HEALTH AND SAFETY POLICY

Under section 2 (3) of the HSWA every employer must prepare, and bring to the notice of his employees, a written statement of his general policy with respect to the health and safety at work of his employees. (See further Leaflet No HSC 6, *Guidance Notes on Employers' Policy Statements for Health and Safety at Work* and booklet *Writing your Health and Safety Policy Statement: How to prepare a safety policy statement for a small business* (HMSO).)

There is no standard format for a statement of health and safety policy. However, it should take into account the following aspects:

- management intent;
- the organization and arrangements for implementing the policy;
- individual responsibilities and accountabilities of directors, line managers, employees and other groups, such as contractors working on site; and
- the role and function of health and safety specialists, such as health and safety advisers, occupational health nurses, occupational physicians and trade union safety representatives.

A statement of health and safety policy has a number of objectives:

- it should affirm long-range purpose;
- it should commit management at all levels and reinforce this purpose in the decision-making process; and
- it should indicate the scope left for decision making by junior managers.

The 'core' or key elements of a statement are:

- **A general statement of intent.** This should indicate in broad terms the organization's overall philosophy in relation to the management of health and safety with particular reference to an employer's duties under section 2 of the HSWA.
- **Organization.** This part is concerned with people and their duties, outlining the chain of responsibility and accountability from the top downwards with respect to the management of health and safety. It might also include a number of other aspects, such as the system for safety monitoring, risk assessment, joint consultation procedures and the system for providing information.

- **Arrangements.** This is a very broad area of policy and deals with the systems and procedures for ensuring and maintaining appropriate levels of health and safety performance. It could include, for instance, the system for identifying training needs and procedures for ensuring health and safety training is undertaken, procedures for operating safe systems of work, health surveillance arrangements, arrangements for reporting, recording and investigating accidents and ill health, emergency procedures in the event of fire and the regulation of contractor activities on site.
- This part of the statement is very much a 'living document' and is subject to regular revision and updating in the light of new legislation and changes in the organization's operations.

Many statements of health and safety policy incorporate appendices. These could include, for example:

- a list of the relevant statutory provisions that apply to the organization;
- individual responsibilities of the various levels of management and of employees;
- specific policies dealing with, for instance:
  - smoking at work;
  - sickness absence;
  - the provision of personal protective equipment; and
  - health surveillance procedures for employees.
- fatal accident procedure;
- joint consultation procedures, eg the role and function of the safety committee;
- procedures to protect visitors; and
- the hazards that could be encountered by employees and the precautions necessary.

MANAGEMENT OF HEALTH AND SAFETY AT WORK REGULATIONS (MHSWR) 1999

The original 1992 version of these regulations implemented in the UK the European Framework Directive 'on the introduction of measures to encourage improvements in the safety and health of workers at work'. These regulations are very important in that:

- the regulations do not stand alone – all other modern health and safety legislation, such as the Workplace (Heath, Safety and Welfare) Regulations 1992 and the Provision and Use of Work Equipment Regulations 1998, must be read in conjunction with the general duties under the MHSWR;

- duties on employers under the MHSWR are of an absolute or strict nature compared with duties under, for instance, the HSWA, which are qualified by 'so far as is reasonably practicable' (see 'The hierarchy of duties under health and safety law' earlier in this chapter).

The regulations are accompanied by an approved code of practice and HSE guidance. Important definitions:

- **New or expectant mother** means an employee who is pregnant; who has given birth within the previous six months; or who is breastfeeding.
- **The preventive and protective measures** means the measures which have been identified by the employer in consequence of the assessment as the measures he needs to take to comply with the requirements and prohibitions imposed upon him by or under the relevant statutory provisions and by Part II of the Fire Precautions (Workplace) Regulations (FPWR) 1997.
- **Young person** means any person who has not attained the age of 18.

Under the regulations, an employer must:

- make a suitable and sufficient assessment of:
  (a) the risks to the health and safety of his employees to which they are exposed whilst at work;
  (b) the risks to the health and safety of other persons not in his employment arising out of or in connection with the conduct by him of his undertaking;
  for the purpose of identifying the measures he needs to take to comply with the requirements and prohibitions imposed upon him by or under the relevant statutory provisions and by Part II of the FPWR;
- when carrying out a risk assessment, take into account specific factors with regard to young persons including their inexperience, lack of awareness of risks and immaturity;
- where five or more employees are employed, record the significant findings of the assessment and any group of employees identified as being especially at risk;
- where implementing any preventive and protective measures, do so on the basis of the principles specified in Schedule 1;
- make and give effect to such arrangements as are appropriate, having regard to the nature of his activities and the size of his undertaking, for the effective planning, organization, control, monitoring and review of the preventive and protective measures, recording such arrangements where five or more employees are employed;

- ensure that his employees are provided with such health surveillance as is appropriate having regard to the risks to their health and safety which are identified by the assessment;
- appoint one or more competent persons to assist him in undertaking the measures he needs to take to comply with the requirements and prohibitions imposed upon him by or under the relevant statutory provisions and by Part II of the FPWR;
- establish and where necessary give effect to appropriate procedures to be followed in the event of serious and imminent danger to persons at work in his undertaking;
- nominate a sufficient number of competent persons to implement those procedures in so far as they relate to the evacuation from premises of persons at work in his undertaking;
- ensure that none of his employees has access to any area occupied by him to which it is necessary to restrict access on grounds of health and safety unless the employee concerned has received adequate health and safety instruction;
- so far as is practicable, require any persons at work who are exposed to serious and imminent danger to be informed of the nature of the hazard and of the steps taken or to be taken to protect them from it;
- ensure that any necessary contacts with external services are arranged, particularly as regards first aid, emergency medical care and rescue work;
- provide his employees with comprehensible and relevant information on:
  (a) the risks to their health and safety identified by the assessment;
  (b) the preventive and protective measures;
  (c) the procedures referred to in Regulation 8 (1) (a) and the measures referred to in Regulation 4 (2) (a) of the FPWR; and
  (d) the risks notified to him in accordance with Regulation 11 (1) (c);
- where two or more employers share a workplace (whether on a temporary or permanent basis):
  (a) cooperate with the other employers concerned so far as is necessary to enable them to comply with the requirements and prohibitions imposed upon them by or under the relevant statutory provisions and by Part II of the FPWR;
  (b) (taking into account the nature of his activities) take all reasonable steps to coordinate the measures he takes to comply with the requirements and prohibitions imposed upon him by or under the relevant statutory provisions and Part II of the FPWR with the measures the other employers concerned are taking to comply with the requirements and prohibitions imposed upon them by that legislation; and
  (c) take all reasonable steps to inform the other employers concerned of the risks to their employees' health and safety arising out of or in connection with the conduct by him of his undertaking;

- ensure that the employer of any employees from an outside undertaking who are working in his undertaking is provided with comprehensible information on:
  - (a) the risks to those employees' health and safety arising out of or in connection with the conduct by that first-mentioned employer or by that self-employed person of his undertaking; and
  - (b) the measures taken by that first-mentioned employer or by that self-employed person in compliance with the requirements and prohibitions imposed upon him by or under the relevant statutory provisions and by Part II of the FPWR in so far as the said requirements and prohibitions relate to those employees;
- in entrusting tasks to his employees, take into account their capabilities as regards health and safety;
- ensure that his employees are provided with adequate health and safety training:
  - (a) on their being recruited into the employer's undertaking;
  - (b) on their being exposed to new or increased risks because of: (i) their being transferred or given a change of responsibilities within the employer's undertaking; (ii) the introduction of new work equipment into or a change respecting work equipment already in use within the employer's undertaking; (iii) the introduction of new technology into the employer's undertaking; or (iv) the introduction of a new system of work into or a change respecting a system of work already in use within the employer's undertaking;
- provide any person he has employed under a fixed-term contract of employment with comprehensible information on:
  - (a) any special occupational qualifications or skills required to be held by that employee if he is to carry out his work safely; and
  - (b) any health surveillance required to be provided to that employee by or under any of the relevant statutory provisions and shall provide the said information before the employee concerned commences his duties.
- where:
  - (a) the persons working in an undertaking include women of child-bearing age; and
  - (b) the work is of a kind which could involve risk, by reason of her condition, to the health and safety of a new or expectant mother, or to that of her baby, from any processes or working conditions, or physical, biological or chemical agents, including those specified in Annexes I and II of Council Directive 92/85/EEC on the introduction of measures to encourage improvements in the safety and health at work of pregnant workers and workers who have recently given birth or are breastfeeding,

also include an assessment of such risk in the assessment required by Regulation 3 (1).

- where:
  - (a) a new or expectant mother works at night; and
  - (b) a certificate from a registered medical practitioner or a registered midwife shows that it is necessary for her health or safety that she should not be at work for any period of such work identified in the certificate,

  subject to section 67 of the 1996 Act, suspend her from work for so long as is necessary for her health or safety;

- ensure that young persons employed by him are protected at work from any risks to their health or safety which are a consequence of their lack of experience, or absence of awareness of existing or potential risks or the fact that young persons have not yet fully matured;

- not employ a young person at work:
  - (a) which is beyond his physical or psychological capacity;
  - (b) involving harmful exposure to agents which are toxic or carcinogenic, cause heritable genetic damage or harm to the unborn child or which in any other way chronically affect human health;
  - (c) involving harmful exposure to radiation;
  - (d) involving the risk of accidents which it may reasonably be assumed cannot be recognized or avoided by young persons owing to their insufficient attention to safety or lack of experience or training; or
  - (e) in which there is a risk to health from: (i) extreme heat or cold; (ii) noise; or (iii) vibration,

- and in determining whether work will involve harm or risks for the purposes of this paragraph, regard shall be had to the results of the assessment.

Employees must use any machinery, equipment, dangerous substance, transport equipment, means of production or safety device in accordance with any training provided and the instruction respecting that use.

They must further inform their employer or any other employee with specific responsibility for the health and safety of his fellow employees: (a) of any work situation which represents a serious and immediate danger to health and safety; and (b) of any matter which represents a shortcoming in the employer's protection arrangements for health and safety.

Schedule 1 – General principles of prevention

Regulation 4

This schedule specifies the general principles of prevention set out in Article 6 (2) of Council Directive 89/291/EEC:

- avoiding risks;
- evaluating the risks which cannot be avoided;
- combating the risks at source;
- adapting the work to the individual, especially as regards the design of work-places, the choice of work equipment and the choice of working and production methods, with a view, in particular, to alleviating monotonous work and work at a predetermined work rate and to reducing their effect on health;
- adapting to technical progress;
- replacing the dangerous by the non-dangerous or the less dangerous;
- developing a coherent overall prevention policy which covers technology, organization of work, working conditions, social relationships and the influences of factors relating to the working environment;
- giving collective protective measures priority over individual protective measures; and
- giving appropriate instructions to employees.

HEALTH AND SAFETY MANUALS AND EMPLOYEE INSTRUCTIONS

One of the problems, particularly with large multi-site organizations, is that of ensuring consistency of approach by managers in dealing with health and safety-related issues, such as the reporting, recording and investigation of accidents and ill health, risk assessment, the operation of permit-to-work systems, regulating the activities of contractors and the safety vetting of new machinery and plant.

It is standard practice for these procedures to be dealt with as a series of in-house codes of practice incorporated in a health and safety manual, which is held by a senior manager and the safety officer on site.

There is also a duty on employers to advise and inform employees of the hazards they may encounter and the precautions necessary on their part. Here it is common for organizations to produce a set of safety rules, which must be followed by all employees. These health and safety rules are issued at the induction training stage of all new employees.

EMPLOYERS' LIABILITY INSURANCE

The Employers' Liability (Compulsory Insurance) Act 1969 deals with the duties on employers in terms of insuring themselves against claims that may be made by employees.

Every employer carrying on business in Great Britain must insure and maintain insurance against liability for bodily injury or disease sustained by his employees, and arising out of or in the course of their employment in Great Britain in that business.

This insurance must be provided under one or more 'approved policies', that is a policy of insurance not subject to any conditions or exceptions prohibited by regulations.

Cover

Cover is required in respect of liability to employees who either: (a) are ordinarily resident in Great Britain; or (b) though not ordinarily resident in Great Britain, are present in Great Britain in the course of their employment for a continuous period of not less than 14 days.

Issue and display of certificate

The insurer must issue the employer with a certificate of insurance, which has to be issued not later than 30 days after the date on which the insurance was commenced or renewed. The certificate must be prominently displayed.

Employers' Liability (Compulsory Insurance) Regulations 1998

These regulations consolidated with amendments the Employers' Liability (Compulsory Insurance) General Regulations 1971 and subsequent amending regulations made under the Employers' Liability (Compulsory Insurance) Act 1969.

Under these regulations:

- the sum insured must be not less than £5,000,000;
- prescribed wording on a certificate of insurance must provide adequate information about the cover provided;
- certificates must be kept for at least 40 years;
- authorized inspectors are empowered to require not just the production of a current certificate but also the production of past certificates;
- employers of offshore employees are required to produce a copy of the relevant certificate of insurance on request from an employee within 10 days.

Penalties under the Act

- **Failure to insure or maintain insurance** – maximum penalty on conviction £1,000.
- **Failure to display a certificate of insurance** – maximum penalty on conviction £500.

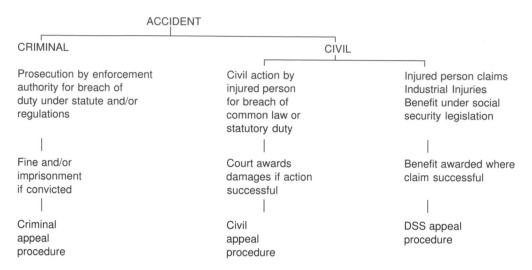

Figure 1.4 *Legal routes following an accident at work*

KEY POINTS

- Health and safety law is concerned with the civil and criminal liabilities of, particularly, employers towards their employees and to other persons who may be affected by their activities.
- The principal statute dealing with criminal law is the HSWA, and all regulations are made under this statute.
- More recent regulations are based on requirements of European Community directives.
- Under the civil law every employer has a duty to take reasonable care to protect the safety of his employees whilst at work.
- Most civil claims are based on the tort of negligence.
- Duties under the criminal law may be absolute or qualified.
- Health and safety matters are dealt with by both the criminal and civil courts.
- Health and safety law is written down in statutes and regulations, which in turn are supported by HSC approved codes of practice. HSE guidance notes, which may also accompany regulations, have no legal status.
- Enforcement of criminal law is by inspectors appointed under the Act.
- Every employer must produce a written statement of health and safety policy and draw the key aspects of same to the attention of all his employees.
- The MHSWR place a wide range of duties on employers, in particular those relating to risk assessment, the installation of management systems and the appointment of competent persons.
- Specific provisions are laid down in the above regulations with respect to pregnant workers and young persons.

2

Health and safety management

There is an implied duty on the part of employers to manage health and safety under the HSWA. This duty, however, is more clearly laid down in the MHSWR (see Chapter 1).

HEALTH AND SAFETY MANAGEMENT

The ACOP to the MHSWR outlines five elements of successful management practice, namely:

- **Planning.** Employers should set up an effective health and safety management system to implement their health and safety policy which is proportionate to the hazards and risks. Adequate planning includes:
  - (a) Adopting a systematic approach to the completion of a risk assessment. Risk assessment methods should be used to decide on priorities and to set objectives for eliminating hazards and reducing risks. This should include a programme, with deadlines for the completion of the risk assessment process, together with suitable deadlines for the design and implementation of the preventive and protective measures which are necessary.
  - (b) Selecting appropriate methods of risk control to minimize risks.
  - (c) Establishing priorities and developing performance standards both for the completion of risk assessment(s) and for the implementation of preventive and protective measures, which at each stage minimizes the risk of harm to

people. Wherever possible, risks are eliminated through selection and design of facilities, equipment and processes.

- **Organization.** This includes:

  (a) Involving employees and their representatives in carrying out risk assessments, deciding on preventive and protective measures and implementing those requirements in the workplace. This may be achieved by the use of formal health and safety committees where they exist, and by the use of teamworking, where employees are involved in deciding on the appropriate preventive and protective measures and written procedures, etc.

  (b) Establishing effective means of communication and consultation in which a positive approach to health and safety is visible and clear. The employer should have adequate health and safety information and make sure it is communicated to employees and their representatives, so informed decisions can be made about the choice of preventive and protective measures. Effective communication will ensure that employees are provided with sufficient information so that control measures can be implemented effectively.

  (c) Securing competence by the provision of adequate information, instruction and training and its evaluation, particularly for those who carry out risk assessments and make decisions about preventive and protective measures. Where necessary this will need to be supported by the provision of adequate health and safety assistance or advice.

- **Control.** Establishing control includes:

  (a) Clarifying health and safety responsibilities and ensuring that the activities of everyone are well coordinated.

  (b) Ensuring everyone with responsibilities understands clearly what they have to do to discharge their responsibilities, and ensure they have the time and resources to discharge them effectively.

  (c) Setting standards to judge the performance of those with responsibilities and ensure they meet them. It is important to reward good performance as well as to take action to improve poor performance.

  (d) Ensuring adequate and appropriate supervision, particularly for those who are learning and who are new to a job.

- **Monitoring.** Employers should measure what they are doing to implement their health and safety policy, to assess how effectively they are controlling risks, and how well they are developing a positive health and safety culture. Monitoring includes:

  (a) Having a plan and making adequate routine inspections and checks to ensure that preventive and protective measures are in place and effective. Active monitoring reveals how effectively the health and safety management system is functioning.

(b) Adequately investigating the immediate and underlying causes of incidents and accidents to ensure that remedial action is taken, lessons are learnt and longer-term objectives are introduced.

In both cases it may be appropriate to record and analyse the results of monitoring activity, to identify any underlying themes or trends which may not be apparent from looking at events in isolation.

- **Review.** Review involves:
  (a) Establishing priorities for necessary remedial action that was discovered as a result of monitoring to ensure that suitable action is taken in good time and is completed.
  (b) Periodically reviewing the whole of the health and safety management system including the elements of planning, organization, control and monitoring to ensure that the whole system remains effective.

Successful Health and Safety Management (HS(G)65)

This HSE publication explains the health and safety management process as, fundamentally, taking place in a series of stages thus:

- **Policy.** Organizations which are successful in achieving high standards of health and safety have health and safety policies which contribute to their business performance, while meeting their responsibilities to people and the environment in a way which fulfils both the spirit and the letter of the law. In this way they satisfy the expectations of shareholders, employees, customers and society at large. Their policies are cost effective and aimed at achieving the preservation and development of physical and human resources and reductions in financial losses and liabilities. The policies influence all their activities and decisions, including those to do with the selection of resources and information, the design and operation of working systems, the design and delivery of products and services, and the control and disposal of waste.

- **Organizing.** Organizations which achieve high health and safety standards are structured and operated so as to put their health and safety policies into effective practice. This is helped by the creation of a positive culture which secures involvement and participation at all levels. It is sustained by effective communication and the promotion of competence which enables all employees to make a responsible and informed contribution to the health and safety effort. The visible and active leadership of senior managers is necessary to develop and maintain a culture supportive of health and safety management. Their aim is not simply to avoid accidents, but to motivate and empower people to work safely. The vision, values and beliefs of leaders become the shared 'common knowledge' of all.

- **Planning.** These successful organizations adopt a planned and systematic approach to policy implementation. Their aim is to minimize the risks created by work activities, products and services. They use risk assessment methods to decide priorities and set objectives for hazard elimination and risk reduction. Performance standards are established and performance is measured against them. Specific actions needed to promote a positive health and safety culture to eliminate and to control risks are identified. Wherever possible, risks are eliminated by the careful selection and design of facilities, equipment and processes or minimized by the use of physical control measures. Where this is not possible systems of work and personal protective equipment are used to control risks.

- **Measuring performance.** Health and safety performance in organizations which manage health and safety successfully is measured against predetermined standards. This reveals when and where action is needed to improve performance. The success of action taken to control risks is assessed through active self-monitoring involving a range of techniques. This includes an examination of both hardware (premises, plant and substances) and software (people, procedures and systems), including individual behaviour. Failures of control are assessed through reactive monitoring which requires the thorough investigation of any accidents, ill health or incidents with the potential to cause harm or loss. In both active and reactive monitoring the objects are not only to determine the immediate causes of substandard performance but, more importantly, to identify the underlying causes and the implications for the design and operation of the health and safety management system.

- **Auditing and reviewing performance.** Learning from all relevant experience and applying the lessons learnt are important elements in effective health and safety management. This needs to be done systematically through regular reviews of performance based on data both from monitoring activities and from independent audits of the whole health and safety management system. These form the basis for self-regulation and for securing compliance with sections 2 to 6 of the HSWA. Commitment to continuous improvement involves the constant development of policies, approaches to implementation and techniques of risk control. Organizations which achieve high standards of health and safety assess their health and safety performance by internal reference to key performance indicators and by external comparison with the performance of business competitors. They often also record and account for their performance in their annual reports.

These elements, featured in Figure 2.1, are relevant in all management situations, not merely those relating to health and safety at work.

The principal recommendations with respect to these five elements of successful health and safety management are summarized below.

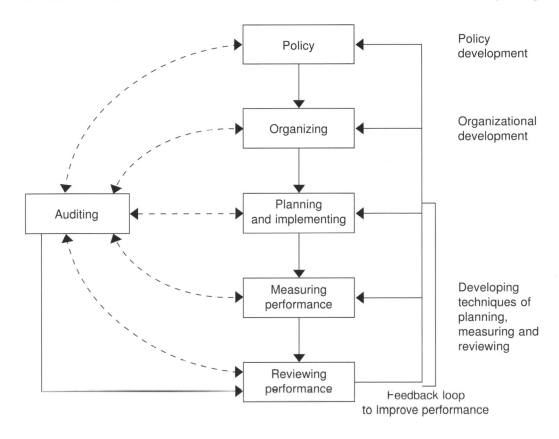

Figure 2.1 *Key elements of successful health and safety management*

Effective health and safety policies

Effective health and safety management demands comprehensive health and safety policies which fulfil the spirit and the letter of the law, which are effectively implemented and which are considered in all business practice and decision making. Organizations achieving high standards of health and safety develop policies that recognize:

- that health and safety can contribute to business performance by preserving and developing human and physical resources, by reducing costs and liabilities and as a means of expressing corporate responsibility;
- that leaders must develop appropriate organizational structures and a culture which supports risk control and secures the full participation of all members of the organization;
- the need to resource and plan policy implementation adequately;
- that the only effective approach to injury, ill health and loss prevention is one based on the systematic identification and control of risk;

- the need for the organization to develop an understanding of risk control and to be responsive to internal and external change;
- the need to scrutinize and review performance so as to learn from experience;
- the connection between quality and health and safety.

Organizing for health and safety

Organizations achieving success in health and safety create and sustain a culture which secures the motivation and involvement of all members of the organization and the control of risks. This leads them to establish, operate and maintain structures and systems that aim at:

- securing control by:
  - employing managers who lead by example;
  - clear allocation of responsibilities for policy formulation and development, for planning and reviewing health and safety activities, for the implementation of plans, and for reporting on performance;
  - the allocation of health and safety responsibilities to people with the necessary authority and competence, who are given the time and resources to carry out their duties effectively;
  - ensuring that individuals are held accountable for their health and safety responsibilities and are motivated by systems of target setting and positive reinforcement;
  - the provision of adequate supervision, instruction and guidance;
  - payment and reward systems which avoid conflict between achieving output targets and health and safety requirements;
- encouraging cooperation of employees and safety representatives by:
  - involving them in policy formulation and development and in planning, implementing, measuring, auditing and reviewing performance;
  - making arrangements for involvement at the operational level to supplement more formal participative arrangements;
- securing effective communication by means of visible behaviour, written material and face-to-face discussion;
- ensuring competence through recruitment, selection, placement, transfer and training and the provision of adequate specialist advice.

Planning and implementing

Organizations achieving success in health and safety minimize risks in their operation by drawing up plans and setting performance standards with the aim of eliminating and controlling risks. They establish, operate and maintain planning systems which:

- identify objectives and targets for their achievement within a specific period;
- set performance standards for management actions designed to initiate, develop, maintain and improve a positive health and safety culture in the four key areas – control, competence, communication and cooperation;
- set performance standards for the control of risks which are based on hazard identification and risk assessment, which take legal requirements as the minimum acceptable standard of performance and which emphasize:
  - the elimination of risks by the substitution of safer premises, plant or substances and, where this is not reasonably practicable,
  - the control of risks by physical safeguards which minimize the need for employees to follow detailed systems of work or to use protective equipment;
- establish priorities for the provision and maintenance of control measures by the use of risk assessment techniques, giving priority to high-risk areas and adopting temporary control measures to minimize risks where satisfactory control cannot be achieved immediately;
- set performance standards for the control of risks both to employees and to others who may be affected by the organization's activities, products and services;
- ensure the adequate documentation of all performance standards, the detail of documentation reflecting the degree of risk.

Measuring performance

Organizations achieving success in health and safety measure their performance against predetermined plans and standards, the implementation and effectiveness of which they assess as a basis for taking appropriate remedial action. This leads them to establish, operate and maintain systems which ensure that performance is measured objectively. Such systems include:

- active monitoring systems which:
  - measure the achievement of objectives and specified standards;
  - reflect risk control priorities by concentrating on high-risk activities which are monitored in more depth and/or more frequently;
- reactive monitoring systems which collect and analyse information suggesting failures in health and safety performance. These require systems for reporting:
  - injuries and cases of ill health;
  - other loss events, eg damage to property;
  - incidents (including all those which had the potential to cause injury, ill health or loss);
  - hazards; and
  - weaknesses or omissions in performance standards;

- reporting and response systems which ensure that information from active and reactive monitoring is evaluated by people competent to identify situations which create an immediate risk to health or safety, and to ensure that appropriate remedial action is taken;
- investigation systems which ensure:
  - the investigation of reports arising from active and reactive monitoring, with priority being given to those circumstances which present the greatest risk;
  - the identification of both the immediate and the underlying causes of events;
  - the referral of information to the level of management with authority to initiate the necessary remedial action, including organizational and policy changes;
  - the adequate analysis of all collected data to identify common features or trends and initiate improvements.

Reviewing performance

Organizations achieving success in health and safety aim to evaluate performance, in order:

- to maximize learning and to ensure that appropriate action is taken to improve the control of specific risks; and
- to improve overall health and safety performance and further develop their health and safety policies.

This leads them to establish, operate and maintain audit and review systems which ensure that:

- information is obtained by the use of in-house auditing systems or external auditors on the validity and reliability of the whole health and safety management planning and control system, and the ability of the organization to develop its health and safety policies and improve the control of risks;
- appropriate remedial action is taken to deal with specific issues arising from measurement activities and to ensure that progress in implementing remedial action is followed through according to plan;
- the overall effectiveness of policy implementation is assessed internally with particular reference to the following four key performance indicators:
  - assessment of the degree of compliance with health and safety performance standards;
  - identification of areas where standards are absent or inadequate;
  - assessment of the achievement of specific objectives;
  - accident, ill-health and incident data together with analyses of immediate and underlying causes, trends and common features;

- health and safety performance is assessed externally by comparison with other organizations.

Fundamentally, organizations need a system for managing health and safety at work. HS(G)65 provides employers with a systematic approach to the subject, including organizing for health and safety and minimum objectives for performance standards.

Further advice is provided in BS 8800: 1996 *Guide to Occupational Health and Safety Management Systems* and in *ISO 14001: The Plan – Do – Act – Check Cycle*.

ACCIDENT PREVENTION

The ACOP to the MHSWR refers to both proactive and reactive monitoring as essential elements of the management system for preventing accidents.

Active monitoring

Proactive or pre-accident strategies are concerned with the prevention of accidents, incidents and ill health. They include the implementation of well-established 'safe place' and 'safe person' strategies dealt with later in this chapter.

Reactive monitoring

Reactive monitoring, on the other hand, involves a number of post-accident strategies, directed at identifying the causes of accidents and ill health and obtaining feedback for incorporation in future proactive strategies. The reporting, recording and investigation of accidents is a common reactive strategy.

Accident definitions

It would be appropriate, at this stage, to define what is meant by an accident:

- An unplanned and uncontrolled event which has led to or could have caused injury to persons, damage to plant or other loss (Royal Society for the Prevention of Accidents).
- An undesired event that results in physical harm to a person or damage to property. It is usually the result of a contact with a source of energy (ie kinetic, electrical, chemical, thermal, ionizing radiation, non-ionizing radiation, etc) above the threshold limit of the body or structure (Frank Bird, Executive Director, American Institute of Loss Control).

- An unexpected, unplanned event in a sequence of events that occurs through a combination of causes. It results in physical harm (injury or disease) to an individual, damage to property, business interruption or any combination of these (Department of Occupational and Environmental Health, University of Aston in Birmingham).

Fundamentally, all accidents are unforeseeable (in the case of the accident victim), unplanned, unintended and unexpected. In the majority of cases, there is a sequence of events which leads to the accidents and there may be a number of direct and indirect causes.

'Safe place' strategies

These strategies are concerned with the actions necessary to prevent accidents and to reduce the objective danger that is a precondition of accidents:

- **Safe systems of work.** A safe system of work is a prerequisite for the prevention of accidents. Safe systems of work involve people, planning the operation, the provision of information, instruction and training, and the removal of hazards at the design stage of work activities. The design and implementation of safe systems of work is a common outcome of risk assessment. In certain cases, safe systems may be formally documented as with a permit-to-work system.
- **Safe processes.** Processes operated in workplaces include manufacturing processes, treatment processes, the conversion of raw materials to finished products, the use of machinery and plant, operation of display screen equipment, processes involving the use of hazardous substances and the use of internal transport equipment, such as lift trucks.
- **Safe premises.** A safe workplace involves consideration of design, layout and structural features, such as floors and windows, structural stability, control of environmental factors, such as lighting, fire protection arrangements and measures for ensuring safe means of escape in the event of fire. The WHSWR and accompanying ACOP provide detailed requirements for workplaces.
- **Safe equipment.** Work equipment includes machinery, plant, mobile equipment, such as lift trucks, and hand tools. Maintenance of this equipment is an essential requirement for ensuring safe working, together with information, instruction, training and supervision in the correct operation and use of equipment.
- **Safe materials.** Consideration must be given to the health and safety requirements for a wide range of substances, such as acids, alkalis, flammable substances, poisons, carcinogenic substances and mutagenic substances, in terms of handling, storage and disposal of waste products. Information provided by suppliers in

safety data sheets is an essential element for ensuring safe use of substances. Health risk assessments must be produced by employers for substances classified as 'substances hazardous to health' under the COSHH Regulations.

- **Safe access and egress.** Access to and egress from the workplace and specific parts of the workplace, such as those at heights above floor and ground level, or confined spaces, must be safe. Access must also be considered in the case of approach roads and the segregation of pedestrians from vehicular traffic leading to and around a workplace. More specific access, in terms of the use of ladders by people working at heights, must be safe.

- **Competent and trained personnel.** There is an urgent need to ensure that people are competent for the tasks they are required to perform, such as the operation of machinery and plant, mobile access equipment and the use of hazardous substances. Systems for the provision of information, instruction and training should feature in the health and safety management system, with particular reference to induction training, on-the-job training and refresher training. In certain cases, the employees of contractors may need information and training in the hazards and precautions necessary whilst working on site prior to commencing contract work.

- **Adequate supervision.** Supervision should extend through senior management to line management. Supervision requirements, including those for ensuring appropriate levels of health and safety performance by employees and others, should be incorporated in job descriptions. Procedures in the event of unsafe behaviour should be written down, including the taking of disciplinary action against offenders.

'Safe person' strategies

People make mistakes which can lead to accidents. Others may have a total disregard for safety procedures. Some people, such as young persons, have a greater potential for accidents, as a result of their immaturity and lack of knowledge and experience of workplace hazards. 'Safe person' strategies are directed at increasing people's perception of risk and to ensuring safe behaviour at work. These strategies include:

- **The provision and use of personal protective equipment.** There is a duty on employers, in certain cases, to provide various forms of personal protective equipment (PPE) under the Personal Protective Equipment at Work Regulations. Employees are required to use and wear PPE in defined work situations. PPE must be carefully selected and appropriate to the risks it is designed to provide protection against (see Chapter 9).

- **Care of the vulnerable.** Certain groups of employees, such as young persons, older workers, pregnant workers, disabled workers, those exposed to specific hazards, such as radiation workers and those involved with lead processes, are more vulnerable to accidents and occupational ill health. In certain cases, there may be a need for medical or health surveillance of these groups. A much greater level of supervision is required for people coming within the 'vulnerable' classification.

- **Personal hygiene.** Personal hygiene is very much a matter of individual training and upbringing. However, certain processes and operations may expose workers to health risks, such as those resulting in occupational dermatitis or metal poisoning through contamination of the hands and other parts of the body. Hand-to-mouth contamination arising from consumption of food contaminated by dirty hands, or the use of contaminated drinking vessels, is a serious risk in some workplaces. There may be a need, therefore, to ban all forms of eating and drinking in workplaces, restricting food and drink consumption to a canteen or dining area.

  Good standards of personal hygiene should be promoted through induction and refresher training, the use of safety propaganda, such as safety posters, and high levels of supervision where hazardous substances are used. This should be supported by the provision and maintenance of adequate welfare facilities, namely washing and showering facilities, separate clothing storage for work clothing and personal clothing not worn at work, and frequent replacement of contaminated overalls and other forms of work clothing.

- **Caution towards danger.** Some people are more careful than others. However, there is a need to promote a general caution towards danger and the use of safe systems of work.

- **Careful conduct.** Horseplay and unsafe behaviour is a contributory factor in many accidents. This may include the removal of machinery guards, failure to use PPE, use of lift trucks by unauthorized persons, such as the employees of contractors, smoking in no-smoking areas, and abuse of equipment, compressed gases and flammable substances. Employees should be regularly reminded of their duties under the HSWA with respect to safe working, and this should be supported by disciplinary action wherever unsafe conduct is identified.

Post-accident strategies

While the emphasis must always be on the prevention of accidents, employers should have a number of systems in place in the event of accidents of varying severity. These include:

- **Feedback strategies.** Feedback from the investigation of accidents is an essential feature of the safety management system. This is how organizations learn by their mistakes, incorporating the recommendations arising from investigation into future pre-accident strategies. The correct use and interpretation of accident statistics are vital here, bearing in mind that, while this form of information may identify trends in accident experience, it is not a true measure of safety performance.
- **Disaster/emergency procedures.** Employers have a duty under the MHSWR to install procedures for serious and imminent danger and for danger areas. A number of questions need to be asked:
  - 'What conditions could create a disaster situation?'
  - 'What is the worst-case scenario bearing in mind the processes undertaken, substances stored and the number of people on site at any one time?'
  - 'Are there parts of this workplace that could be classified as "danger areas"?'

On this basis, an emergency plan should be developed incorporating a range of procedures to be followed by both employers and employees in the event of an emergency arising. See later in this chapter 'Emergency procedures'.

SAFETY MONITORING

Safety monitoring is a proactive area of health and safety practice directed at identifying hazards, and assessing and evaluating safety performance. Safety monitoring systems form part of the 'arrangements' for health and safety in the organization's statement of health and safety policy.

Safety monitoring may take the form of:

- **Safety inspections.** A safety inspection is generally taken to mean a scheduled inspection of a workplace or part of a workplace by a health and safety specialist, a group of safety representatives or a designated manager. A safety inspection has a number of objectives, such as:
  - to identify hazards;
  - to examine compliance with safe systems of work, the use of personal protective equipment, safe use of substances, etc;
  - to examine the workplace as part of an accident investigation;
  - to examine maintenance and housekeeping standards;
  - in the case of trade union safety representatives, to ensure their members are adequately protected against risks to their health and safety.

There is no standard format for a safety inspection, but generally this entails walking the workplace, internally and externally, observing working practices and identifying hazards and shortcomings in the employer's protection arrangements.

- **Safety audits.** A safety audit is defined by RoSPA as the systematic measurement and validation of an organization's management of its health and safety programme against a series of specific and attainable standards. This form of monitoring subjects each area of an organization's activities to a systematic critical examination with the objective of minimizing injury and loss.

  Safety audits place great strength on the examination of management systems for safety, commencing with the statement of health and safety policy and reviewing procedures for risk assessment, the training and appointment of competent persons, documentation arrangements, eg for permit-to-work systems, planned preventive maintenance procedures, environmental monitoring, accident and incident reporting procedures and methods for ensuring legal compliance. As with safety inspections, there is no standard format for a safety audit, but many organizations have developed there own in-house format, which is used to measure management performance.

- **Safety surveys.** A safety survey can comprise:
  - a detailed examination of a number of critical areas of operation; or
  - an in-depth study of the whole health and safety operations of a workplace.

  The outcome of a safety survey is a safety survey report outlining short-term, medium-term and long-term recommendations for health and safety improvement over, for example, a five-year period. The person undertaking the safety survey generally revisits at specified intervals to assess progress in implementation of the recommendations and prepares a progress report for the attention of local management.

- **Safety tours.** Safety tours take the form of an unscheduled examination of a workplace by a group of people, such as a safety committee, with the objective of ensuring, for example, previous committee recommendations for safe working are in place, to hear the views of employees on health and safety, to check current arrangements with respect to fire protection, machinery safety, etc are being maintained and to examine housekeeping levels.

  The purpose of a safety tour should be specified and, to be effective, recommendations made by tour members should be implemented quickly. Safety tours also help to raise interest in the subject among employees if they can see their observations are being noted and acted upon by management.

- **Safety sampling exercises.** Safety sampling is a technique designed to measure, by random sampling, the accident potential in specific parts of a workplace, or premises of a similar nature, such as offices, shops, workshops and kitchens, by identifying specific safety defects or omissions.

  Many multi-site organizations use safety sampling exercises as a means of comparing safety performance across their various locations, with a view to rewarding good or improved performance by managers and taking remedial action in the event of poor performance.

Safety sampling exercises generally incorporate a series of performance indicators, such as fire protection, housekeeping and manual handling, whereby these selected areas of performance are ranked numerically, say from 1 to 5 or from 1 to 20, according to significance. Safety specialists check individual location performance against these performance indicators during an inspection of each workplace, awarding scores appropriately (see Figure 2.2).

Safety sampling exercises commonly form the basis for a safety award scheme directed at raising the profile of health and safety within an organization.

		Locations				
		| A |	B |	C |	D |	E |
1. Housekeeping	Max 20					
2. Fire protection	Max 20					
3. Machinery safety	Max 20					
4. Electrical safety	Max 15					
5. Internal storage arrangements	Max 10					
6. Use of hazardous substances	Max 10					
7. Manual handling operations	Max 10					
8. Personal protection	Max 10					
9. Welfare amenities	Max 10					
10. Lift truck operations	Max 15					
11. Lighting	Max 10					
12. Access and egress	Max 10					
13. Dust and fume control	Max 10					
14. Hand tools	Max 10					
15. Structural safety	Max 20					
TOTALS	Max 200					

Figure 2.2 *Safety sampling exercise*

HAZARD IDENTIFICATION AND RISK ASSESSMENT

The identification of hazards and subsequent assessment of the risks arising from these hazards is a legal requirement and an essential part of the health and safety management system. Before considering these aspects, however, it would be appropriate to define the terms 'hazard' and 'risk'.

'Hazard' is defined as:

- exposure to risk;
- something with the potential to cause harm – this can include substances or machines, methods of work and other aspects of work organization (ACOP to the MHSWR);
- the result of a departure from the normal situation, which has the potential to cause death, injury, damage or loss.

'Risk' is variously defined as:

- a chance of bad consequences;
- exposure to chance of injury or loss;
- the probability of a hazard leading to personal injury and the severity of that injury;
- the likelihood of potential harm;
- the likelihood of potential harm from that hazard being realized.

The *extent* of the risk will depend upon:

- the likelihood of that harm occurring;
- the potential severity of that harm, ie of any resultant injury or adverse health effects; and
- the population which might be affected by the hazard, ie the number of people who might be exposed (ACOP to the MHSWR).

Hazard identification

The identification of hazards is the starting point of the health and safety management process. It can take place in a number of ways:

- **Routine observation.** This is the process of observing working practices, such as manual handling operations, fork-lift truck movements, the correct use of hazardous substances and contractors working on a roof. Fundamentally, managers need to 'keep their eyes open', when moving round the workplace, to unsatisfactory practices that could lead to accidents and ill health arising from work.

- **Safety monitoring.** One of the principal functions of a safety inspection is to identify hazards. Other forms of safety monitoring, such as audits, surveys and sampling exercises will, in turn, identify hazards.

- **Accident investigation.** Investigation of an accident will, in many cases, identify hazards that actually contributed to the accident and other hazards which could be the cause of further accidents.

- **Hazard reports.** Under the MHSWR employees have a duty to report to their employer any hazards and shortcomings in the employer's protection arrangements. There should be a formal procedure for this reporting process, including certification by the safety adviser when a hazard has been eliminated or controlled.

Risk assessment

Once hazards have been identified, the risks arising from these hazards should be assessed. Details of the risk assessment process are specified in the ACOP to the MHSWR thus:

General principles and purpose of risk assessment

9.   Regulation 3 of the MHSWR requires all employers and self-employed people to assess the risks to workers and any others who may be affected by their work or business. This will enable them to identify the measures they need to take to comply with health and safety law.

Note: In order to undertake risk assessment satisfactorily, it is essential that persons undertaking risk assessments are fully familiar with the relevant statutory provisions, such as the Workplace (Health, Safety and Welfare) Regulations (WHSWR) 1992, which apply in the circumstances.

All employers should carry out a systematic general examination of the effects of their undertaking, their work activities and the condition of the premises. Those who employ five or more employees should record the *significant findings* of the risk assessment.

10.   A risk assessment is carried out to identify the risks to health and safety to any person arising out of, or in connection with work, or the conduct of their undertaking. It should identify how the risks arise and how they impact on

those affected. This information is needed to make decisions on how to manage those risks so that the decisions are made in an informed, rational and structured manner, and the action taken is proportionate.

11. A risk assessment should usually involve identifying the hazards present in any working environment or arising out of commercial activities and work activities, and evaluating the extent of the risks involved, taking into account existing precautions and their effectiveness.

12. The purpose of the risk assessment is to help the employer or self-employed person to determine what measures should be taken to comply with the employer's or self-employed person's duties under the *'relevant statutory provisions'* and Part II of the FPWR. This covers the general duties in the HSWA and the requirements of Part II of the Fire Regulations and the more specific duties in the various acts and regulations (including these regulations) associated with the HSWA. Once the measures have been determined in this way, the duty to put them into effect will be defined in the statutory provisions. For example a risk assessment on machinery would be undertaken under the MHSWR, but the Provision and Use of Work Equipment Regulations determine what precautions must be carried out. A risk assessment carried out by a self-employed person in circumstances where he or she does not employ others does not have to take into account duties arising under Part II of the Fire Regulations.

'Suitable and sufficient'

13. A suitable and sufficient risk assessment should be made. 'Suitable and sufficient' is not defined in the regulations. In practice it means the risk assessment should do the following:

    (a) The risk assessment should identify the risks arising from or in connection with work. The level of detail in a risk assessment should be proportionate to the risk. Once the risks are assessed and taken into account, insignificant risks can usually be ignored, as can risks arising from routine activities associated with life in general, unless the work activity compounds or significantly alters those risks. The level of risk arising from the work activity should determine the degree of sophistication of the risk assessment.

Five Steps to Risk Assessment (Ind(G)163)

This HSE leaflet provides guidance to firms in the commercial, service and light-industrial sectors. The principal elements of this leaflet are outlined in the box.

Five steps to risk assessment: how to assess the risks in your workplace

Follow the five steps in this leaflet:

- Step 1: Look for the hazards.
- Step 2: Decide who might be harmed and how.
- Step 3: Evaluate the risks and decide whether the existing precautions are adequate or whether more should be done.
- Step 4: Record your findings.
- Step 5: Review your assessment and revise it if necessary.

- **Step 1: Hazard.**
  Hazard means anything that can cause harm (eg chemicals, electricity, working from ladders, etc).
  Look only for hazards which you could reasonably expect to result in significant harm under the conditions in your workplace. Use the following examples as a guide:
  - slipping/tripping hazards, eg poorly maintained floors or stairs;
  - fire, eg from flammable materials;
  - chemicals, eg battery acid;
  - moving parts of machinery;
  - work at a height, eg from mezzanine floors;
  - ejection of material, eg from plastic moulding;
  - pressure systems, eg steam boilers;
  - vehicles, eg fork-lift trucks;
  - electricity, eg poor wiring;
  - dust, eg from grinding;
  - fumes, eg welding;
  - manual handling;
  - noise;
  - poor lighting;
  - low temperature.
- **Step 2: Who might be harmed?**
  There is no need to list individuals by name – just think about the groups of people doing similar work or who might be affected, eg:
  - office staff;
  - maintenance personnel;

    – contractors;

    – people sharing your workplace;

    – operators;

    – cleaners;

    – members of the public.

Pay particular attention to:

    – staff with disabilities;

    – visitors;

    – inexperienced workers;

    – lone workers.

They may be more vulnerable.

- **Step 3: Is more needed to control the risks?**

  Risk is the chance, high or low, that somebody will be harmed by the hazard. For the hazards listed, do the precautions already taken:

      – meet the standard set by a legal requirement?

      – comply with a recognized industry standard?

      – represent good practice?

      – reduce risk as far as is reasonably practicable?

  Have you provided:

      – adequate information, instruction or training?

      – adequate systems or procedures?

  If so, then the risks are adequately controlled, but you need to indicate the precautions you have in place. (You may refer to procedures, company rules, etc.)

  Where the risk is not adequately controlled, indicate what more you need to do (the 'action list').

- **Step 4: Record your findings.**

- **Step 5: Review and revision.**

  Set a date for review of the assessment.

  On review check that the precautions for each hazard still adequately control the risk. Note the outcome. If necessary, complete a new page for your risk assessment.

  Making changes in your workplace, eg when bringing in new:

      – machines,

      – substances,

      – procedures,

  may introduce significant new hazards. Look for them and follow the five steps.

Risk assessment

Risk assessment for
Company Name

Company Address

Postcode

Assessment
undertaken
Date
Signed
Date

Assessment
review
Date

Step 1	Step 2	Step 3
List the significant hazards here.	List groups of people who are at risk from the significant hazards you have identified.	List existing controls or note where the information may be found. List risks which are not adequately controlled and the action needed.

Figure 2.3 *HSE risk assessment document*

SAFE SYSTEMS OF WORK

The need for employers to ensure, so far as is reasonably practicable, the provision and maintenance of systems of work that are safe and without risks to health is incorporated in the HSWA, s 2 (2) (a).

What is a safe system of work?

A safe system of work can be defined as:

- the integration of men, machinery and materials in a correct environment to provide the safest possible working conditions in a work area;
- the integration of personnel, articles and substances in a suitable environment and workplace to produce and maintain an acceptable standard of safety; due consideration must also be given to foreseeable emergencies and the provision of adequate rescue facilities.

Safe systems of work may be formally written procedures, on a stage-by-stage basis, indicating the stages of the operation, the hazards that can arise and the precautions necessary. Information, instruction and training must be provided in these aspects of safe systems. Where there may be a high degree of foreseeable risk, it may be necessary to operate a permit-to-work system.

Fundamentally, safe systems of work incorporate five basic elements:

1. **The workplace.** Workplaces should be safe in terms of, for example, structural safety, fire protection arrangements, access and egress, layout and arrangement of working areas.
2. **Work equipment.** Many forms of work equipment are used in workplaces – machinery, mobile work equipment and hand tools. Work equipment should be appropriate for the task, with sound design and safety specification. People may need to be informed and trained in the correct use of work equipment.
3. **People at work.** The design of safe systems of work needs to consider the need for safe behaviour, the potential for human error, sound knowledge and skills, willingness to conform on the part of employees, job experience and the training needs of employees.
4. **Materials.** Materials must be safe, must not create risks to health during processing and should meet recommended quality assurance standards, which may incorporate safety specifications. Waste products should be safe for disposal.
5. **Environmental factors.** The control of the working environment, in terms of temperature, lighting, ventilation, noise control and the prevention of airborne pollution, is an essential feature of safe systems of work.

Permit-to-work systems

A permit-to-work system is a form of safe system of work operated where there may be a high degree of foreseeable risk. It incorporates a series of defined stages, each of which must be successfully completed before the next stage can commence, and is dependent on a high level of supervision at all stages of the operation. The decision to operate a permit-to-work system may be one of the outcomes of a work activity risk assessment.

Only a limited number of 'authorized persons' should be nominated for the issue of permits to work, and for overseeing the correct operation of same. 'Authorized persons' could include senior managers and specialist managers, such as a chief engineer.

The fundamental stages of the operation of a permit-to-work system are:

- **Assessment.** The assessment of the situation, including the work to be carried out, the hazards that could arise, the precautions necessary and the methods, materials and equipment to be used, should be undertaken by a senior manager assisted by a health and safety practitioner. The principal objective is to determine the steps to be taken to make the operation safe and the precautions necessary at each stage of the work.

- **Withdrawal from service.** Much will depend upon the nature of the work to be carried out, but this stage entails the withdrawal of any plant, or area of the workplace, from service and entry by unauthorized personnel. This may entail the use of physical barriers, displaying specific notices and the use of personnel to prevent people entering a particular area where, for instance, fumigation is to be undertaken. A declaration that the plant or area has been withdrawn from service should be made on the permit-to-work document.
- **Isolation of sources of energy.** Plant and machinery may need to be mechanically and electrically isolated. Where a complicated isolation procedure is necessary for plant and machinery, it is common to attach an instruction indicating the stages of isolation to the permit to work. A declaration that all sources of energy have been isolated should be made on the document.
- **Cancellation.** After satisfactory completion of the work, a declaration to this effect should be made on the permit by the senior manager overseeing the operation.
- **Return to service.** The manager responsible for the plant or area should check that the work has been completed satisfactorily and that the permit has been cancelled before accepting same back into service. He should then sign to that effect on the form.

At completion of the exercise, the permit to work should be filed for subsequent review of permits issued over a period, such as six months.

Permit-to-work situations

A permit-to-work system is commonly operated in the following situations:

- work on certain electrical systems;
- work in the vicinity of, or requiring the use of, highly flammable, explosive or toxic substances;
- entry into confined spaces, closed vessels and vessels containing agitators or other moving parts;
- welding and cutting operations in workplaces other than workshops;
- work in isolated locations, with difficult access or at high level;
- certain work involving commissioning of new plant;
- certain fumigation activities using hazardous substances;
- certain work involving ionizing radiation;

- work which could cause atmospheric pollution of the workplace; and
- any activities involving contractors in the above operations.

COMPETENT PERSONS

Traditionally, health and safety law has promoted the concept of 'competent persons' for a number of work activities which entail varying degrees of risk. Competent persons are appointed by an employer for certain examination, inspection and testing tasks with respect to work equipment, for undertaking a range of activities where there may be a high degree of foreseeable risk, and for various physical inspection activities involving scaffolds, excavations and lifting operations in construction work.

Fundamentally, a competent person should be appointed by an employer. He should have the appropriate skill, knowledge and experience to, for example, identify defects in equipment, ensure safe working, plan operations involving risk, inspect, examine and test equipment and draw up certain documentation.

In many cases, duties of competent persons are identified in regulations, such as the MHSWR and the Lifting Operations and Lifting Equipment Regulations.

EMERGENCY PROCEDURES

The duty on employers with respect to procedures to be followed in the event of serious or imminent danger is detailed in Regulation 8 of the MHSWR (see Chapter 1).

A well-organized emergency procedure takes account of four stages:

1. **Preliminary action.** This is, perhaps, the most important part of an emergency procedure and refers to:
   (a) the preparation of a plan tailored to meet the specific requirements of the site, products and surroundings;
   (b) briefing of employees on details of the plan, including the position of essential equipment;
   (c) the training of personnel involved and appointment of competent persons for certain actions;
   (d) the implementation of a programme of inspections of potentially hazardous areas, testing of warning systems and specification of evacuation procedures; and
   (e) specifying the date at which the plan will be re-examined and updated.

2. **Action when emergency is imminent.** When there is evidence that an emergency is imminent, this stage will feature procedures for assembly of key personnel, advance warning to external authorities and testing of systems connected with the emergency scheme.

3. **Action during the emergency.** Subject to satisfactory implementation of phases 1 and 2, phase 3 should proceed according to plan. There may however, be unexpected variations in a predicted emergency. Decision-making personnel, selected beforehand for this purpose, will need to make precise and rapid judgements to ensure that appropriate action follows the decisions made.

4. **Ending the emergency.** There must be a procedure for declaring plant, systems and specific areas safe, together with the reoccupation of premises where possible.

Implementing the emergency procedure

The following points must be considered in the implementation of an emergency procedure:

- liaison with external authorities and other organizations;
- the appointment of an emergency controller;
- the designation of an emergency control centre;
- authority for initiating the emergency procedure;
- notification to local authorities;
- call-out of competent persons;
- the taking of immediate action on site;
- evacuation of premises;
- access to records;
- alternative means of communication;
- public relations;
- catering and temporary shelter arrangements;
- contingency arrangements; and
- training of everyone on site in the procedure.

VULNERABLE GROUPS

Certain groups of employees are classed as 'vulnerable' to the risk of injury or disease by virtue of their condition. These groups include new and expectant mothers, young persons, and elderly and disabled workers. Special provisions may need to be made for such persons in addition to those providing protection to a workforce generally.

New or expectant mothers

Risks specific to new or expectant mothers, associated with, for example, exposure to hazardous substances or when undertaking manual handling tasks, must be taken into account in a risk assessment.

Young persons

The MHSWR make specific provisions for the protection of young persons based on their lack of experience, or absence of awareness of existing or potential risks, or the fact that such persons have not yet fully matured (see Chapter 1).

As with new and expectant mothers, the needs and limitations of young persons must be taken into account in any risk assessment undertaken. Similarly, their capabilities as regards health and safety must be taken into account by an employer when entrusting tasks. Fundamentally, young persons need a higher degree of supervision than adult employees, and employers must bear this fact in mind when considering work systems and practices.

Elderly and disabled workers

These groups of workers may be limited in their ability to move swiftly in the event of an emergency and may suffer a range of disabilities which prevent them from undertaking certain tasks, such as manual handling, work at heights and even the operation of machinery. Their capability for work should be assessed by an occupational physician or occupational health nurse on a regular basis.

The limitations of this group of workers should be taken into account in the risk assessment process.

ACCIDENT AND ILL-HEALTH REPORTING AND RECORDING REQUIREMENTS

Reporting of Injuries, Diseases and Dangerous Occurrences Regulations (RIDDOR) 1995

These regulations cover the requirements for employers to report to the relevant enforcing authority, ie the HSE or local authority, specified categories of injury and disease sustained by both people at work and people not at work, along with certain events, known as 'dangerous occurrences', and incidents involving gas and gas appliances.

Important definitions:

- **Accident** includes: (a) an act of non-consensual physical violence done to a person at work; and (b) an act of suicide which occurs on, or in the course of operation of, a relevant transport system.
- **Disease** includes a medical condition.
- **Major injury** (listed in Schedule 1) means:
  - (i) any fracture, other than to the fingers, thumbs and toes;
  - (ii) any amputation;
  - (iii) dislocation of shoulder, hip, knee or spine;
  - (iv) loss of sight (whether temporary or permanent);
  - (v) any chemical or hot metal burn to the eye or any penetrating injury to the eye;
  - (vi) any injury resulting from an electric shock or electrical burn (including any electrical burn caused by arcing or arcing products;
  - (vii) any other injury: (a) leading to hypothermia, heat-induced illness or unconsciousness; (b) requiring resuscitation; or (c) requiring admittance to hospital for more than 24 hours;
  - (viii) loss of consciousness caused by asphyxia or by exposure to a harmful substance or biological agent;
  - (ix) either of the following conditions which result from the absorption of any substance by inhalation, ingestion or through the skin: (a) acute illness requiring medical treatment; or (b) loss of consciousness;
  - (x) acute illness which requires medical treatment where there is reason to believe that this resulted from exposure to a biological agent or its toxins or infected material.
- **Relevant transport system** means a railway, tramway, trolley vehicle system or guided transport system.

Under these regulations:

- The responsible person, ie the employer or a person in control of premises, must *notify* the relevant enforcing authority, ie by telephone or fax, and subsequently make a *report* within 10 days on the approved form, ie Form 2508 (see Figure 2.4):
  - (a) of the death of any person at work as a result of an accident arising out of or in connection with work;
  - (b) of any person at work suffering a specified major injury as a result of an accident arising out of or in connection with work;

Health & Safety at Work etc. Act 1974
The Reporting of Injuries, Diseases and Dangerous Occurrences Regulations 1995

HSE
Health & Safety
Executive

Report of an injury or dangerous occurrence

Filling in this form
This form must be filled in by an employer or other responsible person

Part A

About you
1. What is your name?

2. What is your job title?

3. What is your telephone number?

About your organisation
4. What is the name of your organisation?

5 What is its address and postcode?

6. What type of work does the organisation do?

Part B

About the incident
1. On What date did the incident happen?

/ /

2. At what time did the incident happen
please use the 24- hour clock eg 0600

3. Did the incident happen at the above address?
Yes ☐ Go to question 4

No ☐ Where did the incident happen?

☐ elsewhere in your organisation – give the name address and postcode

☐ at someone else's premises – give the name address and postcode

☐ in a public place - give details of where it happened

If you do not know the postcode, what is the name of the local authority?

4. In what department, or where on the premises, did the incident happen?

Part C

About the injured person
If you are reporting a dangerous occurrence, go to part F.
If more than one person was injured in the same incident, please attach the details asked for in Part C and Part D for each injured person.

1. What is their full name?

2. What is their home address and postcode?

3. What is their home phone number?

4. How old are they?

5. Are they
☐ male?
☐ female?

6. What is there job title?

7. Was the injured person (tick only one box)
☐ one of your employees?

☐ on a training scheme? Give details:

☐ on work experience?

☐ employed by someone else? Give details of the employer:

☐ self-employed and at work?

☐ a member of the public?

Part D

About the injury
1. What was the injury? (eg fracture, laceration)

2. What part of the body was injured?

F2508 (01/96)

continued overleaf

Figure 2.4 *Report of an injury or dangerous occurrence*

3. Was the injury (tick one box that applies)

☐ a fatality?

☐ a major injury or condition? (see accompanying notes)

☐ an injury to an employee or self-employed person which prevented them doing their normal work for more than 3 days?

☐ an injury to a member of the public which meant they had to be taken from the scene of the accident to a hospital for treatment?

4. Did the injured person (tick all boxes that apply)

☐ Become unconscious?

☐ need resuscitation?

☐ remain in hospital for more than 24 hours?

☐ none of the above?

Part E

About the kind of accident
Please tick the one box that best describes what happened, then go to Part G.

☐ contact with moving machinery or material being machined

☐ Hit by a moving, flying or falling object

☐ Hit by a moving vehicle

☐ Hit by something fixed or stationery

☐ Injured while handling, lifting or carrying

☐ Slipped, tripped or fell on the same level

☐ Fell from a height
How high was the fall?

| metres |

☐ Trapped by something collapsing

☐ Drowned or asphyxiated

☐ Exposed to, or in contact with, a harmful substance

☐ Exposed to fire

☐ Exposed to an explosion

☐ Contact with electricity or an electrical discharge

☐ Injured by an animal

☐ Physically assaulted by a person

☐ Another kind of accident (describe it in Part G)

Part F

Dangerous occurrences
Enter the number of the dangerous occurrence you are reporting. (The numbers are given in the the Regulations and in the notes which accompany this form).

Part G

Describing what happened
Give as much detail as you can. For instance
• the name of any substance involved
• the name and type of any machine involved
• the events that led to the incident
• the part played by any people
If it was a personal injury, give details of what the person was doing. Describe any action that has since been taken to prevent a similar incident. Use a separate piece of paper if you need to.

Part H

Your signature
Signature

Date
| / / |

Where to send the form
Please send it to the Enforcing Authority for the place where it happened. If you do not know the Enforcing Authority, send it to the nearest HSE office.

Figure 2.4 *Continued*

(c) of any person who is not at work suffering an injury as a result of an accident arising out of or in connection with work and where that person is taken from the site of the accident to a hospital for treatment in respect of that injury;

(d) of any person who is not at work suffering a major injury as a result of an accident arising out of or in connection with work at a hospital; or

(e) where there is a dangerous occurrence.

- The responsible person must further report as soon as practicable, and in any event within 10 days of the accident, using the approved form, any situation where a person at work is incapacitated for work of a kind which he might reasonably be expected to do, either under his contract of employment or, if there is no such contract, in the normal course of his work, for more than three consecutive days (excluding the day of the accident but including any days which would have not been working days) because of an injury resulting from an accident arising out of or in connection with work.

- Where any employee, as a result of an accident at work, has suffered a reportable injury which is a cause of his death within one year of the date of that accident, the employer must inform the relevant enforcing authority in writing as soon as it comes to his knowledge, whether or not the accident has been reported.

- Where:

  (a) a person at work suffers from any of the occupational diseases specified in column 1 of Part I of Schedule 3 and his work involves one of the activities specified in the corresponding entry in column 2 of that part, or

  (b) a person at an offshore installation suffers from any of the diseases specified in Part II of Schedule 3,

  the responsible person shall forthwith send a report thereof to the relevant enforcing authority on the approved form (Form 2508A), unless he forthwith makes a report thereof to the HSE by some other means so approved (see Figure 2.5).

  The above requirement applies only if:

  (a) in the case of an employee, the responsible person has received a written statement prepared by a registered medical practitioner diagnosing the disease as one of those specified in Schedule 3; or

  (b) in the case of a self-employed person, that person has been informed by a registered medical practitioner that he is suffering from a disease so specified.

- Whenever a conveyor of flammable gas through a fixed pipe distribution system, or a filler, importer or supplier (other than by means of retail trade) of a refillable container containing liquefied petroleum gas receives notification of any death or any major injury which has arisen out of or in connection with the gas distributed, filled, imported or supplied, as the case may be, he must forthwith notify the HSE of the incident and within 14 days send a report on the approved form (Form 2508G).

- Whenever an employer or self-employed person who is a member of a class of person approved by the HSE for the purposes of preamp 3 of the Gas Safety (Installation and Use) Regulations 1994 (ie a CORGI-registered gas installation business) has in his possession sufficient information for it to be reasonable for him to decide that a gas fitting or any flue or ventilation used in connection with that fitting, by reason of its design, construction, manner of installation, modification or servicing, is or has been likely to cause death, or any major injury by reason of:

  (a) accidental leakage of gas,

  (b) inadequate combustion of gas, or

  (c) inadequate removal of the products of combustion of gas,

  he must within 14 days send a report of it to the HSE on the approved form (Form 2508G), unless he has previously reported such information.

- Records must be maintained by the responsible person of all reportable injuries, diseases and dangerous occurrences. This may take the form of a register or, commonly, photocopies of Forms 2508 and 2508A.

Dangerous occurrences

A dangerous occurrence is an event which has significant potential for death, major injury and, in some cases, an adverse effect on the surrounding community. Included in this wide list of events or occurrences are major fires, failure of lifting machinery, explosions, accidents and incidents at level crossings, sinking of craft, insecure tips and the loss of stability or buoyancy of an offshore platform.

Dangerous occurrences are classified in Schedule 2 in five groups, namely:

1. general;
2. mines;
3. quarries;
4. relevant transport systems;
5. offshore workplaces.

Reportable diseases

Reportable diseases are those listed in Schedule 3 of RIDDOR and which relate to a specified activity. They are listed under three groups:

Health & Safety at Work etc. Act 1974
The Reporting of Injuries, Diseases and Dangerous Occurrences Regulations 1995

HSE
Health & Safety
Executive

Report of a case of disease

Filling in this form
This form must be filled in by an employer or other responsible person.

Part A

About you

1. What is your name?

2. What is your job title?

3. What is your telephone number?

About your organisation

4. What is the name of your organisation?

5 What is its address and postcode?

6. Does the affected person usually work at this address?

7. What type of work does the organisation do?

Part B

About the affected person

1. What is their full name?

2. What is their date of birth?

  / /

3. What is their job title?

4. Are they
  ☐ male?
  ☐ female?

5. Is the affected person (tick one box)
  ☐ one of your employees?
  ☐ on a training scheme? Give details:

  ☐ on work experience?
  ☐ employed by someone else? Give details:

  ☐ other? Give details:

F2508A (01/96)

continued overleaf

Figure 2.5 *Report of a case of disease*

Part C

The disease you are reporting

1. Please give:
   - The name of the disease, and the type of work it is associated with: or
   - The name and number of the disease (from schedule 3 of the regulations – see the accompanying notes).

2. What is the date of the statement of the doctor who first diagnosed or confirmed the disease?

    / /

3. What is the name and address of the doctor?

Part D

Describing the work that led to the disease

Please describe any work done by the affected person which might have led to them getting the disease

If the disease is thought to have been caused by exposure to an agent at work (eg a specific chemical) please say what that agent is.

Give any other information which is relevant

Give your description here

Continue your description here

Part E

Your signature

Signature

Date

    / /

Where to send the form
Please send it to the Enforcing Authority for the place where it happened. If you do not know the Enforcing Authority, send it to the nearest HSE office.

For official use
Client number   Location

Event number
                       ☐ INV REP ☐ Y ☐ N

Figure 2.5 *Continued*

1. conditions due to physical agents and the physical demands of work, eg subcutaneous cellulitis of the hand (beat hand);
2. infections due to biological agents, eg brucellosis;
3. conditions due to substances, eg poisoning by, for example, ethylene oxide or methyl bromide.

THE INVESTIGATION OF ACCIDENTS AND INCIDENTS

The investigation of all accidents, ie those resulting in injury and damage, is a reactive strategy in health and safety management. Accidents may result in injury, lost time and damage to premises, plant and equipment. Incidents, that is those events which do not result in injury but result in interruption or stoppage of the work process, also need investigation as they could be the forerunners of future accidents. Similarly, 'near misses', namely those incidents which are unplanned and unforeseeable that could have resulted, but did not result, in injury, property damage or other form of loss, should be investigated.

The purpose of investigation of all these events is to identify their causes, both direct and indirect, not to apportion blame. Most importantly, the investigation of these events produces feedback for incorporation in future safety strategies, the process of an organization learning by its mistakes.

Many accident investigations identify the need for risk assessment of the work activity, workplace and/or work group's operations in particular.

Effective accident investigation should identify all or some of the following:

- whether there has been a breach of statute or regulations by the organization;
- whether there has been a breach of a common law duty and the potential for the injured party suing the organization for negligence or breach of statutory duty;
- whether the accident is reportable to the enforcing authority under RIDDOR;
- evidence of damage to structures, equipment and materials;
- evidence of unsafe working practices, such as failure to follow a safe system of work or the recommendations in a risk assessment;
- evidence of exposure to hazardous substances or the incorrect use of hazardous substances;
- evidence of faulty work equipment and/or the abuse or misuse of work equipment;
- the events leading up to the accident;
- those persons who witnessed the accident; and
- the remedial action necessary to prevent a recurrence.

In serious accident situations, photographs should be taken of the accident scene, and a line sketch with measurements produced indicating the events prior to the accident.

Where it is necessary for witnesses to produce statements, such persons should be cautioned in accordance with the procedures under the Police and Criminal Evidence Act.

In some cases, it may be appropriate to form an investigating committee to ascertain the causes of the accident.

The above factors should also be considered in the investigation of the causes of occupational diseases and conditions, in particular the need to identify the physical, chemical, biological or work-related agent that caused the disease or condition. (See further Chapter 8.)

Feedback from accident investigation

Feedback from accident investigation is important. The outcomes of feedback could include:

- the redesigning of safe systems of work;
- the issuing of specific safety instructions;
- documentation of safety procedures more specifically;
- the establishment of a working group to review safety procedures;
- the identification of information, instruction and training needs for certain groups;
- improved supervision requirements;
- improvements in environmental control, such as lighting;
- the need to raise general awareness of employees and contractors' employees;
- procedures for regulating contractors' activities more effectively;
- the need for the introduction of a planned maintenance programme; and
- the need to improve levels of housekeeping and cleaning.

THE COSTS OF ACCIDENTS, INCIDENTS AND ILL HEALTH

All accidents, incidents and occupational ill health represent varying degrees of loss to an organization. While many managers may complain about 'the cost or burden of health and safety', what many fail to realize is the costs that arise following these events which tend to get written against the operating costs of the organization. Costs can be classified as direct or indirect costs.

Direct costs

Direct costs, sometimes referred to as 'insured costs', include premiums paid annually to an insurance company to cover the employer's liability in terms of claims made by injured employees. Such premiums are effected, to some extent, on the previous claims history of the organization.

Other direct costs can include fines in the criminal courts for breaches of health and safety law.

Indirect costs

These costs are commonly disregarded or not even considered by some employers. As such, they can include:

- treatment costs – the cost of first aid treatment, transport to hospital, charges made by accident and emergency departments of hospitals;
- attendance costs – those costs for the attendance of a local doctor at an accident scene;
- lost time costs – of the injured person, management, first aid staff and others;
- production costs – the extra production costs as a result of lost production following an accident;
- staff costs – through payment of overtime rates following the stoppage in production sometimes following an accident;
- damage costs – such as the replacement of damaged work equipment, structural repairs and the cost of labour to undertake same;
- training and supervision costs – as a result of the need to provide training and increase supervision;
- representation costs – the cost of being represented in the courts by solicitors, barristers and expert witnesses following prosecution by the enforcement agency; and
- miscellaneous costs – such as the replacement of personal items belonging to the injured person and others, eg spectacles, personal clothing and footwear.

In addition to the indirect costs outlined above, there are further indirect costs which could conceivably add 25 per cent to the calculated indirect costs of accidents and ill health. These may include:

- reduced output and performance due to reduced morale following, particularly, a fatal accident to a member of the workforce;
- reduced sales and business as a result of adverse media publicity;

- trade union activity or reaction; and
- increased attention from enforcement agencies.

The costs to an injured employee

In addition to the cost of pain and suffering considered in a civil claim for negligence by an employee against an employer, other personal costs which might be taken into account in such a claim are:

- loss of earnings for the period of absence from work;
- loss of earning capacity due to mental and/or physical injury;
- reduced earning capacity, due to physical disablement;
- legal costs in pursuing a claim (which may be awarded by a judge against the employer).

THE PROVISION OF INFORMATION, INSTRUCTION AND TRAINING

The duty on employers to provide, so far as is reasonably practicable, information, instruction and training to employees and, in some cases, other persons, such as the employees of contractors, is well established in sections 2 and 3 of the HSWA. This duty is also a standard feature of many regulations, such as the Personal Protective Equipment at Work Regulations and the COSHH Regulations.

In particular, the Health and Safety (Information for Employees) Regulations 1998 require that every employer display the standard poster 'Health and Safety Law – What you should know' in a prominent position in every workplace.

Information and instructions

Information and instructions are commonly incorporated in employee handbooks which are issued to employees at the induction training stage. Written in a straight-forward manner, these handbooks incorporate rules for safe working, procedures for reporting accidents and hazards that may arise in the workplace, instructions on the correct use of personal protective equipment, sickness absence procedures, details of the role of the health and safety adviser and trade union safety representatives, safe manual handling procedures and many other topics relevant to the workplace and working practices.

Training

'Training' is defined as 'the systematic development of attitude, knowledge and skill patterns required by an individual to perform adequately a given task or job'. Under the MHSWR, health and safety training must be provided in a range of situations (see Chapter 1).

It is essential that organizations have a formal health and safety training programme directed at all levels of management, including directors, and employees.

Induction training

All employees should receive induction training. Topics for inclusion in induction training include:

- the organization's statement of health and safety policy, with particular reference to the individual responsibilities of all levels of management and employees;
- procedures for reporting hazards, near misses, accidents and ill health arising from work;
- details of hazards specific to the job and the precautions necessary on the part of employees;
- procedures in the event of fire, including means of escape and assembly points;
- current welfare arrangements, ie sanitation, hand washing, showers, clothing storage, facilities for taking meals and first aid arrangements;
- sources of health and safety information available;
- the correct use of personal protective equipment; and
- the role and function of the health and safety adviser.

Orientation training

Orientation training is required, for example, where people:

- change jobs;
- are given new responsibilities, eg promotion to supervisor;
- are required to operate machinery with which they are unfamiliar;
- are required to use hazardous substances for the first time;
- are required to operate a specific safe system of work; and
- move their job to another part of the workplace.

JOINT CONSULTATION AND HEALTH AND SAFETY

Under the HSWA employers have a duty to consult with safety representatives.

Safety Representatives and Safety Committees Regulations 1977

Employers have a duty to consult with trade union appointed safety representatives in the following circumstances and situations thus:

- on the introduction of any measure at the workplace which may substantially affect the health and safety of the employees the safety representatives concerned represent;
- with respect to his arrangements for appointing or, as the case may be, nominating persons (ie competent persons) in accordance with Regulation 6 (1) of the MHSWR;
- with respect to any health and safety information he is required to provide to the employees and safety representatives concerned by or under the relevant statutory provisions;
- on the planning and organization of any health and safety training he is required to provide to employees the safety representatives concerned represent by or under the relevant statutory provisions; and
- on the health and safety consequences for the employees the safety representatives concerned represent of the introduction (including the planning thereof) of new technologies into the workplace.

Functions of safety representatives

Safety representatives have certain functions, namely:

- to make representations to the employer on matters arising from the investigation of hazards, causes of accidents and ill health, and complaints from his members;
- to undertake workplace inspections;
- to investigate hazards and the causes of accidents, incidents and ill health involving the members of his trade union;
- to receive information from inspectors;
- to represent his members in consultation with inspectors; and
- to attend meetings of a safety committee.

Safety committees

Where requested in writing by at least two safety representatives, an employer must form a safety committee. When establishing a safety committee, an employer must:

- consult with the safety representatives making this request and with representatives of the trade union whose members work in any workplace where it is proposed that the safety committee will function;
- post a notice stating the composition of the committee and the workplaces to be covered by same, in a place where it can be easily read by employees;
- establish the committee within three months following the request for its formation.

Health and Safety (Consultation with Employees) Regulations 1996

These regulations brought into operation changes in the law with respect to consultation on health and safety in workplaces where there is no trade union involvement.

Under these regulations employers must consult with employees who are not covered by the Safety Representatives and Safety Committees Regulations. This may be by direct consultation with employees or through representatives of employee safety (ROES).

HSE guidance accompanying the regulations details:

- which employees must be involved;
- the information they must be provided with;
- procedures for the election of ROES;
- the training, time off and facilities they must be provided with; and
- their function in office.

SAFETY PROPAGANDA

Safety propaganda includes all those measures directed at increasing awareness of employees to hazards and the precautions necessary on their part to be safe at work. Much will depend upon the method of communication.

Safety posters

Safety posters are commonly used in workplaces to convey a range of messages about safe working and to be effective:

- they must be appropriate to the hazards to which employees are exposed and the measures necessary on their part to avoid these hazards, eg the wearing of head protection;
- they rapidly lose significance if displayed for periods longer than four weeks and, therefore, must be changed on a regular basis;

- they should relate to any particular safety measures being developed in the organization at that point in time, eg the safe use of hand tools or the introduction of a particular safe system of work; and
- the use of 'horror posters' depicting people with injuries, in many cases, causes employees to 'switch off' to the message being conveyed and is not recommended.

KEY POINTS

- The need for organizations to have clearly documented health and safety management systems is clearly required under health and safety law.
- Accident prevention is concerned with the development and implementation of a range of 'safe place' and 'safe person' strategies.
- All organizations should operate a system for monitoring safety in the workplace.
- The development and implementation of safe systems of work is a prerequisite for good standards of health and safety performance.
- Where there is a high degree of foreseeable risk in certain processes and activities, a permit-to-work system should be operated.
- In many cases, employers need to appoint competent persons to oversee high-risk activities and implement certain procedures.
- Organizations should have a formally documented and well-practised emergency procedure.
- Specific provisions for health and safety must be provided in the case of vulnerable groups of employees.
- Procedures for reporting death at work, major injury and dangerous occurrences to the enforcing authority are covered by RIDDOR.
- The organization of feedback on the outcome of accident investigation is an essential part of the health and safety management system.
- All accidents, ill health and incidents represent substantial losses to organizations.
- Employers have a duty to provide information, instruction and training for employees and to consult with employees on health and safety issues.

3

The working environment

INTRODUCTION

The term 'environment' is of French origin meaning 'the surroundings; that which surrounds us'. The duty on an employer under the HSWA 'to provide and maintain a working environment for his employees that is, so far as is reasonably practicable, safe, without risks to health, and adequate as regards facilities and arrangements for their welfare at work' is well established. This duty is further reinforced by more specific duties under, for example, the Workplace (Health, Safety and Welfare) Regulations (WHSWR) 1992 and in the ACOP to same.

The working environment covers a broad range of issues, including the design of the workplace, structural aspects, control over environmental stressors, such as extremes of temperature, poor lighting and inadequate ventilation, the maintenance of a range of welfare amenity provisions, such as sanitation and washing facilities, and the prevention of overcrowding.

This chapter examines the various aspects of the working environment, in particular duties under the WHSWR and the ACOP to the regulations, and the management systems necessary to ensure a safe and healthy working environment.

THE WORKPLACE REQUIREMENTS

The law relating to health, safety and welfare in the workplace is incorporated in the Workplace (Health, Safety and Welfare) Regulations 1992. These regulations should be read in conjunction with the general duties placed on employers and the self-employed under the MHSWR. The majority of duties under the WHSWR are of an absolute nature.

Regulation 2 – interpretation:

- **Disabled person** has the meaning given by section 1 of the Disability Discrimination Act 1995.
- **Traffic route** means a route for pedestrian traffic, vehicles or both and includes any stairs, staircase, fixed ladder, doorway, gateway, loading bay or ramp.
- **Workplace** means any premises or part of premises which are not domestic premises and are made available to any person as a place of work and includes:
    (a) any place within the premises to which such a person has access while at work; and
    (b) any room, lobby, corridor, staircase, road or other place used as a means of access to or egress from the workplace or where facilities are provided for use in connection with the workplace other than a public road.

Under the WHSWR, employers must:

- ensure that where a workplace is in a building, the building has a stability and solidity appropriate to the nature of the use of the workplace;
- ensure that the workplace and the equipment, devices and systems to which this regulation applies are maintained (including cleaned as appropriate) in an efficient state, in efficient working order and in good repair;
- ensure the equipment, devices and systems are subject to a suitable system of maintenance;

    Note: The equipment, devices and systems to which this regulation applies are:
    (a) equipment and devices a fault in which is liable to result in a failure to comply with any of these regulations;
    (b) mechanical ventilation systems provided pursuant to Regulation 6; and
    (c) equipment and devices intended to prevent or reduce hazards.

- ensure effective and suitable provision is made to ensure that every enclosed workplace is ventilated by a sufficient quantity of fresh or purified air;
- ensure any plant used for complying with the above requirements includes an effective device to give visible or audible warning of any failure of the plant where necessary for reasons of health or safety;
- ensure that, during working hours, the temperature in all workplaces inside buildings is reasonable;

- ensure that the method of heating or cooling is not used which results in the escape into the workplace of fumes, gas or vapour of such character and to such extent that they are likely to be injurious or offensive to any person;
- ensure that a sufficient number of thermometers are provided to enable persons at work to determine the temperature in any workplace inside a building;
- ensure every workplace shall have suitable and sufficient lighting;
- provide and maintain suitable and sufficient emergency lighting in any room in circumstances in which persons at work are specially exposed to danger in the event of failure of artificial lighting;
- keep every workplace and the furniture, furnishings and fittings therein sufficiently clean;
- ensure the surfaces of the floor, wall and ceiling of all workplaces inside buildings are capable of being kept sufficiently clean;
- so far as is reasonably practicable, not allow waste materials to accumulate except in suitable receptacles;
- ensure every room where persons work shall have sufficient floor area, height and unoccupied space for the purposes of health, safety and welfare;
- ensure every workstation is so arranged that it is suitable both for any person at work in the workplace who is likely to work at that workstation and for any work of the undertaking which is likely to be done there;
- provide a suitable seat for each person at work in the workplace whose work includes operations of a kind that the work (or a substantial part of it) can or must be done sitting;
- ensure every floor in a workplace and the surface of every traffic route in a workplace is of a construction that is suitable for the purpose for which it is used;
- so far as is reasonably practicable, ensure every floor in a workplace and the surface of every traffic route in a workplace is kept free from obstructions and from any article or substance which may cause a person to slip, trip or fall;
- provide on all traffic routes suitable and sufficient handrails and, if appropriate, guards;
- so far as is reasonably practicable, take suitable and effective measures, other than by the provision of personal protective equipment and the provision of information, instruction, training and supervision, to prevent either of the events specified below:
  - any person falling a distance likely to cause personal injury;
  - any person being struck by a falling object likely to cause personal injury;
- indicate, where appropriate, any area where there is a risk to health or safety from either of the above events;
- securely fence every traffic route over, across or in an uncovered tank, pit or structure;

- so far as is reasonably practicable, securely cover or fence every tank, pit or structure where there is a risk of a person in the workplace falling into a dangerous substance in the tank, pit or structure;

  Note: 'Dangerous substance' means:
  (a) any substance likely to scald or burn;
  (b) any poisonous substance;
  (c) any corrosive substance;
  (d) any fume, gas or vapour likely to overcome a person; or
  (e) any granular or free-flowing solid substance, or any viscous substance which, in any case, is of a nature or quantity which is likely to cause danger to any person.

- ensure every window or other transparent or translucent surface in a wall or partition and every transparent or translucent surface in a door or gate is, where necessary for reasons of health or safety:
  (a) of safety material or protected against breakage of the material; and
  (b) appropriately marked or incorporating features so as, in either case, to make it apparent;

- ensure no window, skylight or ventilator which is capable of being opened is likely to be opened, closed or adjusted in a manner which exposes any person performing such operation to a risk to his health or safety;

- ensure no window, skylight or ventilator is in a position which is likely to expose any person in the workplace to a risk to his health or safety;

- ensure all windows and skylights in a workplace are of a design or so constructed that they may be cleaned safely (in considering whether a window or skylight is safe, account may be taken of equipment used in conjunction with the window or skylight or of devices fitted to the building);

- ensure every workplace is organized in such a way that pedestrians and vehicles can circulate in a safe manner;

- provide traffic routes that are suitable for the persons or vehicles using them, sufficient in number, in suitable positions and of sufficient size; all traffic routes must be suitably indicated;

- provide doors and gates which are suitably constructed (including being fitted with any necessary safety devices);

- ensure escalators and moving walkways:
  (a) function safely;
  (b) are equipped with any necessary safety devices;
  (c) are fitted with one or more emergency stop controls which are easily identifiable and readily accessible;

- provide suitable and sufficient sanitary conveniences at readily accessible places;

- provide suitable and sufficient washing facilities, including showers if required by the nature of the work or for health reasons, at readily accessible places;

- provide an adequate supply of wholesome drinking water for all persons at work in the workplace;
- provide suitable and sufficient accommodation:
  (a) for any person at work's own clothing which is not worn during working hours; and
  (b) for special clothing which is worn by any person at work but which is not taken home;
- provide suitable and sufficient facilities for any person at work in the workplace to change his clothing in all cases where:
  (a) he has to wear special clothing for the purposes of his work; and
  (b) he cannot, for reasons of health or propriety, be expected to change elsewhere;
- provide suitable and sufficient rest facilities and facilities for taking meals at readily accessible places;
- provide suitable facilities for any person at work who is a pregnant woman or nursing mother to rest; and
- organize, where necessary, those parts of the workplace (including in particular doors, passageways, stairs, showers, wash basins, lavatories and workstations) used or occupied directly by disabled persons at work to take account of such persons.

SAFETY SIGNS AND SIGNALS IN THE WORKPLACE

A safety sign is commonly defined as 'a sign that gives a message about health or safety by a combination of geometric form, safety colour and symbol or text, or both'.

Health and Safety (Safety Signs and Signals) Regulations 1996

These regulations apply to all workplaces, including offshore installations, and work activities where people are employed, but exclude signs and labels used in connection with the supply of substances, products and equipment or the transport of dangerous substances.

The regulations cover the various means of communicating health and safety information, including the use of illuminated signs, hand and acoustic signals, for example fire alarms, spoken communication and the marking of pipework containing dangerous substances. These requirements are in addition to traditional signboards, such as prohibition and warning signs, and include fire safety signs. The signboards specified in the regulations are covered by BS 5378, Parts 1 and 3: *Safety Signs and Colours*.

Safety sign classification

- **Prohibition signs.** These are circular with a red band enclosing a crossed-out symbol on a white background, for example 'No Smoking'.
- **Warning signs.** These signs are triangular in shape with a yellow background and black borders, symbols and text, for example 'LPG – Highly flammable'.
- **Mandatory signs.** These are circular in shape incorporating a white mandatory symbol and/or text on a blue background, for example 'Wear ear protectors'.
- **Safe condition signs.** These are indicated by a green square or rectangle with symbols and lettering in white, such as 'Emergency stop'.

Principal requirements

- Safety signs must be provided where the risk assessment made under the MHSWR indicates that the risk cannot be avoided or adequately controlled in other ways. Where a safety sign would not help to reduce that risk, or where the risk is not significant, a sign is not required. The regulations extend the term 'safety sign' to include hand signals, pipeline markings, acoustic signals and illuminated signs.
- Safety signs, including fire exit, fire fighting and fire alarm signs, must convey the message instead of relying solely on text. Fire exit signs must incorporate the 'running man' pictogram. (The display of the sign 'Fire Exit' without the pictogram is illegal.)
- Signs must be maintained, and employees must receive adequate instruction and training in the meaning of safety signs and the measures to be taken in connection with same.
- The regulations also require, where necessary, the use of road traffic signs within workplaces to regulate road traffic.
- Employers are required to mark pipework containing dangerous substances, for example by identifying and marking pipework at sampling and discharge points. The same symbols or pictograms need to be shown as those commonly seen on containers of dangerous substances, but using the triangular-shaped warning sign.
- Although the regulations specify a code of hand signals for mechanical handling and directing vehicles, they permit other equivalent codes to be used such as BS 6736: *Code of Practice for Hand Signalling Use in Agricultural Operations*, and BS 7121: Part 1: *Code of Practice for the Safe Use of Cranes*.
- Dangerous locations, for example where people may slip, or fall from heights, or where there is low headroom, and traffic routes may need to be marked to meet the requirements of the WHSWR.
- Although these regulations require stores and areas containing significant quantities of dangerous substances to be identified by the appropriate warning sign, ie the same signs used for marking pipework, they mainly have effect in

smaller stores. This is because the majority of sites on which 25 tonnes or more of dangerous substances are stored can be expected to be marked in accordance with the Dangerous Substances (Notification and Marking of Sites) Regulations 1990. These have similar marking requirements for storage of most dangerous substances. Stores need not be marked if they hold very small quantities and the labels on containers can be seen clearly from outside the store.

- Where evacuation from a building is needed, the regulations require the fire alarm signal to be continuous.

MANAGEMENT SYSTEMS

In order to ensure a safe and healthy working environment, a number of management systems are essential. In some cases, the management systems outlined below may well feature as part of the preventive and protective measures arising from a workplace risk assessment.

Workplace safety inspections

In many organizations, managers are expected to inspect their working areas on a daily basis with a view to taking instant remedial action where necessary.

The principal objective of a safety inspection is the identification of hazards and subsequent specification of measures to eliminate or control same. However, a safety inspection may also identify areas of good safety practice and compliance with safe systems of work, and examine maintenance standards, working practices and environmental conditions, along with compliance or otherwise with legal requirements.

Hazard reporting

Under the MHSWR, employees have a duty to inform their employer of situations which represent 'a serious and immediate danger to health and safety' and 'shortcomings in their employer's protection arrangements for health and safety'.

To ensure this process works effectively, employees should be regularly reminded of their duties in this respect. A standard 'hazard report' form should be readily available for employees to record the hazard. The report should also incorporate the following information (see Figure 3.1):

- the nature of the hazard, date and time;
- the verification of the hazard or otherwise by a line manager;
- the remedial action necessary, including financial approval where appropriate;
- the priority of action required;

Hazard Report

1. Report (to be completed by the person identifying a hazard)

Date		Time		Location	

Reported to: Verbal		Written	

Description of hazard (including location, plant machinery, etc)

Signature		Position	

2. Action (to be completed by manager / supervisor)

Hazard Verified:		Yes / No	Date		Time	

Remedial action (including changes in system of work)

Action to be taken by: Name		Signature	

Priority rating   1   2   3   4   5   Estimated cost

Completion: Date   Time

Interim precautions

Signature		(Departmental Manager)

3. Financial Approval (to be completed by authorizing manager)

The expenditure necessary to eliminate or control the above hazard is approved

Signature		Manager/Assistant Manager	Date	

4. Completion

The remedial action described above is complete	Actual cost	

Date		Signatures		Persons completing work
				Departmental manager

5. Safety Advisor Check

I have checked completion of the above and confirm the hazard has been eliminated or controlled

Signature		Safety advisor	Date	

Priority ratings   1 – Immediate
                         2 – 48 hours
                         3 – 1 week
                         4 – 1 month
                         5 – 3 months

Figure 3.1 *Hazard report*

- any interim precautions to be taken;
- notification of the completion of remedial action; and
- verification by the safety adviser that the hazard has been eliminated or controlled.

Hazard reports should be serial-numbered. Regular reviews of the hazards notified and action taken should be carried out to provide feedback for future action prevention strategies.

Planned preventive maintenance

The duty to maintain the workplace, equipment, systems and devices in an efficient state, in efficient working order and in good repair is well recognized. In addition, the need for well-documented management procedures to put this requirement into practice can be identified in the MHSWR.

Documented procedures should take the form of a planned preventive maintenance system which incorporates the following features:

- a description or statement of the structural item, item of equipment or safety system and devices to be maintained;
- the detailed maintenance procedure to be followed;
- the frequency of maintenance necessary;
- individual management responsibility for ensuring the maintenance work is completed satisfactorily; and
- any precautions necessary in the maintenance work.

Planned preventive maintenance procedures should be reviewed on a regular basis.

Cleaning procedures

There is a general duty on employers under the WHSWR to ensure that the workplace and the furniture, furnishings and fittings are kept sufficiently clean. Similar provisions apply in the case of food premises under the Food Safety (General Food Hygiene) Regulations 1995.

As with planned preventive maintenance, cleaning procedures should be documented in the form of cleaning schedules. A cleaning schedule should incorporate the following elements:

- a description or statement of the workplace area, structural surface or item to be cleaned;
- the cleaning procedure, equipment and materials to be used;

- the frequency of cleaning;
- individual management responsibility for ensuring satisfactory completion of the cleaning task; and
- any precautions necessary in, for example, the use of chemical-based cleaning compounds.

A cleaning schedule may further incorporate arrangements for the removal and disposal of waste materials

Environmental monitoring and standards

The quality of the working environment has a significant effect on the well-being of people at work. Poorly controlled working environments can result in a range of health-related conditions, such as heatstroke. Regular monitoring of environmental elements, such as temperature, lighting, ventilation and humidity, is, therefore, an important aspect in the maintenance of a healthy working environment.

Other forms of environmental stressor, such as those arising from the presence of airborne contaminants in the form of dusts, gases, mists, vapours and fumes, or noise and vibration, may be present in a workplace. These can contribute to a range of occupational diseases, such as occupational cancers, noise-induced hearing loss and chemical poisonings. In certain cases, there may be a requirement under regulations, such as the COSHH Regulations and the Noise at Work Regulations, to undertake regular monitoring of the workplace environment.

Formal procedures should be established to ensure environmental monitoring is undertaken and the recommendations arising from such monitoring implemented.

Traffic management on site

The risk of both vehicular traffic accidents and of people being killed or badly injured whilst walking, for example from a car park to a reception area, is a common feature of many workplaces. The regulation of both vehicular and pedestrian traffic is, thus, a critical feature of workplace safety.

Particular attention must be given to providing and maintaining a safe system of work for the loading and unloading of vehicles, together with the operation of lift trucks in loading areas, and for regulating the activities of drivers in terms of internal and external routes taken, parking locations used, speed and the potential for coming into contact with pedestrians, cyclists and other vehicles. Disciplinary action may need to be taken against drivers who exceed established workplace speed limits and restrictions.

Consideration must be given to the number of vehicles, of all classes, using the workplace external and internal traffic routes, with particular attention to the widths of roads and gangways, obstructions arising from overhead structures, parked vehicles, plant and machinery and spillages, and the presence of corners, bends and junctions.

Roadways should be constructed in hard-wearing materials with suitable gradients and drainage for storm water. They should incorporate standard road signs and markings, be well lit, particularly during the winter, and be maintained in a good state of repair.

There should be adequate segregation of pedestrian routes from vehicular routes, by the provision of designated footpaths or walkways, crossings, barriers, bridges and subways, where appropriate. Workshops and production areas should have separate entrances and exits, along with separate personnel entrances.

Internal gangways should be at least 1 metre wide and as straight as possible, marked out, and maintained clear at all times. They should be well lit and all doors connecting with same should open outwards. In many cases a gangway may also be the designated means of escape from a workplace and should be clearly marked as such.

All on-site drivers should receive formal training prior to the use of any form of site transport. Training should incorporate:

- the nature of the site and layout of the main and subsidiary roads, along with internal traffic routes and gangways;
- details of one-way systems in operation;
- dangerous points in the road system, together with the locations of speed limiters;
- locations of pedestrian crossings and walkways;
- locations of fire exits;
- current speed restrictions;
- specific parking locations for internal transport;
- loading and unloading areas and bays; and
- details of contractor activities which may affect transport arrangements.

Maintenance, examination and testing of equipment and devices

The procedure for ensuring the regular examination and testing of certain items of equipment, along with safety devices to machinery, should be specified in conjunction with current legal requirements under, for example, the Electricity at Work Regulations and Memorandum of Guidance (see Chapter 6), the Provision and Use of Work Equipment Regulations (see Chapter 4) and the Lifting Operations and Lifting Equipment Regulations (see Chapter 4).

Special precautions for vulnerable groups

Young persons, new and expectant mothers and disabled persons are the more common vulnerable groups who may need particular care and attention. The risks peculiar to these groups need to be taken into account during the risk assessment process and specific preventive and protective measures installed.

KEY POINTS

- The HSWA places a general duty on employers to ensure, so far as is reasonably practicable, a working environment that is safe, without risks to health and adequate as regards arrangements for welfare.
- The working environment incorporates a range of factors or elements, including the design and structure of workplaces, the prevention or control of environmental stressors and the provision and maintenance of welfare facilities.
- The principal requirements relating to the working environment are incorporated in the WHSWR and accompanying HSC approved code of practice.
- There is an absolute duty on employers to maintain the workplace, equipment, systems and devices in an efficient state, in efficient working order and in good repair.
- The requirements of the WHSWR form part of the relevant statutory provisions which must be taken into account when undertaking a workplace risk assessment.
- Safety signs must comply with the requirements of the Health and Safety (Safety Signs and Signals) Regulations 1996.
- To ensure the maintenance of a safe and healthy working environment, operation of a number of management systems, such as planned preventive maintenance, is essential.

4

Engineering safety

INTRODUCTION

This area of safety is concerned with all manner of work equipment – machinery, lifting equipment, pressure vessels and pressure systems, mechanical handling systems and mobile handling equipment, such as lift trucks. Machinery has always been extensively regulated through statutes and regulations, such as the Factories Act 1961, the Provision and Use of Work Equipment Regulations (PUWER) 1998, Lifting Operations and Lifting Equipment Regulations (LOLER) 1998 and the Pressure Systems Safety Regulations 2000.

Fatal and major injury accidents associated with the use of work equipment are common, and the need for well-designed guarding systems, safety devices and systems of work is a prerequisite of engineering safety management systems.

This chapter reviews the principal hazards associated with machinery, machinery guards and safety devices, the safety features of lifting machinery and tackle, pressure vessels and pressure systems, and mechanical and mobile handling systems, together with the legislation relating to these areas of engineering safety.

MACHINERY HAZARDS

What is a machine?

BS EN 292 *Safeguarding of Machinery* defines a machine as 'an apparatus for applying power, having fixed and moving parts, each with definite functions'. Fundamentally, a machine has:

- operational parts, which perform the primary output function of that machine, such as drilling a hole or pressing sheet metal to a particular shape; and
- non-operational parts, which provide the power or motion to the operational parts, such as the drives to motors.

Operational or functional parts of a machine basically include a 'prime mover' and various forms of transmission machinery. These two terms are defined in the Factories Act 1961 thus:

- **Prime mover** means any engine, motor or other appliance which provides mechanical energy derived from steam, water, wind, electricity, the combustion of fuel or other source.
- **Transmission machinery** means every shaft, wheel, pulley, drum, system of fast and loose pulleys, coupling, clutch, driving belt or other devices by which the motion of a prime mover is transmitted to or received by any machine or appliance.

Machinery-related injuries

BS EN 292 outlines the principal causes of machinery-related injuries thus:

- coming into contact with machinery, or being trapped between the machinery and any material in or at the machinery or any fixed structure;
- being struck by, or becoming entangled in motion in the machinery;
- being struck by parts of the machinery ejected from it;
- being struck by material ejected from the machinery.

The majority of machinery-related hazards are associated with the design features of machinery. These hazards can be classified thus:

- **Traps.** Traps may take three forms:
  - **Reciprocating traps.** This type of trap is featured in the horizontal or vertical movement of machinery, such as power presses and machines incorporating rams, such as compacting machinery. At the point where the injury occurs, the limb is stationary.
  - **Shearing traps.** This form of trap involves a guillotine motion where a moving part of the machine traverses a fixed part, or where two moving parts traverse each other, as with a pair of scissors or shears. Various forms of metal cutting machinery incorporate this form of trap.
  - **In-running nips.** Nips are created for instance, where a moving belt meets a roller, where a moving belt meets a pulley, and where two moving rollers, drums or toothed wheels meet (see Figure 4.1).

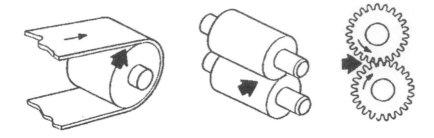

Figure 4.1 *In-running nips*

- **Entanglement.** Hair, clothing, such as sleeves, and limbs can become entangled in rotating shafts, drills or the chucks to drilling machinery (see Figure 4.2).

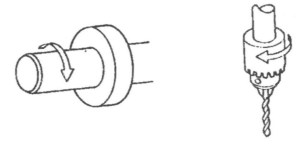

Figure 4.2 *Examples of risk of entanglement*

- **Ejection.** Metal particles from items being machined and the actual parts of a machine may be ejected from a machine. Grinders, for instance, can emit metal particles and grindstone particles. In some cases, a grinding wheel, or abrasive wheel, may burst. Drilling machines may emit part of a broken drill after breakage of the drill.
- **Contact.** Hand or body contact with certain parts of machinery can result in injury, for instance direct burns from hot surfaces, friction burns from moving belts and grinding wheels, and hand injuries from projecting metal fasteners on moving belts.

Events leading to injury

Common examples of events leading to machinery-related injury include:

- unexpected start-up or movement of machinery;
- a person reaching into a feed device;

- uncovenanted stroke by a machine; and
- actual machine failure.

HAND TOOLS

Approximately 10 per cent of all lost-time injuries are associated with the abuse and misuse of hand tools, commonly causing a range of injuries, such as deep cuts, amputations of fingers, blinding and severing of veins and arteries.

The duty to maintain hand tools 'in an efficient state, in efficient working order and in good repair' is a basic requirement of the PUWER. This implies the need for frequent inspections of hand tools to ensure their relative safety. The correct use of hand tools should be ensured through training and constant supervision of users. Hand tools used by contractors and their employees should also be subject to regular inspection.

PROVISION AND USE OF WORK EQUIPMENT REGULATIONS 1998

The original version of these regulations implemented the European Council directive 'concerning the minimum health and safety requirements for the use of work equipment by workers at work', generally known as the 'Machinery Safety' Directive.

The regulations are supported by guidance prepared by the HSE and HSC. The majority of the requirements are of an absolute nature.

Important definitions:

- **Work equipment** means any machinery, appliance, apparatus or tool or installation for use at work (whether exclusively or not).
- **Use** in relation to work equipment means any activity involving work equipment and includes starting, stopping, programming, setting, transporting, repairing, modifying, maintaining, servicing and cleaning.

Under the regulations, employers must:

- ensure that work equipment is so constructed or adapted as to be suitable for the purpose for which it is used or provided;
- in selecting work equipment, have regard to the working conditions and to the risks to health and safety of persons which exist in the premises or undertaking in which that work equipment is to be used and any additional risk posed by the use of that work equipment;

- ensure that work equipment is used only for operations for which, and under conditions for which, it is suitable;
  Note: 'Suitable' means suitable in any respect which it is reasonably foreseeable will affect the health or safety of any person.
- ensure that work equipment is maintained in an efficient state, in efficient working order and in good repair;
- ensure that where any machinery has a maintenance log, the log is kept up to date;
- ensure that where the safety of work equipment depends on the installation conditions, it is inspected:
  (a) after installation and before being put into service for the first time; or
  (b) after assembly at a new site or in a new location,

  to ensure that it has been installed correctly and is safe to operate;
- ensure that work equipment exposed to conditions causing deterioration which is liable to result in dangerous situations is inspected:
  (a) at suitable intervals, and
  (b) each time that exceptional circumstances which are liable to jeopardize the safety of the work equipment have occurred,

  to ensure that health and safety conditions are maintained and that any deterioration can be detected and remedied in good time;
- ensure that the result of an inspection made under this regulation is recorded and kept until the next inspection under this regulation is recorded;
- ensure that no work equipment:
  (a) leaves his undertaking; or
  (b) if obtained from the undertaking of another person, is used in his undertaking,

  unless it is accompanied by physical evidence that the last inspection required to be carried out under this regulation has been carried out;
- where the use of work equipment is likely to involve a specific risk to health or safety, ensure that:
  (a) the use of that work equipment is restricted to those persons given the task of using it; and
  (b) repairs, modifications, maintenance or servicing of that work equipment is restricted to those persons who have been specifically designated to perform operations of that description (whether or not they are also authorized to perform other operations);
- ensure that the persons designated for the purposes of the above paragraph have received adequate training related to any operations in respect of which they have been so designated;

- ensure that all persons who use work equipment have available to them adequate health and safety information and, where appropriate, written instructions pertaining to the use of that work equipment;
- ensure that any of his employees who supervises or manages the use of work equipment has available to him adequate health and safety information and, where appropriate, written instructions pertaining to the use of that work equipment;
- ensure that the information and instructions required by either of the above paragraphs shall include information and, where appropriate, written instructions on:
  (a) the conditions in which and the methods by which the work equipment may be used;
  (b) foreseeable abnormal situations and the action to be taken if such a situation were to occur; and
  (c) any conclusions to be drawn from experience in using the work equipment;
  Note: Information and instruction required by this regulation shall be readily comprehensible to those concerned.
- ensure that all persons who use work equipment have received adequate training for the purposes of health and safety, including training in the methods which may be adopted when using the work equipment, any risks which such use may entail and the precautions to be taken;
- ensure that any of his employees who supervises or manages the use of work equipment has received adequate training for purposes of health and safety, including training in the methods which may be adopted when using the work equipment, any risks which such use may entail and precautions to be taken;
- ensure that an item of work equipment conforms at all times with any essential requirements, other than requirements which, at the time of its being first supplied or put into service in any place in which these regulations apply, did not apply to work equipment of its type;
  Note: 'Essential requirements', in relation to an item of work equipment, means requirements relating to the design and construction of work equipment of its type in any of the instruments listed in Schedule 1 (being instruments which give effect to Community directives concerning the safety of products).
- ensure that measures are taken in accordance with paragraph 2 which are effective:
  (a) to prevent access to any dangerous part of machinery or to any rotating stock-bar; or
  (b) to stop the movement of any dangerous part of machinery or rotating stock-bar before any part of a person enters a danger zone;

The measures required by paragraph 1 shall consist of:

(a) the provision of fixed guards enclosing every dangerous part or rotating stock-bar where and to the extent that it is practicable to do so, but where or to the extent that it is not, then

(b) the provision of other guards or protection devices where and to the extent that it is practicable to do so, but where or to the extent that it is not, then

(c) the provision of jigs, holders, push-sticks or similar protection appliances used in conjunction with the machinery where and to the extent that it is practicable to do so, and the provision of information, instruction, training and supervision as is necessary.

Note: All guards and protection devices provided under sub-paragraph (a) or (b) of paragraph 2 shall:

(a) be suitable for the purpose for which they are provided;

(b) be of good construction, sound material and adequate strength;

(c) be maintained in an efficient state, in efficient working order and in good repair;

(d) not give rise to any increased risk to health or safety;

(e) not be easily bypassed or disabled;

(f) be situated at sufficient distance from the danger zone;

(g) not unduly restrict the view of the operating cycle of the machinery, where such a view is necessary;

(h) be so constructed or adapted that they allow operations necessary to fit or replace parts and for maintenance work, restricting access so that it is allowed only to the area where the work is to be carried out and, if possible, without having to dismantle the guard or protection device.

All protection appliances provided under sub-paragraph (c) of paragraph 2 shall comply with sub-paragraphs (a) to (d) and (g) of paragraph 3.

In this regulation:

– **danger zone** means any zone in or around machinery in which a person is exposed to a risk to health or safety from contact with a dangerous part of machinery or a rotating stock-bar;

– **stock-bar** means any part of a stock-bar which projects beyond the head-stock of a lathe.

● take measures to ensure that the exposure of a person using work equipment to any risk to his health or safety from any hazard specified in paragraph 3 is either prevented or, where that is not reasonably practicable, adequately controlled;

Note: The measures required by paragraph 1 shall:

(a) be measures other than the provision of personal protective equipment or of information, instruction, training and supervision, so far as is reasonably practicable; and

(b)   include, where appropriate, measures to minimize the effects of the hazard as well as to reduce the likelihood of the hazard occurring.

The hazards referred to in paragraph 1 are:

(a)   any article or substance falling or being ejected from work equipment;

(b)   rupture or disintegration of parts of work equipment;

(c)   work equipment catching fire or overheating;

(d)   the unintended or premature discharge of any article or of any gas, dust, liquid, vapour or other substance which, in each case, is produced, used or stored in the work equipment;

(e)   the unintended or premature explosion of the work equipment or any article or substance produced, used or stored in it.

Note: **Adequate** means adequate having regard only to the nature of the hazard and the nature and degree of exposure to the risk, and **adequately** shall be construed accordingly.

- ensure that work equipment, parts of work equipment and any article or substance produced, used or stored in work equipment which, in each case, is at a high or very low temperature shall have protection where appropriate so as to prevent injury to any person by burn, scald or sear;

- ensure that, where appropriate, work equipment is provided with one or more controls for the purposes of:

(a)   starting the work equipment (including restarting after a stoppage for any reason); or

(b)   controlling any change in the speed, pressure or other operating conditions of the work equipment where such conditions after the change result in risk to health and safety which is greater than or of a different nature from such risks before the change;

- ensure that, where a control is required by the above paragraph, it shall not be possible to perform any operation mentioned in sub-paragraph (a) or (b) of that paragraph except by a deliberate action on such control;

- ensure that, where appropriate, work equipment is provided with one or more readily accessible controls the operation of which will bring the work equipment to a safe condition in a safe manner;

Note: Any control shall bring the work equipment to a complete stop where necessary for reasons of health and safety.

Any control shall, if necessary for reasons of health and safety, switch off all sources of energy after stopping the functioning of the work equipment.

Any control shall operate in priority to any control which starts or changes the operating conditions of the work equipment.

- ensure that, where appropriate, work equipment is provided with one or more emergency stop controls unless it is not necessary by reason of the nature of the hazards and the time taken for the work equipment to come to a complete stop as a result of the action of any control;

- ensure that all controls for work equipment are clearly visible and identifiable, including by appropriate marking where necessary;
- except where necessary, ensure that no control for work equipment is in a position where any person operating the control is exposed to risk to his health or safety;
- ensure where appropriate:
  (a) that, so far as is reasonably practicable, the operator of any control is able to ensure from the position of that control that no person is in a place where he would be exposed to any risk to his health or safety as a result of the operation of that control, but where or to the extent that it is not reasonably practicable
  (b) that, so far as is reasonably practicable, systems of work are effective to ensure that, when work equipment is about to start, no person is in a place where he would be exposed to a risk to his health or safety as a result of the work equipment starting, but where neither of these is reasonably practicable
  (c) that an audible, visible or other suitable warning is given by virtue of Regulation 24 whenever work equipment is about to start;
- ensure, so far as is reasonably practicable, that all control systems of work equipment are:
  (a) safe; and
  (b) are chosen making due allowances for the failures, faults and constraints to be expected in the planned circumstances of use;
  Note: A control system shall not be safe unless:
  (a) its operation does not create an increased risk to health or safety;
  (b) it ensures, so far as is reasonably practicable, that any fault in or damage to any part of the control system or the loss of supply of any source of energy used by the work equipment cannot result in additional or increased risk to health or safety;
  (c) it does not impede the operation of any other control.
- ensure that, where appropriate, work equipment is provided with suitable means to isolate it from all its sources of energy;
  Note: The means mentioned in the above paragraph shall not be suitable unless they are clearly identifiable and readily accessible.
- take appropriate measures to ensure that reconnection of any energy source to work equipment does not expose any person using the work equipment to any risk to his health or safety;
- ensure that work equipment or any part of work equipment is stabilized by clamping or otherwise where necessary for purposes of health or safety;

- ensure that suitable and sufficient lighting, which takes account of the operations to be carried out, is provided at any place where a person uses work equipment;
- take appropriate measures to ensure that work equipment is so constructed or adapted that, so far as is reasonably practicable, maintenance operations which involve a risk to health or safety can be carried out while the work equipment is shut down or, in other cases:
  (a) maintenance operations can be carried out without exposing the person carrying them out to a risk to his health or safety; or
  (b) appropriate measures can be taken for the protection of any person carrying out maintenance operations which involve a risk to his health or safety;
- ensure that work equipment is marked in a clearly visible manner with any marking appropriate for reasons of health and safety;
- ensure that work equipment incorporates any warnings or warning devices which are appropriate for the reasons of health and safety;
  Note: Warnings given by warning devices on work equipment shall not be appropriate unless they are unambiguous, easily perceived and easily understood.
- ensure that no employee is carried by mobile work equipment unless:
  (a) it is suitable for carrying persons; and
  (b) it incorporates features for reducing to as low as is reasonably practicable risks to his safety, including risks from wheels and tracks;
- ensure that, where there is a risk to an employee riding on mobile work equipment from its rolling over, it is minimized by:
  (a) stabilizing the work equipment;
  (b) a structure which ensures that the work equipment does no more than fall on its side;
  (c) a structure giving sufficient clearance to anyone being carried if it overturns further than that; or
  (d) a device giving comparable protection;
- where there is a risk of anyone being carried by mobile work equipment being crushed by its rolling over, ensure that it has a suitable restraining system for him;
- ensure that a fork-lift truck which carries an employee is adapted or equipped to reduce to as low as is reasonably practicable the risk to safety from its overturning;
- ensure that where self-propelled work equipment may, while in motion, involve risk to the safety of persons:
  (a) it has facilities for preventing it being started by an unauthorized person;
  (b) it has appropriate facilities for minimizing the consequences of a collision where there is more than one item of rail-mounted work equipment in motion at the same time;
  (c) it has a device for braking and stopping;

(d) where safety constraints so require, emergency facilities operated by readily accessible controls or automatic systems are available for braking and stopping the work equipment in the event of failure of the main facility;

(e) where the driver's direct field of vision is inadequate to ensure safety, there are adequate devices for improving his vision so far as is reasonably practicable;

(f) if provided for use at night or in dark places: (i) it is equipped with lighting appropriate to the work being carried out; and (ii) it is otherwise sufficiently safe for such use;

(g) if it, or anything carried or towed by it, constitutes a fire hazard and is liable to endanger employees, it carries appropriate fire-fighting equipment unless such equipment is kept sufficiently close to it;

- ensure that where remote-controlled self-propelled work equipment involves a risk to safety while in motion:
  (a) it stops automatically once it leaves its control range; and
  (b) where the risk is of crushing or impact it incorporates features that guard against such risk unless other appropriate devices are able to do so;

- where the seizure of the drive shaft between mobile work equipment and its accessories or anything towed is likely to involve a risk to safety:
  (a) ensure that the work equipment has a means of preventing such seizure; or
  (b) where such seizure cannot be avoided, take every possible measure to avoid an adverse effect on the safety of an employee;

- ensure that where:
  (a) mobile work equipment has a shaft for the transmission of energy between it and other mobile work equipment; and
  (b) the shaft could become soiled or damaged by contact with the ground while uncoupled;
  the work equipment has a system for safeguarding the shaft.

- ensure that a power press is not put into service for the first time after installation, or after assembly at a new site or in a new location, unless:
  (a) it has been thoroughly examined to ensure that it: (i) has been installed correctly; and (ii) would be safe to operate; and
  (b) any defect has been remedied;

- ensure that a guard, other than one to which the paragraph below relates, or protection device is not put into service for the first time on a power press unless:
  (a) it has been thoroughly examined when in position on that power press to ensure that it is effective for its purpose; and
  (b) any defect has been remedied;

- ensure that a part of a closed tool which acts as a fixed guard is not used on a power press unless:

(a) it has been thoroughly examined when in position on any power press in the premises to ensure that it is effective for its purpose; and

(b) any defect has been remedied;

- for the purpose of ensuring that health and safety conditions are maintained, and that any deterioration can be detected and remedied in good time, ensure that:

(a) every power press is thoroughly examined, and its guards and protection devices are thoroughly examined when in position on that power press: (i) at least every 12 months, where it has fixed guards only; or (ii) at least every 6 months, in other cases; and (iii) each time that exceptional circumstances have occurred which are liable to jeopardize the safety of the power press or its guards or protection devices; and

(b) any defect is remedied before the power press is used again.

- ensure that a power press is not used after the setting, resetting or adjustments of its tools, save in trying out its tools or save in die proving, unless:

(a) its every guard and protection device has been inspected and tested while in position on the power press by a person appointed in writing by the employer who is: (i) competent; or (ii) undergoing training for that purpose and acting under the immediate supervision of a competent person, and who has signed a certificate which complies with the paragraph below; or

(b) the guards and protection devices have not been altered or disturbed in the course of the adjustment of its tools;

- ensure that a power press is not used after the expiration of the fourth hour of a working period unless its every guard and protection device has been inspected and tested while in position on the power press by a person appointed in writing by the employer who is:

(a) competent; or

(b) undergoing training for that purpose and acting under the immediate supervision of a competent person,

and who has signed a certificate that complies with the paragraph below;

Note: A certificate shall:

(a) contain sufficient particulars to identify every guard and protection device inspected and tested and the power press on which it was positioned at the time of the inspection and test;

(b) state the date and time of the inspection and test; and

(c) state that every guard and protection device on the power press is in position and effective for its purpose.

Working period, in relation to a power press, means:

(a) the period in which the day's or night's work is done; or

(b) in premises where a shift system is in operation, a shift.

A person making a thorough examination for an employer shall:

(a) notify the employer forthwith of any defect in a power press or its guard or protection device which in his opinion is or could become a danger to persons;

(b) as soon as is practicable make a report of the thorough examination to the employer in writing authenticated by him or on his behalf by signature or equally secure means and containing the information specified in Schedule 3; and

(c) where there is in his opinion a defect in a power press or its guard or protection device which is or could become a danger to persons send a copy of the report as soon as is practicable to the enforcing authority for the premises in which the power press is situated.

A person making an inspection and test for an employer shall forthwith notify the employer of any defect in a guard or protection device which in his opinion is or could become a danger to persons and the reason for his opinion.

- ensure that the information in every report is kept available for inspection for two years after it is made;
- ensure that a certificate is kept available for inspection:
   (a) at or near the power press to which it relates until superseded by a later certificate; and
   (b) after that, until six months have passed since it was signed.

Implications for employers

The implications for employers are systems related, namely:

- the assessment of risks at the selection stage of new work equipment in terms of:
   – the actual construction of the equipment;
   – the intended use of the equipment;
   – its suitability for use in the workplace; and
   – the conditions under which it is to be used;
- ongoing safety assessment of existing work equipment;
- the implementation of formally documented planned maintenance systems;
- designation of certain trained persons to undertake identified high-risk activities, such as maintenance or fault finding without guards in position;
- the provision of information, instruction and training for staff using any form of work equipment; and
- the development, documentation and implementation of management procedures aimed at ensuring safe use of work equipment in all work situations, including requirements for the inspection of work equipment.

WORK EQUIPMENT RISK ASSESSMENT

Under the MHSWR and the PUWER, there may be a need for employers to assess the risks arising from the use or operation of work equipment. In this exercise, in addition to considering the 'relevant statutory provisions', ie the requirements of the PUWER, the following factors should be taken into account:

- design features of the equipment – the form and distribution of harm;
- the actual persons at risk and the general circumstances of operation; and
- specific events leading to injury.

One of the main outcomes of a work equipment risk assessment may be the need to provide a better standard of guarding, in conjunction with a safety device, in some cases.

MACHINERY GUARDING

Machinery guards can be largely classified under five headings in order of relative safety. In many cases, the guard will be linked with a safety device.

Fixed guards

These are the most effective form of guard. They have no moving parts associated with them, or dependent on the mechanism of any machinery, and when in position they prevent access to a danger point or area (see Figure 4.3).

They are principally used to prevent access to non-operational parts and may take the form of a solid casting, sheet metal (minimum 18 SWG – 1.22 millimetres), perforated or expanded metal, 'Weldmesh' (minimum 14 SWG), safety glass panels or polycarbonate panels.

Interlocking guards

These are guards that have a movable part so connected with the machinery controls that:

- the part(s) of the machinery causing danger cannot be set in motion until the guard is closed;
- the power is switched off and the motion braked before the guard can be opened sufficiently to allow access to the dangerous parts; and
- access to the danger point or area is denied while the danger exists.

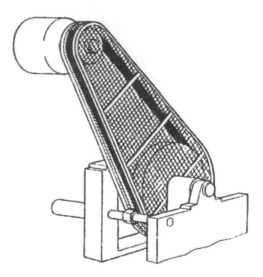

Figure 4.3 *Fixed guard to transmission machinery*

An interlocking guard is further defined as 'a moving guard which, in the closed position, prevents all access to the dangerous parts'. The control gear for starting up cannot be operated until the guard is fully closed and the guard cannot be opened until the dangerous moving parts have come to rest.

For a true interlock system, all moving parts must be at rest before the guard or gate can be opened. Some interlocks control only the power supply, and others, the power supply and movement of parts. In order to achieve the same level of safety as with a fixed guard, the reliability and maintenance of interlocking guards are significant.

Methods of interlocking include:

- mechanical;
- electromechanical;
- pneumatic (compressed air);
- hydraulic (electro) – the use of hydraulic fluid to vary pressure;
- key exchange (electrical); and
- simple electrical.

Automatic guards

These are guards that are associated with, and dependent upon, the mechanism of the machinery and operate so as to remove physically from the danger area any part of a person exposed to danger. This form of guard incorporates a device so fitted in relation to the dangerous parts that the operator is automatically prevented from

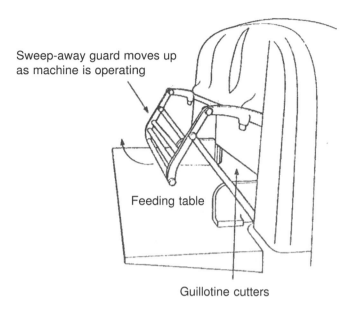

Sweep-away guard moves up
as machine is operating

Feeding table

Guillotine cutters

Figure 4.4   _Guarding to a power-operated guillotine_

coming into contact with same. Typical machines using this system of guarding are power presses, press brakes and certain types of guillotine (see Figure 4.4).

Here the guard is totally independent of the operator, and the function of the guard is to remove the operator from the dangerous action of the machine by means of a moving barrier or arm which sweeps outwards. There may be some degree of risk in that the operator can be injured by the moving barrier, and this type of guard is only suitable for large, slow-moving barriers, as with presses. These guards operate on a side-to-side, sweep-away or push-out motion.

Automatic guards have a number of disadvantages:

- risk of injury to the operator as a result of the sweep-away motion;
- the linkages to the motion must be rigidly connected as they can become loose through constant use;
- when the linkages become worn the guard is often racing the tools to maintain safe operation; and
- they need extensive maintenance and frequent inspection.

Distance guards

These are guards which do not completely enclose a danger point or area but which place it out of normal reach. The guard may incorporate a tunnel, fixed grill or rail positioned at sufficient distance so that access to the moving parts cannot be gained except through a deliberately unsafe act.

Adjustable guards

These guards incorporate an adjustable element which, once adjusted, remains in that position during a particular operation. This is the least reliable form of guard in that it requires the operator to adjust same to the safe position prior to the operation of the machine. Adjustable guards are commonly used in conjunction with vertical drilling machinery and certain types of woodworking machinery, such as circular saws (see Figure 4.5) and bandsaws (see Figure 4.6).

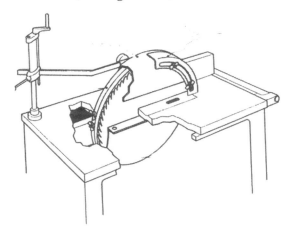

Figure 4.5   *Guards for a floor-mounted circular saw*

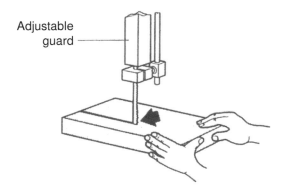

Figure 4.6   *Adjustable guard to a bandsaw blade*

SAFETY DEVICES

A safety device is a protective appliance, other than a guard, which eliminates or reduces danger before access to a danger point or area can be achieved. Most safety devices operate on a trip system.

Trip devices

A trip device operates on the basis whereby any approach by a person beyond the safe limit of machinery causes the device to actuate and stop the machinery, or reverse its motion, thus preventing or minimizing injury at the danger point.

Trip devices take a number of forms (see Figures 4.7 and 4.8):

- mechanical;
- photoelectric;
- pressure-sensitive mat;
- ultrasonic devices;
- two-hand control devices;
- overrun devices; and
- mechanical restraint devices.

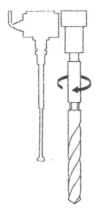

Figure 4.7   *Telescopic trip device for a drilling machine*

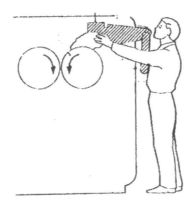

Figure 4.8   *Safety trip bar on a horizontal two-roll mill*

SAFETY MECHANISMS

Various forms of safety mechanism are commonly used in conjunction with guards and safety devices. The detailed design of the mechanism affects the safety of the operator. When assessing machinery, the following factors should be considered:

- **Reliability.** Given the conditions a mechanism or single component is subjected to over a period of time, it must perform in a reliable way all the time. Warning systems must also be reliable to the extent that they operate for the purposes for which they are designed. They should be reliable when exposed to workplace conditions, such as vibration, shock, water, steam, etc.
- **Precise operation.** The mechanism should operate positively, eg precise linkages between rams and guards. The transmission angle on linkages must be minimal, and control over wear on linkages is essential.
- **Protection against operator abuse and misuse.** Abuse is associated with the operator trying to open a guard before it is due to open, causing wear, and as a result of harsh treatment. Misuse, on the other hand, implies a calculated attempt to defeat the safety mechanism. Mechanisms must, therefore, be designed to prevent both abuse and misuse.
- **Fail-safe.** When the component or mechanism fails, it must do so in such a way that the machine stops and the guard stays closed. This cannot always be achieved, however.
- **Correct method of assembly.** Correct assembly of the safety mechanism is vital.

SECOND-HAND, HIRED AND LEASED WORK EQUIPMENT

Second-hand equipment

In situations where existing work equipment is sold by one company to another and brought into use by the second company, it becomes 'new equipment' and must meet the requirements for such equipment, even though it is second-hand. This means that the purchasing company will need to ascertain that the equipment meets the specific hardware provisions of the PUWER before putting it into use.

Hired and leased equipment

Such equipment is treated in the same way as second-hand equipment, namely that it is classed as 'new equipment' at the hire/lease stage. On this basis, organizations hiring or leasing an item of work equipment will need to check that it meets the requirements of Regulations 11 to 24 before putting it into use.

MOBILE HANDLING EQUIPMENT

Mobile handling equipment includes lift trucks, telescopic materials handlers and certain vehicles used in construction and allied work, such as dumpers and tipper lorries. The majority of accidents are associated with lift trucks of various types. The principal hazards are outlined below.

The principal hazards

Hazards to drivers include:

- overturning through overloading of the forks, or skidding on wet and slippery surfaces;
- contact with structural items, such as doorways, walls and pillars;
- collapse of pallet stacks and pallet racking systems;
- heavy items falling from high-level storage;
- collision with other trucks and vehicles; and
- electric shock from battery-charging equipment and acid burns from battery fluids.

In addition, other persons may be seriously injured through contact with these vehicles, perhaps as pedestrians or as drivers of other trucks.

Safe driving requirements

In any consideration of safe truck driving, the following aspects must be considered.

The driver

Drivers should be in good health, with a good level of hearing and vision. They should normally be over 18 years, and have taken an approved training course.

A number of basic rules should apply with all lift truck operations. Drivers should:

- regulate speed with visibility;
- use the horn where necessary;
- look out for pedestrians and other vehicles;
- drive in reverse when the load obscures the vision;
- travel with the forks down with no movement of the forks when in motion;
- use prescribed lift truck routes only;
- not carry passengers;
- comply with site speed limits, eg 10 mph;
- take care when reversing, using the horn as necessary;

- not park in front of fire exits or appliances;
- slow down on wet or bad surfaces;
- use the hand brake and tilt mechanism correctly;
- take care on ramps and not turn on ramps; and
- when leaving the truck, set the controls in neutral with the forks down, power off and brakes on.

Unauthorized use of trucks should result in disciplinary action.

The truck

Trucks should be serviced regularly, including a 12-monthly examination of the chains. The driver should undertake a daily check, prior to starting or handover, of brakes, lights, horn, steering, battery, hydraulics and speed controls. Any defects should be reported immediately. Defective or damaged trucks should not be used.

The system of work

The following rules are necessary to ensure a safe system of work, namely:

- no exceeding the maximum-rated load capacity;
- loads should be placed dead centre;
- drive with the forks well under the load, with the load firmly located against the fork carriage and the mast tilted to suit the load being carried;
- sling loads only at designated slinging points;
- take care at overhead openings and where there is pipework, ducting and conduits;
- never move a load which looks unsafe;
- no use of broken or defective pallets or pallets of inadequate strength for the load;
- move tines gently into the pallet before lifting and check the stability of the stack before removal of the tines; and
- when stacking, take care to position the pallet load safely; use the inching facility when necessary.

MECHANICAL HANDLING EQUIPMENT

Mechanical handling commonly entails the operation of different forms of conveyor system in a workplace. The following are the more commonly used types of conveyor system:

- **Belt conveyors.** Belt conveyors may be flat or troughed and are frequently used for transporting materials over long distances, for example from a quarry to a processing plant, in the case of limestone and clay. The flat type is commonly used for transporting bulky items or boxed goods, whereas the trough type conveys loose materials, such as grain, coal and aggregates.
- **Roller conveyors.** These operate on the gravity principle, or may be powered, for the transfer of standard loads. The powered type of roller conveyor is commonly used where level or slightly inclined runs are installed, where manual pushing of loads along a conveyor is impracticable, or where the incline necessary for gravity movement is not possible.
- **Chain conveyors.** These may be of the scraper type, used for pushing materials along a fixed trough. Overhead chain conveyors employ hangers attached to the chain from which are suspended the items needing transfer. Trolley-type conveyors incorporate specially designed trolleys mounted on a guide or rail system and are used in, for instance, the movement of vehicle bodies in vehicle assembly.
- **Screw conveyors.** This form of conveyor comprises a rotating screw or auger contained inside a fixed or portable housing. It is used for the transfer of loose or free-flowing materials, such as grain, solid fuels and flour, over short distances.
- **Slat conveyors.** These conveyors comprise a series of wooden or metal slats moving on side chains. They are commonly used for the transfer of boxed or sacked goods and can incorporate inclined levels for the transfer of goods between floors in a workplace.

The principal hazards

The more common hazards associated with all types of conveyor are:

- traps or nips between moving parts, eg between a conveyor chain and chain wheels, or between a moving belt and rollers;
- traps between moving and fixed parts, eg between the screw of a screw conveyor and the edge of the feed opening in the transfer tube;
- hazards associated with sharp edges arising from worn conveyor chains and belts, which may be exposed;
- traps and nips created by drive mechanisms, as with V-belts and pulleys, chains and sprockets; and
- traps created at transfer points between two conveyors, eg between a belt conveyor and a roller conveyor.

The guarding of conveyors

Conveyors generally require guards at identified danger points. Wherever practicable, fixed guards should be installed. Interlocked guards should be installed for dangerous parts of the system where operators need frequent access. In some cases, a tunnel guard, a form of distance guard, may be appropriate at, for example, feed points to the conveyor system. Tunnel guards may be fixed or interlocking.

LIFTING OPERATIONS AND LIFTING EQUIPMENT REGULATIONS (LOLER) 1998

These regulations apply to all sectors of industry. They apply over and above the general requirements of the PUWER in dealing with the specific hazards associated with lifting equipment and lifting operations. The regulations are accompanied by an ACOP and HSE guidance, *Safe Use of Lifting Equipment*.

Under the regulations, employers must:

- ensure that:
  - (a) lifting equipment is of adequate strength and stability for each load, having regard in particular to the stress induced at its mounting or fixed point; and
  - (b) every part of a load and anything attached to it and used in lifting it is of adequate strength;
- ensure that lifting equipment for lifting persons:
  - (a) subject to paragraph (b), is such as to prevent a person using it being crushed, trapped or struck or falling from the carrier;
  - (b) is such as to prevent so far as is reasonably practicable a person using it, while carrying out activities from the carrier, being crushed, trapped or struck or falling from the carrier;
  - (c) subject to the paragraph below, has suitable devices to prevent the risk of a carrier falling;
  - (d) is such that a person trapped in any carrier is not thereby exposed to danger and can be freed;
- ensure that if the risk described in paragraph (c) above cannot be prevented for reasons inherent in the site and height differences:
  - (a) the carrier has an enhanced safety coefficient suspension rope or chain; and
  - (b) the rope or chain is inspected by a competent person every working day;
- ensure that lifting equipment is positioned or installed in such a way as to reduce to as low as is reasonably practicable the risk:
  - (a) of the lifting equipment or a load striking a person; or
  - (b) from a load: (i) drifting; (ii) falling freely; or (iii) being released unintentionally,

and is otherwise safe;

- ensure that there are suitable devices to prevent a person from falling down a shaft or hoistway;
- ensure that:
  (a) subject to paragraph (b), the machinery and accessories for lifting loads are clearly marked to indicate their safe working loads (SWLs);
  (b) where the SWL of machinery for lifting depends upon its configuration: (i) the machinery is clearly marked to indicate its SWL for each configuration; or (ii) information which clearly indicates its SWL for each configuration is kept with the machinery;
  (c) accessories for lifting are clearly marked in such a way that it is possible to identify the characteristics necessary for their safe use;
  (d) lifting equipment which is designed for lifting persons is appropriately and clearly marked to this effect;
  (e) lifting equipment which is not designed for lifting persons but which might be so used in error is appropriately and clearly marked to the effect that it is not designed for lifting persons;
- ensure that every lifting operation is:
  (a) properly planned by a competent person;
  (b) appropriately supervised; and
  (c) carried out in a safe manner;
- ensure that before lifting equipment is put into service for the first time by him it is thoroughly examined by him for any defect unless either:
  (a) the lifting equipment has not been used before;
  (b) in the case of lifting equipment for which an EC declaration of conformity could or (in the case of a declaration under the Lifts Regulations 1997) should have been drawn up, the employer has received such declaration made not more than 12 months before the lifting equipment is put into service,

  or, if obtained from the undertaking of another person, it is accompanied by physical evidence of thorough examination under the regulations;
- ensure that, where the safety of lifting equipment depends upon the installation conditions, it is thoroughly examined:
  (a) after installation and before being put into service for the first time;
  (b) after assembly and before being put into service at a new site or in a new location,

  to ensure that it has been installed correctly and is safe to operate;
- ensure that lifting equipment which is exposed to conditions causing deterioration which is liable to result in dangerous situations is:
  (a) thoroughly examined: (i) in the case of lifting equipment for lifting persons or an accessory for lifting equipment, at least every six months; (ii) in the

case of other lifting equipment, every 12 months; (iii) in either case, in accordance with an examination scheme; and (iv) each time that exceptional circumstances which are liable to jeopardize the safety of the lifting equipment have occurred;

(b) if appropriate for the purpose, inspected by a competent person at suitable intervals between thorough examinations;

- ensure that no lifting equipment:

(a) leaves his undertaking; or

(b) if obtained from the undertaking of another person, is used in his undertaking, unless it is accompanied by physical evidence that the last thorough examination required to be carried out under this regulation has been carried out.

Note: A person making a thorough examination for an employer shall:

(a) notify the employer forthwith of any defect in the lifting equipment which in his opinion is or could become a danger to persons;

(b) as soon as is practicable make a report of the thorough examination in writing authenticated by him or on his behalf by signature or equally secure means and containing the information specified in Schedule 1 to: (i) the employer; (ii) any person from whom the lifting equipment has been hired or leased;

(c) where there is in his opinion a defect in the lifting equipment involving an existing or imminent risk of serious personal injury send a copy of the report as soon as is practicable to the relevant enforcing authority.

A person making an inspection for an employer shall:

(a) notify the employer forthwith of any defect in the lifting equipment which in his opinion is or could become a danger to persons; and

(b) as soon as is practicable make a record of his inspection in writing.

Every employer who has been notified under the above paragraph shall ensure that the lifting equipment is not used:

(a) before the defect is remedied; or

(b) in a case to which sub-paragraph (c) of paragraph 8 of Schedule 1 applies, after a time specified under that sub-paragraph and before the defect is remedied.

Relevant enforcing authority means:

(a) where the defective lifting equipment has been hired or leased by the employer, the HSE;

(b) otherwise, the enforcing authority for the premises in which the defective lifting equipment was thoroughly examined.

Where an employer obtaining lifting equipment to which these regulations apply receives an EC declaration of conformity relating to it, he shall keep the declaration for so long as he operates the lifting equipment.

The employer shall ensure that the information contained in:

(a) every report made to him is kept available for inspection: (i) in the case of a thorough examination of lifting equipment other than an accessory for lifting, until he ceases to use the lifting equipment; (ii) in the case of a thorough examination of an accessory for lifting, for two years after the report is made; (iii) in the case of a thorough examination under paragraph 2 of Regulation 9, until he ceases to use the lifting equipment at the place it was installed or assembled; (iv) in the case of a thorough examination under paragraph 3 of Regulation 9, until the next report is made under that paragraph or the expiration of two years, whichever is later;

(b) every record is kept available until the next such record is made.

SCHEDULE 1: INFORMATION TO BE CONTAINED IN A REPORT OF A THOROUGH EXAMINATION

1. The name and address of the employer for whom the thorough examination was made.
2. The address of the premises at which the thorough examination was made.
3. Particulars sufficient to identify the lifting equipment including where known its date of manufacture.
4. The date of the last thorough examination.
5. The SWL of the lifting equipment or (where its SWL depends upon the configuration of the lifting equipment) its SWL for the last configuration in which it was thoroughly examined.
6. In relation to the first thorough examination of lifting equipment after installation or after assembly at a new site or in a new location:
    (a) that it is such thorough examination;
    (b) (if such be the case) that it has been installed correctly and would be safe to operate.
7. In relation to a thorough examination of lifting equipment other than a thorough examination to which paragraph 6 relates:
    (a) whether it is a thorough examination: (i) within an interval of 6 months under Regulation 9 (3) (a) (i); (ii) within an interval of 12 months under Regulation 9 (3) (a) (ii); (iii) in accordance with an examination scheme under Regulation 9 (3) (a) (iii); or (iv) after the occurrence of exceptional circumstances under Regulation 9 (3) (a) (iv);
    (b) (if such be the case) that the lifting equipment would be safe to operate.
8. In relation to every thorough examination of lifting equipment:
    (a) identification of any part found to have a defect which is or could become a danger to persons, and a description of the defect;

(b)   particulars of any repair, renewal or alteration required to remedy a defect found to be a danger to persons;

(c)   in the case of a defect which is not yet but could become a danger to persons: (i) the time by which it could become such danger; (ii) particulars of any repair, renewal or alteration required to remedy it;

(d)   the latest date by which the next thorough examination must be carried out;

(e)   where the thorough examination included testing, particulars of any test;

(f)   the date of the thorough examination.

9.   The name, address and qualifications of the person making the report; that he is self-employed or, if employed, the name and address of the employer.

10.   The name and address of the person signing or authenticating the report on behalf of its author.

11.   The date of the report.

SAFE LIFTING OPERATIONS

Lifting operations entail the use of lifting machinery such as cranes, which may be fixed, overhead or mobile, chains, ropes and lifting tackle. The following points need consideration to ensure safe crane lifting operations:

- **Fixed cranes**. This type of crane is generally fixed in one location and may incorporate a fixed-angle or adjustable-angle jib, in some cases rotating through 360 degrees. Crane collapses can arise through failure to lift vertically, in particular through attempting to drag a load sideways. In addition, the 'snatching' of a load, as opposed to the slow and steady lifting of same, may cause crane failure. In the case of cranes with an adjustable-angle jib, the reduction in the safe working load as the jib moves towards a horizontal position must be appreciated by crane drivers.

- **Tower cranes.** Failure may arise through incorrect assembly and unsafe modifications to the crane. Falls from a height have resulted through the driver not being able to reach the cab safely and during inspection, maintenance and repair operations. Considerable care is required during the erection and dismantling of tower cranes.

- **Mobile cranes.** There are several different designs of mobile crane. However, most mobile cranes incorporate a telescopic or articulated boom and rotate through 360 degrees. They may be mounted on a specifically designed road vehicle or run on a fixed track. Crane overturns can arise through lifting on soft or uneven ground and failing to use outriggers, which spread the load.

- **Overhead travelling cranes.** This type of crane is commonly used in foundries, steelworks and dockyards. The crane may be fixed or rotate through 360 degrees. Risk of derailment can arise through overloading of the crane, obstructions on the track and the failure of stops located at the end of the rails or traverse. In cases where people are working on a crane track or traverse, effective measures are required to prevent the crane coming into contact. This entails the operation of a permit-to-work system incorporating the complete isolation and locking off of the electrical supply to the crane prior to work commencing.

Requirements for safe lifting

- Packing or other means should be used to prevent the edges of a load coming into contact with slings, ropes or chains used for lifting.
- The angle between the legs of a multiple sling must not be so great that the SWL is exceeded. Reference must be made to the manufacturer's information on the maximum safe working loads for slings at various angles.
- Every part of a load must be securely suspended, supported and secured to prevent displacement of slipping.
- Slings must be attached securely to the lifting appliance and not in a way likely to cause damage to the slings.
- Under no circumstances should the safe working load of a crane be exceeded.
- The radius of the load must not exceed the maximum working radius of the jib.
- Where the load is equal to, or approaching, the SWL, lifting must be halted for a moment after the load has been raised a short distance.
- All practicable measures must be taken to prevent a load coming into contact, and displacing, any other object.
- No load must be left suspended unless a competent person is in charge of the lifting appliance.
- No crane must be used for raising or lowering unless it is either securely anchored or adequately weighted with ballast properly placed and secured. Under no circumstances must the rails on which cranes are mounted be used as anchorages.

PRESSURE VESSELS

The potential for death and major injury arising from the explosion of pressure vessels, such as steam boilers, has always been a major feature of safety legislation, such as the various Factories Acts.

The principal hazards associated with pressure vessels are: overheating caused by low water level, the principal cause of boiler explosions; and the long-term effects of corrosion, which results in boiler failure and, in some cases, explosion.

Overheating in boilers

A number of factors can contribute to overheating, including:

- lack of testing and maintenance of controls and alarms, leading to malfunction;
- inadequate standards of control; and
- isolation of control chambers.

Boiler corrosion

Corrosion in boilers can be extensive, resulting in: wastage (loss of metal thickness and, therefore, strength); and 'grooving', a form of mechanical corrosion, due to expansion and contraction, and accelerated by a build-up of solids, at various points in a vessel.

SIMPLE PRESSURE VESSELS (SAFETY) REGULATIONS 1991

These regulations apply to:

- simple pressure vessels, that is welded vessels made of certain types of steel or aluminium, intended to contain air or nitrogen under pressure and manufactured in series; and
- relevant assembly, that is an assembly incorporating a pressure vessel.

Important definitions:

- **Manufacturer's instructions** are instructions issued by or on behalf of the manufacturer, including the following information:
  - (a) manufacturer's name and mark;
  - (b) the vessel type, batch identification or other particulars identifying the vessel to which the instructions relate;
  - (c) particulars of maximum working pressure in bar, maximum and minimum working temperatures in °C, and capacity in litres;
  - (d) intended use of the vessel;
  - (e) maintenance and installation requirements for vessel safety, and written in the official language of the member state accordingly.
- **Series manufacture** means where more than one vessel of the same type is manufactured during a given period by the same continuous manufacturing process, in accordance with a common design.

- **Vessel** means a simple pressure vessel being a welded vessel intended to contain air or nitrogen at a gauge pressure greater than 0.5 bar, not intended for exposure to flame, and having the following characteristics:
  (a) the components and assemblies contributing to the strength of the vessel under pressure are made either of non-alloy quality steel, or of non-alloy aluminium, or of non-age-hardening aluminium alloy;
  (b) the vessel consists either: (i) of a cylindrical component with a circular cross-section, closed at each end, each end being outwardly dished or flat and being also co-axial with the cylindrical component; or (ii) of two co-axial outwardly dished ends;
  (c) the maximum working pressure (PS) is not more than 30 bar, and the PS.V not more than 10,000 bar litres;
  (d) the minimum working temperature is not lower than –50 °C and the maximum working temperature is not higher than 300 °C in the case of steel vessels, and 100 °C in the case of aluminium or aluminium alloy vessels.

The regulations apply only to vessels manufactured in series, and do not apply to:
  (a) vessels designed specifically for nuclear use, where vessel failure might or would result in the emission of radioactivity;
  (b) vessels specifically intended for installation in, or for use as part of the propulsive system of, a ship or aircraft; or
  (c) fire extinguishers.

Principal requirements

Vessels with a stored energy of _over 50 bar litres_ when supplied in the UK must:

- meet the essential health and safety requirements, ie with regard to materials used in construction, vessel design, manufacturing processes and placing in service of vessels;
- have safety clearance, ie checks made by an approved body;
- bear the CE mark and other specified inscriptions;
- be accompanied by manufacturer's instructions; and
- be safe (as defined).

Vessels with a stored energy _up to 50 bar litres_ when supplied in the UK must:

- be manufactured in accordance with engineering practice recognized as sound in the Community country;
- bear specific inscriptions (not the CE mark); and
- be safe.

Similar requirements to the above apply to such vessels when taken into service in the UK by a manufacturer or importer.

Categories of vessels

Different provisions are made for different categories of vessels depending upon their stored energy expressed in terms of the product of the maximum working pressure in bar and its capacity in litres (PS.V).

Category A vessels

Vessels are graded according to PS.V range thus:

- A.1 – 3,000 to 10,000 bar litres;
- A.2 – 200 to 3,000 bar litres;
- A.3 – 50 to 200 bar litres.

Category B vessels

These are vessels with a PS.V of 50 bar litres or less.

Safety clearance

A vessel in Category A has safety clearance once an approved body has issued an EC verification certificate or an EC certificate of conformity in respect of that vessel.

Approved bodies

These are bodies designated by member states, in the case of the UK by the Secretary for Trade and Industry.

EC mark and other specified inscriptions

Where an approved body has issued an EC verification certificate, that approved body has responsibility for the application of the CE mark to every vessel covered by the certificate.

Where a manufacturer has obtained an EC certificate of conformity, he must apply the CE mark to any vessels covered by the certificate where he executes an EC declaration of conformity that they conform with a relevant national standard or the relevant prototype.

The CE mark must consist of the appropriate symbol, the last two digits of the year in which the mark is applied and, where appropriate, the distinguishing number assigned by the EC to the approved body responsible for EC verification or EC surveillance.

Other specified inscriptions to be applied to Category A and B vessels are:

- maximum working pressure in bar;
- maximum working temperature in °C;
- minimum working temperature in °C;
- capacity of the vessel in litres;
- name or mark of the manufacturer; and
- type and serial or batch identification of the vessel.

PRESSURE SYSTEMS

Pressure systems are regulated by the Pressure Systems Safety Regulations 2000. Under these regulations, 'pressure system' is defined as:

- a system comprising one or more pressure vessels of rigid construction, any associated pipework and protective devices;
- the pipework with its protective devices to which a transportable pressure receptacle is, or is intended to be, connected; or
- a pipeline and its protective devices,

which contains or is liable to contain a relevant fluid, but does not include a transportable pressure receptacle.

Under these regulations:

- anyone who designs any pressure system or any component part thereof, or supplies (whether as a manufacturer, importer or in any other capacity) shall provide written information concerning its design, construction, examination, operation and maintenance;
- the employer of a person who modifies or repairs any pressure system shall provide sufficient written information concerning the modifications or repair;
- any person who manufactures a pressure vessel shall ensure that before it is supplied by him the information specified in Schedule 3 is marked on the vessel, or on a plate attached to it, in a visible, legible and indelible form; and no person shall import a pressure vessel unless it is so marked;

- the employer of a person who installs a pressure system at work shall ensure that nothing about the way in which it is installed gives rise to danger or otherwise impairs the operation of any protective device or inspection facility;
- the user of an installed system and owner of a mobile system shall not operate the system or allow it to be operated unless:
  - he has established the safe operating limits of that system; and
  - he has a written scheme for the periodic examination, by a competent person;
- the user of an installed system and the owner of a mobile system shall ensure that those parts of the pressure system included in the scheme of examination are examined by a competent person at regular intervals;
- if the competent person carrying out the examination is of the opinion that the pressure system or part of the pressure system will give rise to danger unless certain repairs or modifications have been carried out, he shall forthwith make a written report to that effect and, within 14 days of the completion of the examination, send a written report containing the same particulars to the enforcing authority;
- users and owners shall ensure that the system is properly maintained in good repair so as to prevent danger;
- the employer of a person who modifies or repairs a pressure system at work shall ensure that nothing in the way that it is modified or repaired gives rise to danger or otherwise impairs the operation of any protective device or inspection facility;
- users and owners shall keep the last report relating to the system made by a competent person and any such previous reports if they contain information which will materially assist in assessing whether the system is safe to operate or any repairs or modifications to the system can be carried out safely.

INTERNAL TRANSPORT

Numerous fatal and serious accidents are associated with transport operations in workplaces. These include accidents associated with, in particular, reversing vehicles, together with those involving vehicles under repair or maintenance in workshops, loading and unloading operations and overturning incidents, particularly those involving lift trucks. On this basis a formal traffic management system may be necessary, taking into account the requirements of the WHSWR (see Chapter 3).

The HSE guidance to the regulations makes the following recommendations with respect to reversing vehicles.

Where large vehicles have to reverse, measures for reducing risks to pedestrians and any people in wheelchairs should be considered, such as:

- restricting reversing to places where it can be carried out safely;
- keeping people on foot or in wheelchairs away;
- providing suitable high-visibility clothing for people who are permitted in the area;
- fitting reversing alarms to alert, or with a detection device to warn the driver of an obstruction or applying the brakes automatically; and
- employing banksmen to supervise the safe movement of vehicles.

Whatever measures are adopted, a safe system of work should operate at all times. Account should be taken of people with impaired sight or hearing.

If crowds of people are likely to overflow on to roadways, for example at the end of a shift, consideration should be given to stopping vehicles from using the routes at such times.

KEY POINTS

- The law relating to engineering safety is extensive and incorporated in the Provision and Use of Work Equipment Regulations (PUWER) and other regulations, such as the Pressure Systems Safety Regulations.
- Machinery-related hazards are commonly associated with the design features of same.
- The HSE has classified the dangerous parts of machinery.
- Under the PUWER work equipment must be 'suitable' and 'maintained in an efficient state, in efficient working order and in good repair'.
- In certain cases, a work equipment risk assessment may need to be undertaken by an employer.
- Employers must ensure that precautionary measures are taken in respect of dangerous machinery.
- Specific provisions apply in the case of mobile work equipment and power presses.
- Most machinery should feature some form of guard and/or safety device.
- Organizations should lay down and enforce safe working procedures for lift truck operations.
- Under the Lifting Operations and Lifting Equipment Regulations (LOLER) lifting equipment must be thoroughly examined and inspected on a regular basis by a competent person.
- Pressure systems must be designed and constructed to ensure integrity of the system.
- Employers must ensure the provision and maintenance of safe traffic operations on site.

5

Fire prevention and protection

INTRODUCTION

Every year fire and its effects cause substantial losses of life and property. It is essential that everyone at work is familiar with the main causes of fire, how fire spreads and the fire procedures and measures to prevent fire. This chapter deals with the principles of combustion, the classification of fires and fire appliances, procedures for the safe use and storage of flammable substances and the process of fire risk assessment.

Current legislation is principally incorporated in the Regulatory Reform (Fire Safety) Order 2005. Fire authorities have extensive powers for ensuring fire protection in the workplace is adequate.

What is fire?

'Fire' can be defined in several ways:

- a spectacular example of a fast chemical reaction between a combustible substance and oxygen accompanied by the evolution of heat;
- a mixture in gaseous form of a combustible substance and oxygen with sufficient energy put into the mixture to start a fire;
- an unexpected combustion generating sufficient heat or smoke resulting in damage to plant, equipment, goods and/or buildings.

PRINCIPLES OF COMBUSTION

The three requirements for a fire to start and continue are the presence of a fuel, an ignition source of sufficient energy to set the fuel alight and air or oxygen to maintain combustion. If one of these three components is removed, combustion cannot take place. This is the concept of the 'fire triangle':

- **Oxygen/air.** A fire always requires oxygen for it to take place or, having commenced, to continue. The chief source of oxygen is air. A number of substances can be a source of oxygen in a fire, eg oxidizing agents.
- **Combustible substance (fuel).** This includes many substances, eg natural gas (methane), butane, petrol, plastics, natural and artificial fibres, wood, paper, coal and living matter. Inorganic substances are also combustible, eg hydrogen, sulphur, sodium, phosphorus, magnesium and ammonium nitrate.
- **Ignition source.** This is the energy that has to be applied to the oxygen/fuel mixture to start the fire. Usually this energy is in the form of heat or flame or that contained in the substance. Electrical energy is a common ignition source, as in the lightning of a thunder storm, or when an electrical contact, such as a switch, is made or broken.

HEAT TRANSMISSION

Fire involves the three means of heat transmission:

- **Conduction.** Conduction of heat takes place in solids, such as metals, timber, concrete and glass. Some solids, such as metals, are better conductors than, for instance, timber.
- **Convection.** This takes place in liquids and gases by the circulation of convection currents. In a fire, sparks can be conveyed by convection currents, which results in secondary fires being established.
- **Radiation.** Radiation is the process of heat transmission through air and gases.

SOURCES OF IGNITION

Sources of ignition of fire in both domestic and industrial premises are outlined below:

- **Electrical equipment.** Arcing can arise as a result of electrical faults and this results in the production of sparks. Hot surfaces produced by defective electrical equipment are a common source of ignition.

- **Spontaneous ignition.** When some liquids are heated or sprayed on to a very hot surface, they may ignite spontaneously without an ignition source actually present.
- **Spontaneous combustion.** When materials react with oxygen an exothermic reaction takes place, ie one emitting heat, and with materials which readily oxidize there may be some degree of heat accumulation which eventually causes the material to ignite or burst into flames.
- **Smoking.** In many workplaces and work situations, smoking by employees, members of the public and customers can be a source of fire, principally from discarded cigarette ends and matches, but also from smoking in areas where flammable materials are stored or where flammable vapour may be present.
- **Friction.** Sparks can be created by friction between surfaces, for instance where the moving part of a machine comes into contact with a fixed part, or two moving surfaces may rub or slide together during routine machine operation.
- **Hot work processes.** Hot work processes, such as welding, soldering, hot cutting and brazing, can be a source of ignition, particularly where flammable vapours are present.
- **Static electricity.** In situations where electrostatic charging is produced by induction or friction, the charge, in the form of static electricity, can be carried away from the point of origin and, in the event of accumulation of charge, sparks can be produced.
- **Engines, vehicle emissions and hot surfaces.** In vehicle maintenance and parking areas, diesel- and petrol-operated engines, vehicle emissions and hot surfaces of, for example, exhaust systems can be a source of ignition.
- **Open flame sources.** Many open flame sources are encountered in workplaces, eg boilers, furnaces, portable heating appliances and pilot lights to same.
- **Lightning.** In limited cases, lightning can be a source of ignition and this may require the installation of lightning protection by direct earthing.

FIRE SPREAD CONTROL

Fire spread control is directed at eliminating one or more of the three elements which maintain the fire. The ultimate objective is the extinction of the fire, using one or more of the following:

- **Starvation.** There are three ways that starvation can be achieved:
  - take the fuel away from the fire;
  - take the fire away from the fuel; and
  - reduce the quantity or bulk of the fuel.

The first is achieved every day on a gas hob when the tap is turned off. For industrial installations this means isolating the fuel feed at the remote isolation valve. Examples of taking the fire away from the fuel include breaking down stacks and dragging away the burning debris. Breaking down a fire into smaller units is an example of reducing the quantity or bulk of the fuel.

- **Smothering.** Smothering can be achieved by:
  - allowing the fire to consume the oxygen while preventing the inward flow of more oxygen; and
  - adding an inert gas to the burning mixture.
- **Cooling.** This is the most common means of fighting a fire, water being the most effective and cheapest medium. For a fire to be sustained, some of the heat output from the combustion is returned to the fuel, providing a continuous source of ignition energy. When water is added to a fire, the heat output serves to heat and vaporize the water, that is, the water provides an alternative heat sink. Ultimately, insufficient heat is added to the fuel and continuous ignition ceases. In order to assist rapid absorption of heat, water is applied to the fire as a spray rather than a jet, the spray droplets being more efficient in absorbing heat than the stream of water in a jet.

CLASSIFICATION OF FIRES

Fires are commonly classified into four categories according to the fuel type and means of extinction:

- **Class A.** Fires involving solid materials, normally of organic nature, in which the combustion occurs with the formation of glowing embers, eg wood, paper, coal and natural fibres. Water applied as a jet or spray is the most effective way of achieving extinction.
- **Class B.** Fires involving liquids and liquefiable solids.
  Liquids fall into two groups:
  (i)   miscible with water: methanol, acetone, acetic acid; and
  (ii) immiscible with water: petrol, benzene, fats and waxes.
  Foam, vaporizing liquids, carbon dioxide and dry powder can be used on both B(i) and B(ii) type fires. Water spray can be used on type B(i) but not on type B(ii) fires. There may also be some restriction on the type of foam which can be used because some foams break down on contact with alcohols. In all cases, extinction is mainly achieved by smothering. However, water on a B(i) fire also acts by cooling, and by removal of the fuel in that the fuel dissolves in the water.

- **Class C.** Fires involving gases or liquefied gases, eg methane, propane and butane. Both foam and dry chemicals can be used on small liquefied gas spillage fires, particularly when backed up by water to cool the leaking container or spillage collector. A fire from a gas leak can be extinguished either by isolating the fuel remotely or by injecting an inert gas into the gas stream. Direct flame extinguishment is difficult and may be counterproductive in that if the leak continues there may be reignition, often in the form of an explosion. Extinguishers used on liquid gas spillage fires work by smothering.
- **Class D.** Fires involving metals, eg magnesium and aluminium. They can only be extinguished by use of dry powders, which include talc, soda ash, limestone and dry sand. All these extinguishers work by smothering.

'Electrical fires' (fires involving electrical equipment)

This is an obsolete classification. Fires which involve electrical equipment must always be tackled by first isolating the electricity supply and then by the use of carbon dioxide, vaporizing liquid or dry powder. The use of these agents minimizes damage to equipment.

FIRE EXTINCTION

Fires may be extinguished through the use of portable fire-fighting appliances and *in situ* fire-fighting equipment, such as hose reel appliances.

Portable fire-fighting appliances

These are appliances designed to be carried and operated by hand. They contain an extinguishing medium which can be expelled by action of internal pressure and directed on to a fire. This pressure may be stored, or obtained by chemical reaction, or by release of gas from a cartridge. The maximum mass of a portable extinguisher in working order is 23 kilograms.

Portable extinguishers must be painted red and are grouped and colour coded as follows (see also Table 5.1):

- **Water appliances.** Water appliances operate on the basis of cooling and reducing the temperature within a fire, thereby slowing down the rate of combustion and preventing reignition from taking place. As a result of the application of water, steam is produced, which has a blanketing or inerting effect, reducing the amount of air to maintain combustion. Water is the most efficient form of extinguishant for use on Class A fires.

Table 5.1 *Grouping and colour coding of fire appliances*

Extinguisher	Colour code
Water	Red
Foam	Cream
Carbon dioxide	Black
Dry chemical powder	Blue
Vaporizing liquid	Green

- **Foam appliances.** Foam applied to a fire has a smothering effect, preventing further air from reaching the combustion area or seat of the fire. In the case of flammable liquids, foam forms a barrier floating on the burning surface, reducing the evaporation rate of the liquid and preventing the ingress of oxygen to maintain combustion.
- **Carbon dioxide appliances.** Carbon dioxide appliances, when operated, produce a snow which is converted to gas in the fire. This has the effect of slowing down the rate of combustion, reducing the available oxygen through the smothering effect created. Carbon dioxide is most effective on Class A and B fires and those involving electrical appliances and equipment. Under no circumstances should carbon dioxide be used as an extinguishant in fires in confined spaces due to the risk of asphyxiation.
- **Dry chemical powder appliances.** These appliances incorporate a specific powder mixture which interferes with the combustion process, reducing the combustion rate until no further ignition and reignition of the fuel can take place. They are principally designed for use on Class A and B fires.
- **Vaporizing liquid appliances.** These appliances contain halogenated hydro-carbons, such as halon. When operated, they produce a heavy vapour which results in extinguishment due to the exclusion of oxygen and interference with chemical combustion reactions. They are particularly effective on fires involving electrical equipment and do not damage sensitive equipment. Vaporizing liquid appliances should not be used on fires in confined spaces.

In situ fire-fighting equipment

This form of fire-fighting equipment is permanently installed in buildings and takes the form of hose reels and sprinkler systems:

- **Hose reel appliances.** A hose reel appliance is a fixed fire-fighting installation comprising a coil of 25-millimetre internal diameter (ID) flexible hose directly connected to a rising water main. The complete installation consists of either a wet rising main or dry rising main (dry riser) and a landing valve or fire hydrant. The main is generally installed in wrought steel pipe of not less than 100 millimetres ID. A wet rising main should contain water at all times and be directly connected into the fire main with the water at fire main pressure. They may be subject to damage by frost if not adequately protected.

With a dry rising main, on the other hand, the pipe has to be charged with water prior to use. This is achieved by opening out the main to the fire main or by charging the dry main by means of a pump. The inlet for a dry rising main must be in a convenient position for the fire brigade to gain access, provided with a hardstanding for pumps, suitably identified and kept clear at all times.

In addition to hose reels, rising mains are fitted with landing valves which allow the connection of a standard fire hose. Both landing valves and hose reels must be kept clear of obstructions at all times and sited not more than 30 metres from a possible fire location.

- **Sprinkler systems.** These systems provide an automatic means of both detecting and extinguishing or controlling a fire in its early stages. A sprinkler system incorporates an overhead piping system with sprinkler heads fitted to the system at strategic points. The installation is supplied with water from a header tank and/or a water main. Each sprinkler head acts as a valve which is pre-set to open at a specific temperature, releasing water on to a fire. To be effective, the water supply must be automatic and not exposed to risk of freezing, in particular. Sprinkler systems can be arranged to operate an alarm on initial release of water.

FIRE ALARM SYSTEMS

A method of giving warning of fire is required in commercial, industrial and public buildings. The purpose of a fire alarm is to give an early warning of fire in a building; to increase the safety of occupants by encouraging them to escape to a place of safety; and to increase the possibility of early extinction of the fire, thus reducing the loss of, or damage to, the premises and its contents.

BS 5839: Part 1: 1988 lays down guidelines to be followed for the installation of fire alarm systems. In larger buildings this may take the form of a mains-operated system with break-glass alarm call points, an automatic control unit and electrically operated bells or sirens. In relatively small buildings, it would be reasonable to accept a manually operated dry battery or compressed air-operated gong, klaxon or bell. To avoid the alarm point being close to the seat of a fire, duplicate facilities are necessary.

However, much will depend upon the nature of the building, in terms of construction, layout and the number of floors, the number of people on site at any time and materials and substances stored, as to the provision of fire alarm systems. The local fire authority may ultimately decide on the nature of such provision.

FIRE INSTRUCTIONS

A fire instruction is a notice informing people of the action they should take in the event of either:

● hearing the alarm; or
● discovering a fire.

Such notices should be displayed in prominent positions on every floor of a building.

FIRE DRILLS AND SOUNDING OF ALARMS

People should receive training in evacuation procedures, namely fire drills, at least quarterly, and the alarm should be sounded weekly.

It is advantageous to have key personnel trained in the correct use of fire appliances.

FLAMMABLE SUBSTANCES

Classification of flammable substances

Under the Chemicals (Hazard Information and Packaging for Supply) (CHIP) Regulations, flammable substances are classified as 'extremely flammable', 'highly flammable' and 'flammable', ie their **category of danger**. The category of danger is largely based on the flash point of the substance.

Flash point is defined as the minimum liquid temperature at which sufficient vapour is given off to form a mixture with air capable of ignition under prescribed test conditions.

See further Chapter 11.

Handling and storage of flammable substances

Under the CHIP Regulations, suppliers of flammable substances are required to produce safety data for use by employers and others to assist them in determining the safety procedures necessary in the handling, storage and use of flammable substances. Certain features of the data provided are important, namely:

- the identification of the substance or preparation;
- the composition of the substance or preparation;
- hazard identification;
- fire-fighting measures;
- accidental release measures;
- handling and storage aspects;
- exposure controls, including the use of personal protective equipment;
- stability and reactivity of the substance or preparation;
- disposal considerations; and
- transport information.

In most cases it would be appropriate for the employer to assess the risks, and then prescribe preventive and protective measures necessary, to ensure the safe use, handling and storage of flammable substances.

In considering the precautions necessary, a number of basic rules apply. Employees must be briefed in these rules with respect to:

- no smoking, eating or drinking when handling flammable substances or in storage areas;
- maintaining a high level of housekeeping in storage areas;
- careful dispensing from bulk;
- storage of the smallest quantities in work areas;
- transporting in closed containers; and
- ensuring fire appliances are available during use and when dispensing.

FIRE SAFETY LAW

Legal requirements

The Regulatory Reform (Fire Safety) Order 2005 replaced all the former legislation dealing with fire safety. The Order is enforced by Area Fire Authorities, except in specified cases.

The Order distinguishes between **relevant persons** and **responsible persons** and places responsibility for fire safety in a workplace on the **responsible person**.

Important definitions

Relevant person means:

(a)   any person (including the responsible person) who is or may be lawfully on the premises; and

(b)   any person in the immediate vicinity of the premises who is at risk from a fire on the premises, but does not include a firefighter who is carrying out his duties in relation to a function of a fire authority.

Responsible person means:

(a)   in relation to a workplace, the employer, if the workplace is to any extent under his control; and

(b)   in relation to any premises not falling within paragraph (a):
   - the person who has control of the premises (as occupier is otherwise) in connection with the carrying on by him of a trade, business is other undertaking (whether for profit of not); or
   - the owner, where the person in control of the premises does not have control in connection with the carrying on by that person of a trade, business is other undertaking.

Special technical and organizational measures include:

- technical means of supervision;
- connecting devices;
   (a)   control and protection systems;
   (b)   engineering controls and solutions;
   (c)   equipment;
   (d)   materials;
   (e)   protective systems; and
   (f)   warning and other communication systems.

General fire precautions

1.   In this Order, **general fire precautions** in relation to premises means, subject to paragraph (2):
   (a)   measures to reduce the risk of fire on the premises and the risk of the spread of fire on the premises;
   (b)   measures in relation to the means of escape from premises;
   (c)   measures for securing that, at all material times, the means of escape can be safely and effectively used;
   (d)   measures in relation to the means for fighting fires on the premises;
   (e)   measures in relation to the means for detecting fire on the premises and giving warning in case of fire on the premises;

    (f)   measures in relation to the arrangements for action to be taken in the event of fire on the premises, including:
- measures relating to the instruction and training of employees; and
- measures to mitigate the effects of fire.

2.   The measures referred to in paragraph 1 do not include **special, technical and organizational measures** required to be taken is observed in any workplace in connection with the carrying on of any work process, where those precautions:

    (a)   are designed to prevent is reduce the likelihood of fire arising from such a work process is reduce its intensity; and

    (b)   are required to be taken is observed to ensure compliance with any requirement of the relevant statutory provisions within the meaning given by section 53(1) of the HASAWA.

Duties of responsible persons

A responsible person must:

- take such general fire precautions as will ensure, so far as is reasonably practicable, the safety of any of his employees;
- in relation to relevant persons who are not his employees, take such general fire precautions as may reasonably be required in the circumstances of the case to ensure that the premises are safe;
- make a suitable and sufficient assessment of the risks to which relevant persons are exposed for the purpose of identifying the general fire precautions he needs to take to comply with the requirements and prohibitions imposed upon him by or under this Order;
- consider implications of the presence of dangerous substances in the risk assessment process;
- review the risk assessment if no longer valid or there has been a significant change in the matters to which it relates;
- record the significant findings of the risk assessment and details of any group being especially at risk;
- not commence a new work activity involving a dangerous substance unless a risk assessment has been made and measures required by the Order have been implemented;
- make and give effect to arrangements for the effective planning, organization, control, monitoring and review of preventive and protective measures;
- record the arrangements in specified cases;
- where a dangerous substance is present, eliminate or reduce risks so far as is reasonably practicable;

- replace a dangerous substance or the use of a dangerous substance with a substance or process which eliminates or reduces risks so far as is reasonably practicable;
- where not reasonably practicable to reduce above risks, apply *measures* to control the risk and mitigate the detrimental effects of fire;
- arrange safe handling, storage and transport of dangerous substances and wastes;
- ensure premises are equipped with appropriate fire-fighting equipment and with fire detectors and alarms and that non-automatic fire-fighting equipment is easily accessible, simple to use and indicated by signs;
- take measures for fire-fighting in the premises, nominate competent persons to implement these measures and arrange any necessary contact with external services;
- ensure routes to emergency exits and the exits themselves are kept clear at all times;
- comply with specific requirements dealing with emergency routes, exits and doors and the illumination of emergency routes and exits in respect of premises;
- establish and, where necessary, give effect to appropriate procedures for serious and imminent danger and for danger zones, including safety drills, nomination of competent persons to implement the procedures and restriction of access to areas on the grounds of safety;
- ensure additional emergency measures are taken in respect of dangerous substances;
- ensure relevant information is made available to emergency services and displayed at the premises;
- in the event of an accident, incident or emergency related to the presence of a dangerous substance, take immediate steps to mitigate the effects of fire, restore the situation to normal, and inform relevant persons;
- ensure only those persons essential for the carrying out of repairs and other necessary work are permitted in an affected area;
- ensure that the premises and any facilities, equipment and devices are subject to a suitable system of maintenance and are maintained in an efficient state, in efficient working order and in good repair;
- appoint one or more competent persons to assist him in undertaking the preventive and protective measures, ensuring adequate cooperation between competent persons;
- ensure that competent persons have sufficient time to fulfil their functions and the means at their disposal are adequate having regard to the size of the premises, the risks and the distribution of those risks;
- ensure competent persons not in his employment are informed of factors affecting the safety of any person and are provided with the same information as employees;

- provide employees with comprehensible and relevant information on the risks identified in the risk assessment, preventive and protective measures, the identities of competent persons for the purposes of evacuation of premises and the notified risks arising in shared workplaces;
- before employing a child, provide the parent with comprehensible and relevant information on the risks to that child, the preventive and protective measures and the notified risks arising in shared workplaces;
- where a dangerous substance is on the premises, provide employees with the details of any such substance and the significant findings of the risk assessment;
- provide information to employers and the self-employed from outside undertakings with respect to the risks to those employees and the preventive and protective measures taken;
- provide non-employees working in his undertaking with appropriate instructions and comprehensible and relevant information regarding any risks to those persons;
- ensure the employer of any employees from an outside undertaking working in or on the premises is provided with sufficient information with respect to evacuation procedures and the competent persons nominated to undertake evacuation procedures;
- ensure employees are provided with adequate safety training at the time of first employment, and on being exposed to new or increased risks arising from transfer or change of responsibilities, introduction of, or change in, work equipment, the introduction of new technology and the introduction of a new system of work or a change respecting an existing system of work;
- in the case of shared workplaces, cooperate with other responsible person(s), take all reasonable steps to coordinate the measures he takes to comply with this Order with the measures taken by other responsible persons, and take all reasonable steps to inform other responsible persons.

Duties of employees

Employees must:

- take reasonable care for the safety of himself and others who may be affected by his acts or omissions while at work;
- cooperate with his employer to enable him to comply with any duty or requirement imposed by this Order; and.
- inform his employer or any other employee with the specific responsibility for the safety of his fellow employees of any work situation which represents a serious and immediate danger to safety, and any other matter which represents a shortcoming in the employer's protection arrangements for safety.

Enforcement arrangements

Inspectors appointed under the Order have powers similar to those under the HASAWA. They are empowered to serve three types of Notice:

1. Alterations Notice
    Where premises constitute a serious risk to relevant persons or may constitute such a risk if any change is made to them or the use to which they are put, the enforcing authority may serve on the responsible person an Alterations Notice.
2. Enforcement Notice
    If the enforcing authority is of the opinion that the responsible person has failed to comply with any provision of this Order or of any regulations made under it, the enforcing authority may serve on that person an Enforcement Notice.
3. Prohibition Notice
    If the enforcing authority is of the opinion that use of premises involves or will involve a risk to relevant persons so serious that use of the premises ought to be prohibited or restricted, the authority may serve on the responsible person a Prohibition Notice, such a Notice to include anything affecting the escape of relevant persons from the premises.

Offences

1. It is an offence for the **responsible person** to:
    (a) fail to comply with any requirement or prohibition imposed by articles 8 to 21 and 38 (fire safety duties) where that failure places one or more **relevant persons** at risk of death or serious injury in case of fire;
    (b) fail to comply with any requirement or prohibition imposed by regulations made under article 24 where that failure places one or more relevant persons at risk of death or serious injury in case of fire;
    (c) fail to comply with any requirement imposed by article 29(3) (alterations notices);
    (d) fail to comply with any requirement imposed by an enforcement notice;
    (e) fail to comply with any prohibition or restriction imposed by a prohibition notice;
    (f) fail, without reasonable excuse, in relation to apparatus to which article 37 applies (luminous tube signs):
        −   to ensure that such apparatus which is installed in premises complies with article 37(3) and (4); and
        −   to give a notice required by article 37(6) is (8).

2. It is an offence **for any person** to:
    (a) fail to comply with article 23 (general duties of employees at work) where that failure places one or more relevant persons at risk of death or serious injury in case of fire;
    (b) make in any register, book, notice or other document required to be kept, served or given by or under this Order, an entry which he knows to be false in a material particular;
    (c) give any information which he knows to be false in a material particular or recklessly give any information which is so false, in purported compliance with any obligation to give information to which he is subject under or by virtue of this Order, or in response to any inquiry by virtue of article 27(1)(b);
    (d) obstruct, intentionally, an inspector in the exercise or performance of his powers or duties under this Order;
    (e) fail, without reasonable excuse, to comply with any requirements imposed by an inspector under article 27(1)(c) and (d);
    (f) pretend, with intent to deceive, to be an inspector;
    (g) fail to comply with the prohibition imposed by article 40 (duty not to charge employees).

Corporate liability

Where an offence under this Order which is committed by a body corporate is proved to have been committed with the consent or connivance of, or to be attributable to any neglect on the part of any director, manager, secretary or other similar officer of the body corporate, or any person purporting to act in any such capacity, he as well as the body corporate is guilty of that offence and is liable to be proceeded against and punished accordingly.

Defence

In any proceedings for an offence under this Order, except for a failure to comply with articles 8(a) (failure to take general fire precautions) or 12 (elimination or reduction of risks from dangerous substances), it is a defence for the person charged to prove that he took **all reasonable precautions and exercised all due diligence** to avoid the commission of such an offence.

Civil liability for breach of statutory duty

Breach of a duty imposed on an employer by or under this Order, so far as it causes damage to an employee, confers a right of action on that employee in civil proceedings.

FIRE RISK ASSESSMENT

The duty on an employer to undertake a suitable and sufficient assessment of the risks to his own employees, and to other persons not in his employment arising out of or in connection with the conduct by him of his undertaking, is well established. Such a risk assessment must identify the measures necessary to comply with the requirements imposed by or under the relevant statutory provisions.

Fire risk assessment, as with other forms of risk assessment, takes a number of steps or stages thus:

- **Step 1 – Identifying the fire hazards.** This first stage of the exercise entails the identification of: (a) sources of fuel that could contribute to a fire; and (b) sources of ignition. The actual identification of same may be undertaken through a fire safety inspection and a review of items purchased by the organization.

  Sources of fuel will depend upon the nature of the undertaking (commercial, industrial), the processes carried out and articles and substances stored. Liquid fuels can take the form of, for instance, paints, solvents, adhesives, paraffin and white spirit. Solid fuels include packaging materials, plastic, rubber and wooden fixtures and fittings, paper and various solid waste products. Fuels may also be in gaseous form stored in cylinders, such as acetylene and LPG.

  Sources of ignition in a workplace can be extensive, taking into account processes carried out, such as welding, equipment in use, such as grinding machines, cookers, heaters and boilers, and situations where a naked flame may be used, as with people smoking, pilot lights to gas appliances and the use of oil heaters. Sources of ignition may also be associated with defective electrical equipment, static electricity and hot surfaces to equipment.

- **Step 2 – Identifying the people at risk.** Fire, heat and smoke can spread rapidly through a workplace. The principal risk is that of smoke and combustion products preventing people from getting to a fire exit. The result is that people become trapped and suffer asphyxiation.

  A fire risk assessment must, therefore, consider the structure and layout of the workplace with respect to the likely spread of heat and smoke, the number of people in a building or on site at any point in time, including visitors, members of the public and contractors' employees, the fire detection and alarm system and the means of escape.

- **Step 3 – Evaluating the risks and recommending future action.** Once the hazards and the people at risk have been recorded, the risk arising must be evaluated taking into account current measures to control fire risks. In some cases, further control measures may be necessary to reduce the risk to an acceptable level.

These measures may include, for example, greater control over ignition sources, measures to assist disabled workers in the event of fire or reducing the quantity of flammable materials, in particular waste materials, on site at any one time.

Other measures for consideration on a medium- to long-term basis include:

- segregating a specific fire hazard created by a process by moving it to a part of the workplace where it only affects a few people;
- providing additional fire exits and/or protected routes to increase the speed of evacuation;
- training selected employees in the correct use of fire appliances;
- upgrading waste storage arrangements; and
- installation of fire detection and sprinkler systems.

- **Step 4 – Recording the findings of the assessment.** Where more than five employees are employed, the significant findings of the risk assessment, together with any groups of people who may be particularly at risk, must be recorded. This may be assisted by the use of a plan of the workplace to indicate fire hazards and existing control measures. The record should also incorporate an action plan indicating immediate, short-term, medium-term and long-term recommendations to reduce fire risks to an acceptable level. Any control measures identified or introduced must remain effective through testing and maintenance.

- **Step 5 – Reviewing and revising the fire risk assessment.** Risk assessment is an ongoing process. Where changes are made to a workplace, either structurally or in the form of revised working practices, it may be necessary to review and revise the risk assessment. These include:

  - an increase in the number of employees, or people on site as a result of project work being undertaken;
  - the introduction of a new manufacturing process; or
  - changes in layout of open-plan offices.

KEY POINTS

- For fire to take place, three essential elements are required, namely an ignition source, fuel to burn and an ample supply of air.
- Heat transmission takes place by way of conduction, convection and radiation.
- There is a wide range of ignition sources in the average workplace which need to be identified as part of a fire prevention strategy.
- Fire spread control takes place through starvation, smothering and cooling.
- Fire appliances are classified on the basis of the types of fire they are designed to extinguish.
- Fire instructions must be prominently displayed in all workplaces.
- Flammable substances are specifically classified under the Chemicals (Hazard Information and Packaging for Supply) Regulations 2002.
- Under the Regulatory Reform (Fire Safety) Order, responsible persons have both general and specific duties with respect to the taking of general fire precautions, the making and giving effect to 'fire safety arrangements' and the appointment of competent persons to assist them in undertaking the preventive and protective measures.
- Fire authorities have a wide range of powers under current fire safety legislation.
- Employers must undertake a suitable and sufficient fire risk assessment, reviewing same on a regular basis.

6

Electrical safety

INTRODUCTION

Electricity is a form of energy. As with other forms of energy, it can be perfectly safe provided it is treated with care and people follow a number of basic principles in its use. Electrical abuse and misuse, however, can result in death, serious injuries, fire and damage to plant and equipment.

THE PRINCIPAL HAZARDS

Hazards associated with the use of electricity can broadly be divided into two categories, namely:

- the risk of injury to people; and
- the risk of fire and/or explosion.

Physical injury is associated with shock, burns and other injuries from explosions, microwaves, accumulators and batteries, and eye injuries.

ELECTRIC SHOCK

This is the effect produced on the body and, in particular, the nervous system, by an electric current passing through it. The effect varies according to the time that it flows and the strength of the current, which in turn varies with the voltage and the electrical resistance of the body. The resistance of the body varies according to the points of entry and exit of the current and other factors, such as current state of health, body weight and/or the presence of moisture.

The heart is particularly susceptible to electric shock. The flow of current disturbs the heart rhythm, upsetting the blood flow and affecting its vital functions. This is the process of ventricular fibrillation which can be brought about by an alternating current of 1 amp flowing for 10 milliseconds.

Ohm's law:

$$R \text{ (resistance in ohms)} = \frac{E \text{ (pressure in volts)}}{I \text{ (current in amps)}}$$

Table 6.1 *Typical responses to current/voltage*

Voltage	Response	Current
15 volts	Threshold of feeling	0.002–0.005 amp
20–25 volts	Threshold of pain	–
30 volts	Muscular spasm (non-release)	0.015 amp
70 volts	Minimum for death	0.1 amp
120 volts	Maximum for 'safety'	0.002 amp
200–240 volts	Most serious/fatal accidents	0.2 amp

Common cause of death is ventricular fibrillation (spasm) of the heart muscle, which occurs at 0.05 amp. The vascular system ceases to function and the victim dies of suffocation.

Remember: IT'S THE CURRENT THAT KILLS!

$$\text{Current (amps)} = \frac{\text{Voltage}}{\text{Resistance}}$$

FIRST AID

- **Electric shock.** First aid for a victim of electric shock must be cardiac massage plus mouth-to-mouth resuscitation until normal breathing and the heart action return. A victim who is 'locked on' to a live appliance must not be approached until the appliance is electrically dead.

- **Burns.** A current passing through a conductor produces heat. Burns can be caused by contact with hot conductors or by the passage of a current through the body at the point of entry and exit.

  Burns can also be produced by an electric arc, which is a high-temperature electric discharge between two electrodes. The arc is over 3,000 °C and can cause extensive and deeply penetrating burns which may be contaminated by electrode material.

  Where high-frequency currents pass through the body, internal burns can result, although little sensation of electric shock may be experienced.
- **Explosions.** Electrical short circuit or sparking from the electrical contacts in switches or other equipment is a common cause of explosions and subsequent human injury or death. This presupposes the presence of a flammable atmosphere, eg vapour, dust or gas.
- **Eye injuries.** These can arise from exposure to ultraviolet rays from accidental arcing in a process such as welding.
- **Microwave apparatus.** Microwaves can damage the soft tissues of the body.
- **Accumulators and batteries.** Hydrogen gas may be produced as a by-product of battery charging, which can cause explosive atmospheres with the risk of burns. Battery acid from exploding batteries is particularly corrosive.

LEGAL REQUIREMENTS

While the duties under section 2 of the HSWA apply generally in the case of electrical systems, installations and appliances, the principal requirements on employers and others are covered by the Electricity at Work Regulations 1989. Attention should also be paid to the IEE Wiring Regulations in considering best practice with regard to electrical safety.

Electricity at Work Regulations 1989

These regulations, which are accompanied by a memorandum of guidance issued by the HSE, impose duties on persons (referred to in the memorandum of guidance as 'duty holders') in respect of systems, electrical equipment and conductors and in respect of work activities on or near electrical equipment.

Important definitions:

- **Electrical equipment** includes anything used, intended to be used or installed for use, to generate, provide, transmit, transform, rectify, convert, conduct, distribute, control, store, measure or use electrical energy.

- **Injury** means death or personal injury from electric shock, electric burn, electrical explosion or arcing, or from fire or explosion initiated by electrical energy, where any such death or injury is associated with the generation, provision, transmission, transformation, rectification, conversion, conduction, distribution, control, storage, measurement or use of electrical energy.
- **System** means an electrical system in which all the electrical equipment is, or may be, electrically connected to a common source of electrical energy, and includes such source and such equipment.

Under the regulations:

- Except where otherwise expressly provided in these regulations, it shall be the duty of every employer and self-employed person to comply with the provisions of these regulations in so far as they relate to matters which are within his control.
- It shall be the duty of every employee while at work:
  (a) to cooperate with his employer so far as is necessary to enable any duty placed on that employer by the provisions of these regulations to be complied with; and
  (b) to comply with the provisions of these regulations in so far as they relate to matters which are within his control.
- All systems shall at all times be of such construction as to prevent, so far as is reasonably practicable, danger.
- As may be necessary to prevent danger, all systems shall be maintained so as to prevent, so far as is reasonably practicable, such danger.
- Every work activity, including operation, use and maintenance of a system and work near a system, shall be carried out in such a manner as not to give rise, so far as is reasonably practicable, to danger.
- Any equipment provided under these regulations for the purpose of protecting persons at work on or near electrical equipment shall be suitable for the use for which it is provided, be maintained in a condition suitable for that use, and be properly used.
- No electrical equipment shall be put into use where its strength and capability may be exceeded in such a way as may give rise to danger.
- Electrical equipment which may reasonably foreseeably be exposed to:
  (a) mechanical damage;
  (b) the effects of the weather, natural hazards, temperature or pressure;
  (c) the effects of wet, dirty, dusty or corrosive conditions; or
  (d) any flammable or explosive substance, including dusts, vapours or gases,
  shall be of such construction or as necessary so protected as to prevent, so far as is reasonably practicable, danger arising from such exposure.

135

- All conductors in a system which may give rise to danger shall either:
  - (a) be suitably covered with insulating material and as necessary protected so as to prevent, so far as is reasonably practicable, danger; or
  - (b) have such precautions taken in respect of them (including, where appropriate, their being suitably placed) as will prevent, so far as is reasonably practicable, danger.
- Precautions shall be taken, either by earthing or by other suitable means, to prevent danger arising when any conductor (other than a circuit conductor) which may reasonably foreseeably become charged as a result of either the use of a system, or a fault in a system, becomes so charged; and, for the purpose of ensuring compliance with this regulation, a conductor shall be regarded as earthed when it is connected to the general mass of earth by conductors of sufficient strength and current-carrying capability to discharge electrical energy to earth.
- If a circuit conductor is connected to earth or to any other reference point, nothing which might reasonably be expected to give rise to danger by breaking the electrical continuity or introducing high impedance shall be placed in that conductor unless suitable precautions are taken to prevent danger.
- Where necessary to prevent danger, every joint and connection in a system shall be mechanically and electrically suitable for use.
- Efficient means, suitably located, shall be provided for protecting from excess of current every part of a system as may be necessary to prevent danger.
- Subject to paragraph 3, where necessary to prevent danger, suitable means (including, where appropriate, methods of identifying circuits) shall be available for:
  - (a) cutting off the supply of electrical energy to any electrical equipment; and
  - (b) isolation of any electrical equipment.

  In paragraph 1, **isolation** means the disconnection and separation of the electrical equipment from every source of electrical energy in such a way that this disconnection and separation is secure.

  Paragraph 1 shall not apply to electrical equipment which is itself a source of electrical energy but, in such a case as is necessary, precautions shall be taken to prevent, so far as is reasonably practicable, danger.
- Adequate precautions shall be taken to prevent electrical equipment, which has been made dead in order to prevent danger while work is carried out on or near that equipment, from becoming electrically charged during that work if danger may thereby arise.
- No person shall be engaged in any work activity on or so near any live conductor (other than one suitably covered with insulating material so as to prevent danger) that danger may arise unless:
  (a) it is unreasonable in all the circumstances for it to be dead; and

(b) it is reasonable in all the circumstances for him to be at work on or near it while it is live; and

(c) suitable precautions (including where necessary the provision of suitable protective equipment) are taken to prevent injury.

- For the purposes of enabling injury to be prevented, adequate working space, adequate means of access and adequate lighting shall be provided at all electrical equipment on which or near which work is being done in circumstances which may give rise to danger.
- No person shall be engaged in any work activity where technical knowledge or experience is necessary to prevent danger or, where appropriate, injury, unless he possesses such knowledge or experience, or is under such degree of supervision as may be appropriate having regard to the nature of the work.
- In any proceedings for an offence under specific regulations, it shall be a defence for any person to prove that he took all reasonable steps and exercised all due diligence to avoid the commission of that offence.

Memorandum of Guidance on the Electricity at Work Regulations 1989

This HSE document provides excellent guidance on the regulations and, although the guidance is based on legal requirements, it is not intended to be an authoritative interpretation of the law. As such, it has no legal status, providing guidance on best practice. Such interpretation can only be made by the courts.

The purpose of the memorandum is to amplify the nature of the precautions in general terms so as to help in the achievement of high standards of electrical safety in compliance with the duties imposed.

The Wiring Regulations

The Institution of Electrical Engineers Regulations for Electrical Installations (the IEE Wiring Regulations) are non-statutory regulations. They 'relate principally to the design, selection, erection, inspection and testing of electrical installations, whether permanent or temporary, in and about buildings generally and to agricultural and horticultural premises, construction sites and caravans and their sites'.

The IEE Wiring Regulations are a code of practice which is widely recognized and accepted in the UK, and compliance with them is likely to achieve compliance with relevant aspects of the 1989 regulations.

THE RISK OF FIRE

Electricity is a common source of ignition for major fires. Some insulating materials and materials used for electrical connections may be flammable and can give rise to small fires in switchgear, distribution boxes or electricity substations. The risk of losses from fire increases when these local fires go undetected and result in major fires.

Sources of electrical ignition include:

- **sparks** – between conductors or conductor and earth;
- **arcs** – are a larger and brighter discharge of electrical energy and are more likely to cause a fire;
- **short circuits** – arise when a current finds a path from live to return other than through apparatus, resulting in high current flow, heating of conductors to white heat and arcing;
- **overloading** – where too much current flows, causing heating of conductors; and
- **old and defective/damaged wiring** – through breakdown of the insulation, resulting in short circuit, or the use of progressively more equipment on an old circuit, resulting in overloading.

PRECAUTIONS AGAINST ELECTRIC SHOCK

The prime objective of electrical safety is to protect people from electric shock, and also from fire and burns, arising from contact with electricity. There are two basic preventive measures against electric shock, namely:

- protection against direct contact, eg by providing proper insulation for parts of equipment liable to be charged with electricity; and
- protection against indirect contact, eg by providing effective earthing for metallic enclosures which are liable to be charged with electricity if the basic insulation fails for any reason.

When it is not possible to provide adequate insulation as protection against direct contact, a range of measures is available, including protection by the use of barriers or enclosures, and protection by position, ie placing live parts out of reach.

- **Earthing.** This implies connection to the general mass of earth in such a manner as will ensure at all times an immediate discharge of electrical energy without danger. Earthing, to give protection against indirect contact with electricity, can be achieved in a number of ways, including the connection of extraneous conductive parts of premises (radiators, taps, water pipes) to the main earthing terminal of the electrical installation. This creates an equipotential zone and eliminates the risk of shock that could occur if a person touched two different parts of the metalwork liable to be charged, under earth fault conditions, at different voltages.

When an earth fault exists, such as when a live part touches an enclosed conductive part, eg metalwork, it is vital to ensure that the electrical supply is automatically disconnected. This protection is brought about by the use of overcurrent devices, ie correctly rated fuses or circuit breakers, or by correctly rated and placed residual current devices. The maintenance of earth continuity is vital.

- **Fuses.** A fuse is basically a strip of metal of such size as would melt at a predetermined value of current flow. It is placed in the electrical circuit and, on melting, cuts off the current to the circuit. A fuse should be of a type and rating appropriate to the circuit and the appliance it protects.
- **Circuit breakers.** These devices incorporate a mechanism which trips a switch from the 'ON' to 'OFF' position if an excess current flows in the circuit. A circuit breaker should be of the type and rating for the circuit and appliance it protects.
- **Earth leakage circuit breakers (residual current devices).** Fuses and circuit breakers do not necessarily provide total protection against electric shock. Earth leakage circuit breakers provide protection against earth leakage faults, particularly at those locations where effective earthing cannot necessarily be achieved.
- **Reduced voltage.** Reduced voltage systems are another form of protection against electric shock, the most commonly used being the 110-volt centre point earthed system. In this system the secondary winding of the transformer providing the 110-volt supply is centre-tapped to earth, thereby ensuring that at no part of the 110-volt circuit can the voltage to earth exceed 55 volts.
- **Safe systems of work.** When work is to be undertaken on electrical apparatus or a part of a circuit, a formally operated safe system of work should always be used. This normally takes the form of a permit-to-work system which ensures the following procedures:
  - switching out and locking off the electricity supply, ie isolation;
  - checking by the use of an appropriate voltage detection instrument that the circuit, or part of same to be worked on, is dead before work commences;
  - high levels of supervision and control to ensure the work is undertaken correctly;
  - physical precautions, such as the erection of barriers to restrict access to the area, are implemented; and
  - formal cancellation of the permit to work once the work is completed satisfactorily and return to service of the plant or system in question.

PORTABLE ELECTRICAL APPLIANCES

Portable appliances include such items as electric kettles, drills, vacuum cleaners, lamps and word processors, in fact anything that can be connected to a 13-amp socket. Also, 100-volt industrial portable electrical equipment should be considered as portable appliances.

Approximately a quarter of accidents involving electrical energy are associated with various forms of portable electrical appliance. To ensure compliance with the Electricity at Work Regulations, there is an implied duty on employers, in particular, to undertake some form of testing and examination of electrical equipment. Further guidance on portable appliance testing is incorporated in the *Memorandum of Guidance on the Electricity at Work Regulations 1989* and in HSE Guidance Note PM32: *The Safe Use of Portable Appliances*.

Safety of portable appliances

The operator or user of an electrical appliance is protected from the risk of electric shock by insulation and earthing of the appliance, which prevent him from coming into contact with a live electrical part. For insulation to be effective it must offer a high resistance at high voltages. In the case of earthing, it must offer a low impedance to any potentially high fault current that may arise.

A principle of electrical safety is that there should be two levels of protection for the operator or user, and this results in two classes of appliance. **Class 1 appliances** incorporate both earthing and insulation (earthed appliances), whereas **Class 2 appliances** are doubly insulated. The testing procedures for Class 1 and Class 2 appliances differ according to the type of protection provided.

Testing should be undertaken on a regular basis and should incorporate the following:

- inspection for any visible signs of damage to or deterioration of the casing, plug terminals and cable sheath;
- an earth continuity test with a substantial current capable of revealing a partially severed conductor; and
- high-voltage insulation tests.

The test results should be recorded, thus enabling future comparisons to determine any deterioration or degradation of the appliance.

The control system should include:

- clear identification of the specific responsibility for appliance testing;

- maintenance of a log or inventory of all portable appliances, serial-numbered and indicating the date of the last test and a record of test results;
- a procedure for labelling appliances with a serial number, the date when inspected and tested and the date for the next inspection and test.

Any appliance that fails the above tests should be removed from service.

An estimation of the frequency of testing must take into account the type of appliance, its usage in terms of frequency of use and the risk of damage, and any recommendations made by the manufacturer or supplier.

The testing of portable appliances

Tests of portable appliances should confirm the integrity or otherwise of earthing and insulation. To simplify this task a competent person may use a proprietary portable appliance testing (PAT) device. In this case, the appliance under test is plugged into the testing device. Some tests are undertaken through the plug, others through the plug and an auxiliary probe to the casing of the appliance.

Two basic tests can be undertaken with a PAT device, namely:

- **Earth bond test.** This applies a substantial test current, typically around 25 amps, down the earth pin of the plug to the earth test probe, which should be connected by the operator to any exposed metalwork on the casing of the appliance under test. From this the resistance of the earth bond is indicated by the PAT device.
- **Insulation test.** This applies a test voltage, typically 500 volts DC, between the live and neutral terminals bonded together and earth, from which the insulation resistance is indicated by the PAT device.

Other tests include:

- **Flash test.** This tests the insulation at a higher voltage, typically 1.5 kilovolts for Class 1 appliances and 3 kilovolts for Class 2 appliances. From this test, the PAT device derives a leakage current indication. This is a more stringent test of the insulation that can provide an early warning of insulation defects developing in the appliance.

  This test should not be undertaken at a greater frequency than every three months to avoid overstressing the insulation.
- **Load test.** This test measures the load resistance between the live and neutral terminals to ensure that it is not too low for safe operation.
- **Operation test.** This is a further level of safety testing which proves the above tests were valid.

141

- **Earth leakage test.** This test is undertaken during the operation test as a further test of the insulation under its true working conditions. It should also ensure that appliances are not responsible for nuisance tripping of residual current devices.
- **Fuse test.** This test will indicate the integrity of the fuse and that the appliance is switched on prior to other tests.

Earthed Class 1 appliances

The following tests are undertaken:

- earth bond test;
- insulation test; and
- in certain cases, flash test.

Double-insulated Class 2 appliances

The following tests are undertaken:

- insulation test; and
- flash test.

ELECTRIC STORAGE BATTERIES

Batteries, particularly those used for vehicles, can be particularly dangerous due to the risk of explosion, resulting in acid burns to the eyes, face and other parts of the body. Electrically operated vehicles, including lift trucks and commercial delivery vehicles, are commonly used for internal operation in factories and warehouses and for local delivery of goods. Vehicle battery charging in charging bays and workshops produces hydrogen, an extremely flammable gas, which can collect in pockets where such areas are inadequately ventilated. Where a source of ignition is present, such as a naked flame or spark, the gas and the battery will explode.

The HSE publication *Electric Storage Batteries: Safe charging and use* (IND(G)139L) recommends a number of general and specific precautions to be taken where batteries are involved.

KEY POINTS

- Electricity is a form of energy and, as such, can be dangerous.
- The risk of electric shock is the principal hazard associated with the use of electricity.
- Legal requirements are covered in the Electricity at Work Regulations 1989, which impose general duties on a range of 'duty holders'.
- In considering the requirements of the regulations, attention must be paid to the HSE memorandum of guidance on the regulations and the latest edition of the Institution of Electrical Engineers Wiring Regulations.
- Electrical discharge can be a significant cause of fire in premises.
- The three principles of electrical safety – insulation, isolation and earthing – should always be followed.
- Well-developed safe systems of work, including the use of permit-to-work systems, are essential for ensuring safe working with electrical installations.
- A formal system for the maintenance, examination and testing of portable electrical appliances is essential.
- Specific precautions are necessary to ensure the safe use and charging of electric storage batteries, particularly those used on vehicles.

7

Health and safety in construction operations

INTRODUCTION

Traditionally, the construction industry is one of the more dangerous industries. Every year people are killed during construction work through falls from heights, contact with site vehicles, collapses of structures and excavations and electric shock. Major injuries include fractures, amputations of limbs, blindings and crushed limbs.

Construction workers are further exposed to a range of occupational diseases and conditions, such as dermatitis through contact with hazardous substances, noise-induced hearing loss, asbestosis, respiratory conditions arising from exposure to dusts, vibration-induced conditions and prolapsed intervertebral discs arising from incorrect handling and lifting.

CONSTRUCTION ACTIVITIES – THE PRINCIPAL HAZARDS

While the hazards associated with construction activities are extensive, the principal hazards and their causative factors are outlined below:

- **Falls from ladders.** Falls are associated with the use of a ladder at an incorrect pitch, resulting in the ladder slipping out at the base or falling away at the top.

The '1 Out: 4 Up Rule' should always be applied in assessing the correct pitch of a ladder.

Falls can further arise from the use of defective wooden and metal ladders and as a result of overreaching situations.

- **Falls from working platforms.** Unfenced or inadequately fenced working platforms, inadequate and defective boarding to working platforms and the absence of toe boards are contributory factors in falls of people from working platforms.

- **Falls of materials.** Small objects, such as bricks, tiles and hammers, dropped from a height can cause fatal head injuries and other forms of serious injury to people below, including members of the public. This can arise through poor standards of housekeeping on working platforms, the absence of toe boards and barriers, incorrect assembly of gin wheel hoists for raising and lowering materials, incorrect or careless hooking and slinging of loads, the failure to install catching platforms (fans) and through demolition materials being thrown to the ground.

- **Falls from pitched roofs or through fragile roofs.** This is, perhaps, the most common type of fatal accident associated with the construction industry and with those involved in the maintenance of buildings. These falls arise through unsafe working practices at heights and on roofs, the use of inappropriate footwear, the failure to provide verge and eaves protection and to use crawl boards on pitched roofs, together with the stacking of roofing materials on fragile roofs.

- **Falls through openings in flat roofs and floors.** This type of accident arises due to the failure to provide or replace covers to openings or edge protection at openings in flat roofs and floors during various stages of construction. All covers should be clearly marked to indicate the presence of an opening below that cover.

- **Collapses of excavations.** Asphyxiation and fatal injury arising from the collapse of a trench or excavation commonly arise through a failure to support adequately a trench or excavation and in shifting sand situations. The presence of large quantities of water arising, perhaps, as a result of a flash flood or water main bursting may also be a contributory factor in collapse.

  Other causes of, particularly, trench collapses include the practice of stacking building materials, such as pallet loads of bricks, heavy concrete sewer pipe sections and heaps of sand too close to the edge of a deep open trench. The failure to reinstate trench timbering or supports following inspection by a competent person has also been indicated as a cause of trench collapses.

- **Transport accidents.** Injuries arising from people falling from vehicles, some of which may not be designed for carrying passengers, such as dumper trucks, are common.

  Other accidents involving transport on site include crushing by reversing vehicles where no banksman is in operation, collision with defective vehicles owing to inadequate maintenance of, for example, brakes and reversing systems, the operation of vehicles and machinery, particularly lifting appliances, by inexperienced and untrained people and overloading of passenger-carrying vehicles. In particular, poor standards of driving on site roads contribute greatly to death and major injuries sustained by employees and members of the public.

Site roads should be well maintained and drained, kept free from mud and debris as far as possible, and marked out.

- **Use of machinery and powered hand tools.** Failure to guard adequately moving and dangerous parts of machinery, such as power take-offs, woodworking machinery, belt drives and cooling fans, results in a wide range of major injuries.

    The use of powered hand tools with rotating heads, such as angle grinders, and the use of defective and uninsulated electric tools commonly result in a range of injuries from amputations of fingers to electrocution.

- **Housekeeping.** Standards of housekeeping on construction sites vary greatly. Slips, trips and falls, resulting in a range of injuries, are common. Site management should ensure a good standard of housekeeping at all times, including provisions for the storage of waste materials prior to removal.

- **Fire.** Inadequate fire protection measures, commonly associated with poor standards of site supervision, contribute greatly to the risk of fire. Uncontrolled 'hot work' activities, such as welding, may create ignition sources together with burning of site refuse.

    Well-established fire safety procedures, including regular fire drills, are an essential feature of site safety.

- **Personal protective equipment (PPE).** Failure on the part of employers to provide, and of employees to use or wear, PPE can be a contributory factor in many of the major injuries sustained by construction workers.

    Employers should have a clear policy on the provision and use of PPE based on the requirements of the Personal Protective Equipment Regulations 1992, including the undertaking of PPE risk assessments and selection of suitable PPE.

- **Work over water and transport across water.** Construction work on bridges, involving work over water, exposes construction employees to the risk of drowning. In these cases safety harnesses should be provided and used at all times.

    Transport over water to a particular workplace, such as a caisson, further exposes employees to the risk of drowning. This may be caused by the overcrowding of boats, defective and inadequate boats and the failure to provide barriers, life jackets or buoyancy aids and other forms of rescue equipment.

- **Work involving hazardous substances.** Construction workers come into contact with a wide range of hazardous substances, including lead, asbestos and chemical compounds. Failure to prevent or control adequately exposure to these substances, linked with poor standards of personal hygiene, can lead to chemical poisonings, dermatitis and, in some cases, asbestosis. Inhalation of hazardous dusts, such as cement dust, and those arising during demolition, due to a failure to use appropriate respiratory protection, can result in a range of respiratory disorders.

Employers are required to comply with the COSHH Regulations in this case, which includes their undertaking health risk assessments in respect of identified substances hazardous to health, to undertake air monitoring, for example, in the case of exposure to dust, and to provide health surveillance of employees where appropriate.

The Control of Lead at Work Regulations must be complied with where employees may be exposed to lead in its various forms. This may entail air monitoring and the provision of appropriate control measures to prevent inhalation of lead fumes in particular.

Many older buildings still contain asbestos in its various forms. In some cases, asbestos may be present in buildings scheduled for demolition. Here the Control of Asbestos at Work Regulations must be complied with, including the sampling of asbestos to ascertain the form of asbestos, such as blue asbestos (crocidolite), the procedures for stripping the asbestos (wet or dry stripping), air monitoring requirements and, in particular, the selection, provision and use of respiratory protective equipment. A pre-demolition survey of a building should identify the presence of asbestos.

- **Manual handling operations.** Manual handling injuries, such as prolapsed intervertebral discs and hernias, are common in the construction industry, arising from incorrect handling techniques and attempting to lift loads which are too heavy. This may arise from the failure to provide and/or use mechanical handling aids, such as hand trucks, barrows and lifting appliances.

  Employers are required to comply with the Manual Handling Operations Regulations with respect to the undertaking of manual handling risk assessments in cases where mechanical handling aids cannot be used. Employees should receive information, instruction and training in correct manual handling techniques, supported by constant supervision of their manual handling activities.

- **Work on underground services.** Damage to underground electricity, gas and water mains can arise during excavation of an existing site. This may be due to the absence, in many cases, of the plans of the site or the failure to consult existing site plans prior to work commencing.

  Cable and service locators should be used to identify existing service lines, and test holes should be made with a view to identifying drains and sewers. Unsafe digging and excavating has led to the electrocution of workers in the past, falls into underground spaces and the risk of flooding.

- **Work in confined spaces.** A 'confined space' is defined in the Confined Spaces Regulations 1997 as a place which is substantially, though not always entirely, enclosed and where there is a risk that anyone who may enter the space could be:
  - (a) injured due to fire or explosion;
  - (b) overcome by gases, fumes, vapour or the lack of oxygen;
  - (c) drowned;
  - (d) buried under free-flowing solids, such as grain; or
  - (e) overcome due to high temperature.

  Some confined spaces, such as closed tanks and vessels, open-topped tanks, silos and wells, are readily identifiable. However, construction operations may entail work in deep trenches and underground rooms where the risks may be less obvious.

  Work in confined spaces exposes operators to the risk, in particular, of both asphyxiation and anoxia (oxygen deficiency), which may be due to the absence of adequate ventilation in these spaces.

  Any work of this type must comply with the requirements of the regulations. Under the regulations employers must:
  - (a) avoid entry to confined spaces, for example by doing the work from outside;
  - (b) ensure employees follow a safe system of work, such as a permit-to-work system, if entry to a confined space is unavoidable; and
  - (c) put in place emergency arrangements before work starts, which will also safeguard any rescuers involved.

CLIENTS AND CONTRACTORS – CIVIL AND CRIMINAL LIABILITY

The interface between:

- owners and occupiers of land and premises, namely clients; and
- contractors, that is those who provide:
  - a contract of service, such as the erection or modification of a building; or
  - a contract for service, namely the provision of a particular service, such as the maintenance of buildings,

must be considered in terms of both civil and criminal liability.

Civil liability

An occupier is a person who is in control of land and premises and, as such, has a duty to ensure the safe management of same. A contractor, on the other hand, is a person or company who is invited by the occupier on to his land or premises to undertake some corporate function, or to whom performance of some duty has been delegated, such as cleaning the premises or maintaining the roadways. A main contractor may, in turn, employ subcontractors, such as electrical contractors, to undertake certain parts of the contract work.

Generally, all three parties, client, main contractor and subcontractor, can be construed as being 'in occupation' for the purposes of the Occupiers' Liability Act 1957 and can be proceeded against accordingly, including, where appropriate, any architect, civil engineer and geotechnical consultant, where it can be proved that they have been negligent. It should be appreciated that, within the concept of 'managerial control', the owner of land or a building may be just as much in control of a construction project as a main contractor and any subcontractors.

Criminal liability

Occupiers and owners (clients), main contractors and subcontractors are said to be 'in joint occupation and control'. Generally, the main contractor has the greatest liability under the criminal law, such as the Construction (Health, Safety and Welfare) Regulations (CHSWR) 1996, as he has the greatest control over operations. In the case of employers, however, the duties of employers under section 3 of the HSWA must be taken into account, namely the general duties of persons concerned with premises to persons other than their employees.

The Construction (Design and Management) (CDM) Regulations 1994 expand this legal relationship between clients, principal contractors and other contractors.

Regulating the contractor

There is a need for organizations to regulate the activities of all sorts of contractors with a view to preventing accidents and ill health arising from construction and allied activities. These activities can cover a wide range of situations, from simple window cleaning and external painting work to the implementation of a major project lasting several years. Not only must the requirements of the CDM Regulations be considered, but also duties under Regulation 11 of the MHSWR. Regulation 11 outlines duties of employers with respect to shared workplaces. A construction site is a typical 'shared workplace' and, on this basis, there must be 'co-operation and co-ordination' between the employers concerned.

Prior to work commencing, many factors must be considered by the parties concerned, including:

- consultation:
  - (a) prior to commencement of the work; and

    (b)   on an ongoing basis, commonly through weekly or fortnightly progress meetings;

- procedures for ensuring the operation of safe systems of work, including the use of permit-to-work systems and method statements;
- procedures for the investigation, reporting and recording of injuries, diseases and dangerous occurrences under RIDDOR;
- arrangements for use of the client's equipment in certain specified cases;
- measures to ensure the safe operation of plant and machinery on site;
- fire prevention and protection arrangements;
- the control of hazardous substances on site;
- noise prevention and control;
- the operation of contractors' vehicles, including parking arrangements;
- the use of personal protective equipment;
- arrangements for site safety inspections;
- first aid arrangements;
- emergency procedures;
- the provision of information, instruction and training for site workers;
- site clearance arrangements.

Contractors' safety regulations

In the light of the interface between clients and main contractors under the HSWA, CDM Regulations and other regulations affecting construction work, it is common practice for organizations to produce their own 'contractors' safety regulations' or 'rules for the safe conduct of project work', which are issued to contractors at the pre-tender stage of any contract work. As such, compliance with these regulations forms part of the contractual arrangements between client and principal contractor.

CONSTRUCTION SAFETY LAW

Construction (Head Protection) Regulations 1989

These regulations impose requirements for the provision of suitable head protection for, and the wearing of suitable head protection by, persons at work on building operations or works of engineering construction within the meaning of the Factories Act 1961.

    'Suitable head protection' means head protection which:

- is designed to provide protection, so far as is reasonably practicable, against foreseeable risks of injury to the head to which the wearer may be exposed;

- after any necessary adjustment, fits the wearer; and
- is suitable having regard to the work or activity in which the wearer may be engaged.

Under these regulations:

- employers must provide and maintain suitable head protection for employees and ensure it is worn;
- controllers of sites must make rules regulating the wearing of head protection;
- employees and self-employed persons must wear head protection when required to do so; and
- employees must further take reasonable care of head protection and report to their employer any loss of, or defect in, that head protection.

Construction (Design and Management) Regulations 1994

These regulations impose requirements and prohibitions with respect to the design and management aspects of construction work as defined.

Construction work means the carrying out of any building, civil engineering or engineering construction work and includes any of the following:

- the construction, alteration, conversion, fitting out, commissioning, renovation, repair, upkeep, redecoration or other maintenance (including cleaning which involves the use of water or an abrasive at high pressure or the use of substances classified as corrosive or toxic for the purposes of Regulation 7 of the Chemicals (Hazard Information and Packaging for Supply) Regulations 1994), decommissioning, demolition or dismantling of a structure;
- the preparation for an intended structure, including site clearance, exploration, investigation (but not site survey) and excavation, and laying or installing the foundations of the structure;
- the assembly of prefabricated elements to form a structure or the disassembly of prefabricated elements which, immediately before such disassembly, formed a structure;
- the removal of a structure or part of a structure or of any product or waste resulting from demolition or dismantling of a structure or from disassembly of prefabricated elements which, immediately before such disassembly, formed a structure;
- the installation, commissioning, maintenance, repair or removal of mechanical, electrical, gas, compressed air, hydraulic, telecommunications, computer or similar services which are normally fixed within or to a structure,

but does *not* include the exploration for or extraction of mineral resources or activities preparatory thereto carried out at a place where such exploration or extraction is carried out.

A project is notifiable to the HSE if the construction phase:

- will be longer than 30 days; or
- will involve more than 500 person days of construction work.

The principal requirements of the regulations are outlined below:

- Clients must appoint:
  (a) a planning supervisor; and
  (b) a principal contractor,
  in respect of each project.
- The same person, including the client, may be appointed as both planning supervisor and principal contractor provided he is competent to carry out the functions under these regulations; designers must be competent to prepare design.
- Clients and other persons making arrangements for project work must be reasonably satisfied that planning supervisors, designers and contractors have allocated, or will allocate, adequate resources to comply with requirements under the regulations or under the relevant statutory provisions.
- Clients must ensure, so far as is reasonably practicable, that the construction phase of any project does not start unless a health and safety plan has been prepared in respect of that project.
- Clients must ensure that the planning supervisor is provided (as soon as is reasonably practicable but in any event before the commencement of the work to which the information relates) with information about the state or condition of any premises at or on which construction work included or intended to be included in the project is or is intended to be carried out.
- Clients must take reasonable steps to ensure that the information in any health and safety file which has been delivered to them is kept available for inspection by any person who may need information.
- No employer shall cause or permit any employee of his to prepare, and no self-employed person shall prepare, a design in respect of any project unless he has taken reasonable steps to ensure that the client for that project is aware of the duties to which the client is subject by virtue of these regulations and of any practical guidance issued from time to time by the Commission (HSC) with respect to the requirements of these regulations.

- Every designer shall:
  - (a) ensure that any design he prepares and which he is aware will be used for the purposes of the construction work includes among the design considerations adequate regard to the need: (i) to avoid foreseeable risks; (ii) to combat at source risks to the health and safety of any person at work; (iii) to give priority to measures which will protect all persons at work over measures which only protect each person carrying out such work;
  - (b) ensure that the design includes adequate information about any aspect of the project or structure or materials (including articles or substances) which might affect the health or safety of any person at work; and
  - (c) cooperate with the planning supervisor.
- The planning supervisor shall:
  - (a) ensure, so far as is reasonably practicable, that the design of any structure comprised in the project: (i) includes among the design considerations adequate regard to the needs specified in heads (i) to (iii) above; and (ii) includes information as specified above;
  - (b) take such steps as it is reasonable for a person in his position to take to ensure cooperation between designers;
  - (c) give adequate advice to any client and any contractor;
  - (d) ensure that the health and safety file is prepared in respect of each structure comprised in the project;
  - (e) review, amend or add to the health and safety file; and
  - (f) ensure that, on completion of the construction work on each structure comprised in the project, the health and safety file in respect of that structure is delivered to the client.
- The planning supervisor shall ensure that a health and safety plan in respect of the project has been prepared and contains the appropriate information (the pre-tender stage health and safety plan).
- The principal contractor shall take such measures as it is reasonable for a person in his position to take to ensure that the health and safety plan (the construction phase health and safety plan) incorporates all the information specified in Regulation 15.
- The principal contractor must:
  - (a) take reasonable steps to ensure cooperation between all contractors on health and safety requirements relating to construction work;
  - (b) ensure, so far as is reasonably practicable, that every contractor, and every employee at work complies with any rules contained within the health and safety plan; and
  - (c) take reasonable steps to ensure that only authorized persons are allowed on site.

- The principal contractor may:
  - (a) give reasonable directions to any contractor so far as is necessary to enable the principal contractor to comply with his duties under these regulations;
  - (b) include in the health and safety plan rules for the management of the construction work.
- The principal contractor shall ensure, so far as is reasonably practicable, that every contractor is provided with comprehensible information on the risks to the health or safety of that contractor or of any employees or other persons.
- The principal contractor must ensure that employees and self-employed persons at work on the construction work are able to discuss, and offer advice to him on, matters connected with the project which it can reasonably be foreseen will affect their health or safety.
- Contractors must cooperate with the principal contractor so far as is necessary to enable each of them to comply with his duties under the relevant statutory provisions, comply with any directions of the principal contractor (to enable compliance with these regulations), comply with any rules applicable to him in the health and safety plan, promptly provide the principal contractor with the information in relation to any death, injury, condition or dangerous occurrence which the contractor is required to notify or report by virtue of RIDDOR, and promptly provide the principal contractor with any information which may be needed for incorporation in the health and safety file.

Construction (Health, Safety and Welfare) Regulations 1996

These regulations apply to all persons engaged in construction work (as defined above), namely employers, the self-employed, people controlling construction work and employees. Duties are largely of an absolute nature.

Under the regulations, employers must:

- ensure safe places of work (above and below ground) with suitable and sufficient safe access to and egress from same;
- so far as is reasonably practicable, take suitable and sufficient steps to prevent people falling from heights by, for example, the provision of safe working platforms to scaffolds;
- take suitable and sufficient steps to prevent any person falling a distance of more than 2 metres through any fragile material, such as asbestos-cement roof coverings;
- take suitable and sufficient steps, so far as is reasonably practicable, to prevent the fall of any material or object which is liable to cause injury;
- take all practicable steps to ensure that any new or existing structure or part of any such structure which may become unstable or in a temporary state of

weakness or instability due to the carrying out of construction work (including any excavation work) does not collapse accidentally;

- take suitable and sufficient steps to ensure that the demolition or dismantling of any structure is planned and carried out in such a way as to prevent, so far as is practicable, danger;
- when using or firing an explosive charge, take sufficient steps to ensure that no person is exposed to risk of injury;
- take all practicable steps to ensure that any new or existing excavation or any part of such excavation which may be in a temporary state of weakness or instability due to the carrying out of construction work (including other excavation work) does not collapse accidentally;
- take suitable and sufficient steps to prevent, so far as is reasonably practicable, any person being buried or trapped by a fall or dislodgement of any material;
- provide suitable and sufficient equipment for supporting an excavation, any installation, alteration or dismantling of any support for an excavation to be carried out only under the supervision of a competent person;
- take suitable and sufficient steps to prevent any person, vehicle or plant and equipment, or any accumulation of earth or other material, from falling into any excavation;
- take suitable and sufficient steps to identify, so far as is reasonably practicable, and prevent any risk of injury arising from any underground cable or other underground service;
- ensure every cofferdam or caisson and every part thereof is of suitable design and construction, of suitable and sound material and of sufficient strength and capacity for the purpose for which it is used, and is properly maintained, the construction, installation, alteration and dismantling of a cofferdam or caisson to take place only under the supervision of a competent person;
- where during the course of construction work any person is liable to fall into water or other liquid with a risk of drowning, take suitable and sufficient steps to protect such persons from risk of drowning or injury;
- take suitable and sufficient steps to ensure safe transport of any person conveyed by water to or from any place of work;
- organize every construction site in such a way that, so far as is reasonably practicable, pedestrians and vehicles can move safely and without risks to health;
- ensure any door, gate or hatch (including a temporary door, gate or hatch), where there may be a risk of injury to persons on site, incorporates or is fitted with suitable safety devices;
- ensure suitable and sufficient steps are taken to prevent or control the unintended movement of any vehicle;
- ensure safe movement of vehicles on site;

- where any vehicle is used for excavating or handling (including tipping) materials, ensure suitable and sufficient measures are taken to prevent such vehicle from falling into any excavation or pit, or into water, or overrunning the edge of any embankment or earthwork;
- take suitable and sufficient steps to prevent, so far as is reasonably practicable, the risk of injury to any person during the carrying out of construction work arising from fire or explosion, flooding or any substance liable to cause asphyxiation;
- provide and maintain a sufficient number of emergency routes and exits to enable any person to reach a place of safety quickly in the event of danger;
- prepare and, when necessary, implement suitable and sufficient arrangements for dealing with foreseeable emergency, which arrangements shall include procedures for necessary evacuation of the site or any part thereof;
- provide suitable and sufficient fire-fighting equipment, fire detectors and alarm systems which shall be suitably located, together with, so far as is reasonably practicable, instruction for persons at work in the correct use of any fire-fighting equipment which it may be necessary for them to use;
- provide:
  - suitable and sufficient sanitary conveniences and washing facilities, including showers if required by the nature of the work or for health reasons, at readily accessible places;
  - an adequate supply of wholesome drinking water;
  - accommodation for clothing which is not worn during working hours and for special clothing which is worn by any person at work but which is not taken home;
  - suitable and sufficient facilities to change clothing; and
  - suitable and sufficient facilities for rest;
- ensure suitable and sufficient steps are taken to ensure, so far as is reasonably practicable, that every workplace or approach thereto has sufficient fresh or purified air;
- take suitable and sufficient steps, so far as is reasonably practicable, to ensure that during working hours the temperature at any indoor place of work is reasonable;
- arrange every place of work outdoors, so far as is reasonably practicable and having regard to the purpose for which that place is used and any protective clothing or equipment provided for the use of any person at work there, to provide protection from adverse weather;
- provide suitable and sufficient lighting in respect of every place of work and approach thereto and every traffic route, which lighting shall, so far as is reasonably practicable, be by natural light;
- keep every part of a construction site, so far as is reasonably practicable, in good order and every part which is used as a place of work in a reasonable state of cleanliness;

- ensure plant and equipment used for the purpose of carrying out construction work, so far as is reasonably practicable, is safe and without risks to health and of good construction, of suitable and sound materials and of sufficient strength and suitability for the purpose for which it is used or provided;
- ensure any person who carries out any activity involving construction work where training, technical knowledge or experience is necessary to reduce the risks of injury to any person has such training, knowledge or experience, or is under such degree of supervision by a person having such training, knowledge or experience, as may be appropriate having regard to the nature of the activity;
- ensure a place of work referred to in Column 1 of Schedule 7 is used to carry out construction work only if that place has been inspected by a competent person at the times set out in the corresponding entry in Column 2 of that schedule and the person who has carried out the inspection is satisfied that the work can be safely carried out in that place.

Schedule 7, Regulation 29 (1), Places of work requiring inspection

Column 1 Place of Work	Column 2 Time of Inspection
1. Any working platform or part thereof or any personal suspension equipment provided pursuant to paragraph 3 (b) or (c) of Regulation 6.	1. (i) Before being taken into use for the first time; and (ii) after any substantial addition, dismantling or other alteration; and (iii) after any event likely to have affected its strength or stability; and (iv) at regular intervals not exceeding seven days since the last inspection.
2. Any excavation which is supported pursuant to paragraphs 1, 2 or 3 of Regulation 12.	2. (i) Before any person carries out work at the start of every shift; and (ii) after any event likely to have affected the strength or stability of the excavation or any part thereof; and (iii) after any accidental fall of rock or earth or other material.
3. Cofferdams and caissons.	3. (i) Before any person carries out work at the start of every shift; and (ii) after any event likely to have affected the strength or stability of the cofferdam or caisson or any part thereof.

CONSTRUCTION ACTIVITIES – THE PRINCIPAL PRECAUTIONS

Safety inspections and risk assessment

Both clients and main contractors should ensure safety inspections of sites are carried out on a frequent basis. Safety inspections are designed to identify hazards and the precautions necessary.

In many cases a client or main contractor, as a result of a safety inspection, may need to undertake risk assessment for certain aspects of construction work prior to work commencing. Risk assessments must take into account, in particular, the requirements of the CHSWR and the various schedules to these regulations for ensuring safety in a range of situations.

One of the outcomes of a risk assessment, for example in dealing with work on a fragile roof or work involving the use of explosives, is the preparation of a safety method statement.

Safety method statements

These are formally written safe systems of work, or a series of integrating safe systems of work, agreed between a client and a main contractor, or between a main contractor and a subcontractor, and produced where work with a foreseeably high level of risk is to be undertaken, for example work below ground level, work at heights, demolition operations, operations involving the use of explosives, the stripping and removal of asbestos and work on fragile roofs.

Under the CDM Regulations the need for contractors to produce safety method statements prior to high-risk operations should be incorporated in the pre-tender stage health and safety plan.

In certain cases, a standard form of safety method statement may be agreed, used and signed by the main contractor as an indication of his intention to follow that particular safe system of work.

The method statement should specify:

- the operations to be carried out;
- the techniques to be used;
- access provisions;
- measures for safeguarding existing locations;
- structural stability requirements, for example shoring arrangements;
- methods for ensuring the safety of others, such as members of the public;
- health precautions, such as the use of local exhaust ventilation systems;
- procedures to prevent local pollution;
- segregation of certain areas, with or without barriers;

- procedures for disposal of toxic and other wastes; and
- procedures for ensuring compliance with specific legislation, such as the Lead at Work Regulations and the Environmental Protection Act.

Further requirements for work involving asbestos

In addition to the above requirements, the following aspects should be incorporated in a specific safety method statement where work entails the removal or stripping of asbestos from a building:

- the specific safe system of work to be operated;
- procedures for segregation and sealing off of the asbestos-stripping area;
- personal protective equipment requirements;
- welfare amenity provisions, including:
  - sanitation arrangements;
  - hand-washing and showering arrangements;
  - arrangements for separating protective clothing from personal clothing;
  - arrangements for separating clean protective clothing from soiled protective clothing; and
  - drinking water arrangements;
- ventilation requirements and arrangements for the working area;
- personal hygiene requirements for operators;
- atmospheric monitoring procedures, including action to be taken in the event of unsatisfactory results from air samples taken; and
- notification requirements under the Control of Asbestos at Work Regulations.

Work above ground level

Basic scaffolding requirements

- Safe means of access to and egress from working platforms.
- Scaffolds provided at working heights above 2 metres.
- Toe boards, intermediate rails and top rails fitted and maintained.
- Working areas adequately lit.
- No materials to be thrown or tipped from working platforms; tipping chutes to be used.
- Rigidly constructed so as to prevent accident displacement and connected to the building unless constructed as an independent scaffold.
- Standards vertical or leaning towards structure; securely fixed and braced.
- Ledgers and transoms horizontal and securely fixed.
- Putlogs straight and securely fixed.

- Gangways and working platforms adequate in width.
- Working platforms completely boarded and with no gaps between boards.
- Stairs fitted with handrails; toe boards fitted on landings.
- Competent and experienced scaffolders employed for erection, modification and dismantling.
- Record of inspections by a competent person.

Movable (mobile) access equipment

This equipment is commonly used for high-level maintenance work, painting and small-scale building work. It commonly takes the form of a movable tower formed from scaffold tubes or pre-formed frames. (Other forms comprise a scissor-lift or telescopic arrangement incorporating a working platform.)

The tower should incorporate a working platform, access by means of an externally fixed ladder or internally placed raking ladders, and casters at the base which permit the tower to be moved with ease. The following requirements are necessary to ensure safe working:

- secure working platform, completely boarded and fitted with toe boards, intermediate rails and handrails;
- height not to exceed three times the smaller base dimension;
- outriggers may be necessary to increase stability during windy weather conditions;
- diagonal bracing on all four elevations and horizontally;
- casters at corners securely fixed and fitted with locking devices;
- moved with considerable care by pushing or pulling at base level;
- no person, equipment or materials to be present on the working platform during movement.

See further BS 5973: 1981 *Code of Practice for Access and Working Scaffolds and Special Scaffold Structures in Steel*.

Ladders

These precautions cover the actual construction and use of ladders:

- sound construction and maintenance;
- wooden ladders:
  - (a) to have the stiles and rungs with the grain running lengthwise;
  - (b) not to be painted or treated as to hide defects; treatment with clear preservative acceptable;
  - (c) fitted with reinforcing ties;

- equally and properly supported on each stile;
- securely fixed near its upper resting place, or at lower end, or footed;
- terminating at least 1 metre above the landing place;
- landing places every 9.14 metres (30 feet) of vertical distance; landing places fitted with handrails, intermediate rails and toe boards;
- openings in landing as small as possible;
- folding ladders to have a level and firm footing.

Roof work

Falls from or through roofs are the principal types of fatal and major injury accident in construction work. In many cases, these falls are associated with work on fragile roofs constructed from corrugated asbestos cement sheeting, corrugated iron sheets and timber which has decayed to the extent that it is no longer safe to walk on.

Generally, falls occur from the edges of roofs, through gaps or holes in roofs or through fragile roof materials and roof lights. Other accidents are associated with materials thrown from roofs or falling off roofs.

To ensure safe working on roofs a number of precautions must be taken:

- All roof work should be subject to risk assessment taking into account the requirements of the CHSWR. A method statement should be prepared covering the hazards and precautions necessary identified by the risk assessment.
- A secure means of access to and egress from the roof should be provided.
- Appropriate edge protection, comprising a guard rail, intermediate rail and toe board, should be installed in most cases, particularly in the case of flat roofs.
- Where it may not be reasonably practicable to provide working platforms and edge protection, fall arrest equipment, such as safety harnesses or safety nets, should be provided.
- Measures must be taken to prevent materials falling from a roof onto people below, particularly where there may be a risk to members of the public. These measures may include the installation of catching fans and covered walkways, and the provision of chutes and skips for waste materials.
- Consideration must be given to prevailing weather conditions and, in some cases, a decision may need to be made to take people off a roof during inclement weather. Similarly, employers must consider the risk of exposure to excessive sunlight during roof work.
- Particular care must be taken where working on or adjacent to fragile roofs. A full examination of the roof surface must be made with a view to identifying the form of safe system of work necessary. This may entail the installation of safety nets and the use of safety harnesses. The practice of 'running the roof' by walking

- along the line of a roof truss or purlin, with no form of protection, should be prohibited.
- Properly designed roof ladders or crawling boards are essential when working on pitched roofs. Such ladders should be long enough and securely placed.
- All employees working on roofs should be trained to recognize the hazards arising during such work and the precautions necessary.

Work below ground level

Work below ground may entail working in trenches and large excavations. The principal hazard is the risk of collapse of the trench or excavation, together with flooding and people, materials and vehicles falling into same. In some cases, operators may come into contact with live electricity cables. The requirements of the CHSWR must be taken into account at the planning stage of an excavation.

Factors to be considered in the support of an excavation are:

- the nature of the subsoil;
- the projected life of the excavation;
- the actual work to be undertaken, including the use of any equipment;
- the potential for flooding;
- the depth of the trench or excavation; and
- the number of people who will be working below ground level at any one time.

The principal safety requirements are as follows:

- sides and ends battered to a safe angle or supported with timber, sheeting or a purpose-designed support system;
- no spoil or other materials stored close to the edge of the excavation;
- barriers and vehicle stops installed;
- no vehicles parked or allowed near the edge of the excavation;
- adequate access by means of ladders placed at regular intervals along trench;
- struts and braces securely fixed;
- timbering of good construction, sound material, free from patent defect and of adequate strength;
- excavations and approaches well lit;
- means for reaching place of safety in the event of sudden flooding;
- mechanical ventilation provided where there may be a risk of asphyxiation from gases, etc;
- record of inspections by competent person.

Demolition

Demolition is the most hazardous operation undertaken in construction activities. The principal hazards are associated with risks arising from:

- falls of people and materials;
- collapses of structures;
- overloading of floors with debris, resulting in floors collapsing;
- incorrect or unsafe demolition techniques;
- explosions in tanks or other confined spaces;
- live electricity cables and gas mains;
- dusty, corrosive and poisonous materials and/or atmospheres; and
- physical hazards arising from broken glass, projecting nails and cast iron fragments which can cause a range of minor injuries.

In addition to supervision of demolition activities by a competent person, including continuing inspections of operations, the precautions necessary prior to and during demolition include:

- a pre-demolition survey to identify, for instance, the nature and method of construction, previous use of the premises, the location of services, the presence of hazardous substances, including asbestos, cantilevered structures which may need special attention, and any steelwork which may need cutting prior to demolition commencing;
- the preparation of safety method statements and the briefing of operators on the precautions detailed in method statements;
- isolation of services;
- installation of fans or catching platforms;
- ensuring the provision and use of appropriate personal protective equipment, including safety boots, safety helmets and respiratory protection;
- use of temporary shoring arrangements between floors;
- effective control when pulling arrangements, a demolition ball, pusher arm and/ or explosives are being used;
- protection against falling items, such as masonry and brickwork;
- control over access to dangerous areas;
- the use of scaffolding where manual demolition is being carried out;
- protection against falling, through the use of safety harnesses and the installation of safety nets;
- a prohibition on work over open joisting;
- prior removal of glass in windows, partitions and doors; and

- the installation of measures to prevent premature collapse, such as the supporting of specific walls with raking shores.

Wherever mechanical demolition is being carried out, drivers and operators must be adequately trained, and banksmen must be in attendance at all times.

KEY POINTS

- The construction industry has always been one of the more dangerous industries and, as such, has always been extensively regulated from a safety viewpoint.
- The principal hazards to construction workers are the risk of falls from a height and from falling materials.
- Clients and contractors have a range of liabilities under both civil and criminal law.
- All organizations should have procedures for regulating the activities of contractors.
- Construction safety law is concerned with both the safety management of construction work and the prevention of accidents and ill health arising from same.
- All persons must use suitable head protection whenever there is a foreseeable risk of head injury.
- Under the CDM Regulations, clients, designers, planning supervisors, main contractors and other contractors have specific duties.
- The term 'construction work' is very broadly defined.
- Most construction projects must be notified to the HSE.
- Certain places of work, such as the working platforms to scaffolds and excavations, must be inspected by a competent person on a regular basis and for specific purposes.
- Safety method statements should be produced for activities where there is a foreseeable risk of injury.
- Specific precautions are required during the stripping and removal of asbestos.
- Demolition is the most dangerous aspect of construction work, resulting in deaths of operators every year.

8

Occupational health

INTRODUCTION

People at work can be exposed to risks to their health and may contract a range of occupational diseases and conditions. Some people may die as a result of contracting, for instance, occupational cancer, pneumoconiosis or some form of chemical poisoning. Others may be permanently incapacitated through conditions such as noise-induced hearing loss (occupational deafness), occupational asthmas, vibration-induced injury and brucellosis.

This chapter examines the very broad area of occupational health and occupational health practice, including stress at work, health surveillance procedures and the legal requirements relating to, for instance, the control of noise, radiation and asbestos in the workplace.

WHAT IS OCCUPATIONAL HEALTH?

Occupational health is a preventive form of medicine concerned with, firstly, the relationship of work to health and, secondly, the effects of work on the worker.

Occupational health practice is, fundamentally, concerned with measures to prevent or reduce the risk of occupational disease and includes a range of health surveillance procedures.

In its wider context, it incorporates:

- systems for the identification, measurement, evaluation and control of occupational health risks;
- advising employers on welfare amenity provisions, including arrangements for washing and showers, sanitation, clothing storage, facilities for taking meals and the provision of drinking water;
- first aid arrangements, including the training of first aid staff and the provision of emergency services in the event of serious injury;
- consideration of the ergonomic aspects of tasks;
- the selection, provision, assessment of suitability, maintenance and use of personal protective equipment;
- the provision of information, instruction, training and constant supervision for all persons exposed to health risks.

OCCUPATIONAL HEALTH PRACTITIONERS

Various specialists have a contribution to make in the field of occupational health.

Occupational physicians

Occupational physicians are registered medical practitioners who have specialized in occupational medicine, namely the diagnosis and treatment of occupational diseases and conditions.

The British Medical Association has identified the role of the occupational physician as encompassing the following:

1. **The effect of health on the capacity to work**, which includes:
    - provision of advice to employees on all health matters relating to their working capacity;
    - examination of applicants for employment and advice as to their placement;
    - immediate treatment of surgical and medical emergencies occurring at the place of employment;
    - examination and continued observation of persons returning to work after absence due to illness or accident and advice on suitable work;
    - health supervision of all employees with special reference to young persons, pregnant women, elderly persons and disabled persons.
2. **The effect of work on health**, which includes:
    - responsibility for nursing and first aid services;

- study of the work and working environment and how they affect the health of employees;
- periodical examination of employees exposed to special hazards in respect of their employment;
- advising management regarding: the working environment in relation to health; occurrence and significance of hazards; accident prevention; and statutory requirements in relation to health;
- medical supervision of the health and hygiene of staff and facilities, with particular reference to canteens, kitchens, etc and those working in the production of food or drugs for sale to the public;
- arranging and carrying out such education work in respect of the health, fitness and hygiene of employees as may be desirable and practicable;
- advising those committees within the organization which are responsible for the health, safety and welfare of employees.

Occupational health nurses

Occupational health nurses are registered general nurses (RGNs) with a specific qualification in occupational health nursing. The occupational health nurse's role incorporates eight main elements:

- health supervision;
- health education;
- environmental monitoring and occupational safety;
- counselling on health-related issues;
- the provision of a treatment service;
- rehabilitation and resettlement;
- unit administration and the record systems;
- liaison with other services, eg employment medical advisers of the Employment Medical Advisory Service (EMAS).

Occupational hygienists

Occupational hygiene is defined as being concerned with the identification, measurement, evaluation and control of contaminants, and other physical phenomena, such as noise and radiation, which may adversely affect the health of employees.

Occupational hygienists are, therefore, frequently involved in the taking of samples of airborne contaminants, such as gases and fumes, together with asbestos fibres, and in the measurement of noise and vibration. In most cases they work in conjunction with a laboratory which undertakes analysis of air samples. The significance of occupational hygiene has increased as a result of recent legislation, such as the Control of Substances Hazardous to Health (COSHH) Regulations and the Control of Asbestos at Work Regulations.

Entry to the profession is regulated by the British Examination Board in Occupational Hygiene (BEBOH).

CLASSIFICATION OF OCCUPATIONAL HEALTH RISKS

Occupational health risks can generally be classified into four main groups, thus:

- **Physical.** This group entails exposure to physical phenomena, such as noise, radiation and vibration, along with extremes of temperature and pressure, inadequate lighting and airborne particulates, such as dust. Exposure to these physical risks can result in a range of conditions, including noise-induced hearing loss, heat stroke, radiation sickness, decompression sickness, pneumoconiosis, vibration-induced white finger and heat cataract.
- **Chemical.** Exposure to chemical substances classified as 'toxic', 'corrosive', 'harmful' and 'irritant' under the CHIP Regulations (see Chapter 11) can result in death along with a wide range of chemical poisonings and occupational cancers. Dermatitis is a classic indication of exposure to hazardous chemicals.
- **Biological.** Certain types of work, for instance in agriculture and hospital laboratories, may expose people to the risk of exposure to bacteria, viruses and other harmful micro-organisms, some of which are transmissible to humans. These include the human version of anthrax, brucellosis, leptospirosis, legionnaires' disease and aspergillosis (farmer's lung). Certain diseases, such as anthrax and brucellosis, are transmissible from animals to humans (zoonoses).
- **Ergonomic (work related).** The effects on people of poorly designed work layouts and workstations, together with excessive and repetitive movements of joints, can lead to visual fatigue, postural fatigue, physical and mental stress and a range of conditions. These include, for example, writer's cramp, various 'beat' disorders, such as beat elbow and beat wrist, and that group of disorders known as the 'work-related upper limb disorders' or repetitive strain injury.

  Conditions arising from manual handling operations, such as prolapsed intervertebral disc (slipped disc), hernias, and muscle and ligamental strains, also come in this category.

  The potential for stress-induced injury must also be considered in the design of tasks.

REPORTABLE DISEASES

Certain diseases and conditions arising from work are reportable by the employer to the enforcement authority under RIDDOR and are listed in Schedule 3. For a disease to be reportable it must be listed in Column 1 of Part 1 of the schedule and must involve one of the activities specified in the corresponding entry in Column 2 of that part.

There are 47 diseases and they are listed under three groups:

1. **conditions due to physical agents and the physical demands of work**, such as malignant disease of the bones due to ionizing radiation, decompression illness and subcutaneous cellulitis of the hand (beat hand);
2. **infections due to biological agents**, such as anthrax, brucellosis, leptospirosis, Q fever and tetanus;
3. **conditions due to substances**, including poisoning by, for instance, carbon disulphide, ethylene oxide and methyl bromide, cancer of a bronchus or lung, bladder cancer, acne (through work involving exposure to mineral oil, tar, pitch or arsenic) and pneumoconiosis (excluding asbestosis).

Reportable diseases must be reported by the employer to the relevant enforcing authority on Form 2508A, 'Report of a disease'.

PRESCRIBED DISEASES

The Social Security (Industrial Injuries) (Prescribed Diseases) Regulations 1985 (as amended) list those diseases which are prescribed for the purpose of payment of disablement benefit.

A prescribed disease is defined in the Social Security Act 1975 as:

- a disease which ought to be treated, having regard to its causes and incidence and other relevant considerations, as a risk of occupation and not a risk common to all persons; and
- such that, in the absence of special circumstances, the attribution of particular cases to the nature of the employment can be established with reasonable certainty.

Schedule 1 to the regulations classifies prescribed diseases and injuries thus:

- **conditions due to physical agents**, such as heat stroke, noise-induced hearing loss, miner's nystagmus and decompression sickness;

- **conditions due to biological agents**, such as viral hepatitis, aspergillosis, brucellosis and glanders fever;
- **conditions due to chemical agents**, such as lead, mercury, phosphorus and arsenic poisoning, occupational cancers and arsine poisoning;
- **miscellaneous conditions**, such as coal worker's pneumoconiosis and non-infective dermatitis.

THE PRINCIPAL OCCUPATIONAL DISEASES AND CONDITIONS

Many occupational diseases and conditions were common in the 18th century and can be traced to the Industrial Revolution. Lead poisoning and mercury poisoning, on the other hand, were recorded as common in Roman times. Many industries are associated with specific diseases. For instance, the coal-mining industry is associated with coal worker's pneumoconiosis, the textile industry with byssinosis and the pottery industry with silicosis. In recent years, considerable attention has been paid to that group of disorders known as the work-related upper limb disorders, to noise-induced hearing loss and to occupational cancers.

Fundamentally, wherever people are at work, they can be exposed to some form of occupational ill-health risk due to exposure to a range of physical, chemical, biological and work-related agents.

Physically induced conditions

The pneumoconioses

Dust in all its forms and particle sizes represents a significant hazard to workers. The pneumoconioses are a range of lung disorders of a chronic fibrotic nature arising from inhalation of a range of dusts, such as silica, and fibres, particularly in the case of asbestosis. In its broadest sense, pneumoconiosis is defined by the International Labour Organization as 'the accumulation of dust in the lungs and the tissue reactions to its presence'.

Temperature-related conditions

Regular exposure to excessive heat from work processes can result in a number of conditions, such as heat stroke and cataracts of the eye.

Noise-induced hearing loss (occupational deafness)

Noise is defined as 'unwanted sound', and the most common condition associated with exposure to noise is occupational deafness. The Social Security (Industrial

Injuries) (Prescribed Diseases) Regulations define occupational deafness as 'substantial sensorineural hearing loss amounting to at least 50 dB in each ear, being due in the case of at least one ear to occupational noise, and being the average of pure tone losses measured by audiometry over the 1, 2 and 3 kHz frequencies'.

For most types of industrial noise, the dose received, ie the intensity of noise related to the duration of exposure, is the principal consideration as to the degree of noise-induced hearing loss. It should be appreciated that the ability to hear reduces with age (presbyacusis) and it may be difficult to distinguish between this condition and the effects of exposure to noise (sociocusis).

Vibration-induced injury

Risks to health are associated with the use of vibratory hand tools, such as hand-held grinders and drilling equipment, and in situations where the whole body is subject to continuing vibration, as with long-distance lorry driving. Users of vibratory hand tools may suffer from vibration-induced white finger. People such as HGV drivers can experience blurred vision, loss of balance and loss of concentration, a contributory factor in road accidents.

Electric shock

Shock is the principal hazard associated with electricity and a number of factors can affect the severity of same. Death and injury are caused through a current flowing through the body and, in particular, the heart.

Radiation

Radiation is a form of energy and may take a number of forms – alpha particles, beta particles, gamma rays, X-rays, neutrons, bremsstrahlung and cosmic rays. Sources of radiation can be classified as non-ionizing and ionizing radiation. (An **ion** is a charged atom or group of atoms.)

Non-ionizing radiation includes lasers, ultraviolet radiation, infra-red radiation and microwaves. Ionizing radiation sources include radioactive gases and X-ray equipment.

The effects of exposure to ionizing radiation vary according to the type of exposure, eg local, that is, affecting only a part of the body surface, or general, affecting the whole body. The duration of exposure determines the severity of body injury.

Local exposure, the more common form of exposure, may cause reddening of the skin, the skin becoming ulcerated in serious cases. Where exposure is local, the dose small but of long duration, this may cause fibrosis of the skin and loss of hair. Acute general exposure, on the other hand, can have a number of effects on the body, ranging from mild nausea to vomiting, diarrhoea, collapse and eventual death. General exposure to small doses can result in chronic anaemia and leukaemia. There may also be effects on the reproductive system in that the ovaries and testes are particularly vulnerable, resulting in reduced fertility and even sterility.

In addition to the increased susceptibility to cancer, exposure to radiation may damage the genetic structure of reproductive cells, causing stillbirths and malformations of babies born.

Pressure

Work in compressed air, eg in pressurized caissons and diving bells, and in diving operations, may expose people to the risk of decompression sickness.

Chemical agents

Many chemical agents are used in workplaces in specific processes, as cleaning compounds and in laboratory work. The effects on the body can vary significantly. However, the main effects can be classified into a number of clear-cut areas, namely chemical poisonings, occupational cancers, dermatitis and the effects of gassing accidents.

Dermatitis

'Dermatitis' fundamentally implies inflammation of the skin and is the most common occupational disease.

'Non-infective dermatitis' is classified as a prescribed disease in relation to exposure to dust, liquid, vapour or other skin irritant. 'Occupational dermatitis' involving specified agents, such as metalworking fluids and organic solvents, is further reportable under RIDDOR.

In any consideration of the causes of occupational dermatitis, it is essential to distinguish between:

- **primary irritants**, such as solvents and strong acids, which cause dermatitis at the site of contact if permitted to act for sufficient length of time in a sufficient concentration; and
- **secondary cutaneous sensitizers**, such as rubber, nickel, certain plants and many chemical compounds, which do not necessarily cause skin changes initially, but result in a specific skin sensitization. If further contact occurs after seven days or more, dermatitis will develop at the site of the second contact.

Occupational cancers

The term 'cancer' implies some form of new growth in the body, namely a tumour (or neoplasm). This consists of a mass of cells which have undergone some form of irreversible change in their structure and physiology which leads to a continuous proliferation of these cells. The rate of growth of tumours varies significantly. Tumours may be benign or malignant. Certain carcinogens or cancer-producing agents have a latent period of between 10 and 40 years. This is the time between the first exposure to an offending agent and the actual discovery and diagnosis of a tumour.

Biological agents

Certain diseases (the zoonoses) are transmissible from animals to humans. This group includes diseases such as leptospirosis (Weil's disease), aspergillosis (farmer's lung), anthrax, brucellosis, Q fever and glanders. Other diseases may be associated with work with body fluids, such as blood, as with viral hepatitis.

Work-related (ergonomic) conditions

Certain movements of a repetitive type can result in cramps, such as writer's cramp. Repeated friction and pressure on a hand or joint, such as the elbow, are causative factors in the range of 'beat' disorders, such as beat hand and beat elbow (tennis elbow). More recently, attention has been paid to that group of disorders known as 'work-related upper limb disorders', which are associated with repetitive strain injury (RSI), a condition caused by frequent forceful, twisting and repetitive movements of the hand or arm.

Users of display screen equipment may be exposed to the risk of RSI in particular.

Work-related upper limb disorders include tenosynovitis, carpal tunnel syndrome, epicondylitis and tendonitis.

OCCUPATIONAL HEALTH PRACTICE

This is a very broad area embracing a range of occupational health practitioners – occupational physicians, occupational health nurses and occupational hygienists – all of whom have varying roles in preventing occupational ill health. It can embrace all or some of the following:

- **Health surveillance.** This is an area of occupational health practice which is concerned with the ongoing or intermittent monitoring of an employee's health. It concentrates on two main groups of employees:

- those at risk of developing further ill health or disability by virtue of their current health state, eg people exposed to noise;
- those actually or potentially at risk by virtue of the type of work they do during their employment, such as people involved in the stripping of asbestos.

The need for health surveillance of specific employees may be one of the outcomes of a risk assessment under, for example, the MHSWR, the COSHH Regulations and the Noise at Work Regulations.

- **Primary and secondary monitoring.** This involves the clinical observation and treatment of sick persons who may seek advice from an occupational physician or occupational health nurse on their condition arising from work. Primary monitoring of these persons will frequently identify new hazards to health which had not previously been taken into account. For instance, a large number of employees may report evidence of skin rashes or dermatitis, which may be associated with the introduction of a new chemical agent in the work process. Immediate action will be required to investigate the cause of dermatitis.

  Secondary monitoring, on the other hand, is concerned with either preventing or controlling exposure to health hazards which have previously been identified. Typical secondary monitoring activities include audiometric testing on a regular basis of those employees exposed to noise in excess of 85 dBA, the first action level under the Noise at Work Regulations 1989.

- **Providing a treatment service.** Many occupational health services provide an ongoing treatment service to employees for a range of injuries and ill health arising from work. This form of service assists in keeping these employees at work and aids their rehabilitation. The recording and analysis of treatments provided provides useful feedback for future accident prevention strategies. A joint approach by occupational health practitioners and safety practitioners can be effective in this case.

- **Placing people in suitable work.** Under the MHSWR, employers need to take account of human capability when allocating tasks. 'Human capability' embraces both physical and mental capability. Pre-employment health screening by an occupational health nurse and, where appropriate, a medical examination may well identify areas of work which may be unsuitable for certain persons in terms of their capability to undertake tasks.

  This area of occupational health practice can include vision screening of future drivers and users of display screen equipment, assessment of general fitness prior to the allocation of manual handling tasks and aptitude testing for certain tasks requiring a high degree of concentration, such as assembly work.

- **Counselling.** Many people have social, emotional and personal problems in addition to health-related conditions. These cause a state of stress, characterized by insomnia, fatigue and the inability to concentrate and to make decisions. In many cases, this stress may be reflected in the quality of their work. Counselling by someone trained in this aspect of occupational health practice, such as an occupational health nurse, can help people come to terms with stressful events in their lives, many of which may not be associated with work.

- **Monitoring for early evidence of non-occupational disease.** Traditionally, certain occupational diseases have been associated with specific industries. For instance, byssinosis is associated with the cotton industry and silicosis with the ceramics industry. The regular health monitoring of employees not exposed to these conditions is a common feature of occupational health practice. In this case, the principal objective is that of controlling diseases and conditions in working populations with a view to their eventual eradication.

- **Supervision of vulnerable groups.** Certain groups of the working population are more vulnerable to health risks than others. Vulnerable groups include pregnant workers, young persons, elderly workers, disabled workers and employees with a past history of extensive sickness absence. Under the risk assessment provisions of the MHSWR, employers have to take into account the risks to the health and safety of pregnant workers and young persons in particular.

  Supervision may entail ongoing health surveillance of these groups, counselling on a wide range of health and personal issues and measures to remove harmful factors in their work operations.

- **Avoiding potential risks.** Here, the principal emphasis is on prevention, through the careful design of jobs to eliminate occupational health risks. This can involve the design of workstations and work area layouts, reducing repetitive tasks as far as possible, eliminating or reducing the fatigue aspects of certain tasks and taking into account ergonomic features of tasks. Consideration must also be given to the potential for stress among those working long hours or undertaking shift work.

FIRST AID

Under the Health and Safety (First Aid) Regulations 1981 all employers are required to make provision for first aid and to ensure that employees are advised of their arrangements for same.

Fundamentally, first aid is a post-accident strategy directed at saving life or subsequent deterioration in health following accidental injury or illness arising from work. One definition of 'first aid' is 'the skilled application of accepted principles of treatment on the occurrence of an accident or in the case of sudden illness, using facilities and materials available at the time'.

Aims of first aid

First aid is administered:

- to sustain life;
- to prevent deterioration in an existing condition;
- to promote recovery.

Principal aspects of first aid treatment

The more important aspects of first aid are:

- restoration of breathing (resuscitation);
- control of bleeding;
- prevention of collapse.

MANUAL HANDLING OPERATIONS

Manual handling injuries are the principal cause of lost time from work and account for over a third of all work-related injuries. Under the Manual Handling Operations Regulations 1992, the term 'manual handling operations' is defined as meaning 'any transporting or supporting of a load (including the lifting, putting down, pushing, pulling, carrying or moving thereof) by hand or by bodily force'. Manual handling, therefore, is not merely involved with the lifting of loads, but includes any movement of a load in a variety of ways. For instance, pushing a trolley along a corridor or lifting a patient out of bed in a hospital would be classed as 'manual handling operations'.

Manual handling injuries

The principal forms of manual handling injury are prolapsed intervertebral discs ('slipped discs'), hernias and ligamental strains. Other more superficial injuries include crush injuries, and bruises, cuts and lacerations to hands, fingers, forearms, ankles and feet, together with damage to shoulder and elbow joints.

NOISE

'Noise' is generally defined as 'unwanted sound'. As such it may cause damage to hearing, the condition known as 'noise-induced hearing loss' or 'occupational deafness'. Noise may also be a nuisance to people, such as that from discotheques, church bells and privately owned stereo equipment which prevents sleep and disturbs people in their enjoyment of normal living.

From a safety viewpoint, noise can distract attention and concentration, mask audible warning signals or interfere with work, becoming a contributory factor in accidents.

Noise sources

Noise in the workplace can arise as a result of:

- noise produced as a result of vibration in machinery and plant;
- noise taking a structure-borne pathway;
- radiation of structural vibration into the air;
- turbulence created by air or gas flow;
- noise taking an airborne pathway;
- noise produced by vibratory hand tools, such as chain saws.

Hearing damage

Overexposure to loud noise can cause hearing damage. Damage takes place in the cochlea, a snail-shaped organ full of liquid. The motion of this liquid is detected by minute hair cells in the organ of Corti and is converted to electrical impulses which are passed to the brain. Hearing damage takes place in the organ of Corti whereby the hair cells cease to respond to stimuli. This damage is irreparable.

The most common condition associated with exposure to noise is noise-induced hearing loss (occupational deafness). Under the Social Security (Industrial Injuries) (Prescribed Diseases) Regulations, this condition is described as 'substantial sensorineural hearing loss amounting to at least 50 dB in each ear, being due in the case of at least one ear to occupational noise, and being the average of pure tone losses measured by audiometry over the 1, 2 and 3 kHz frequencies'.

DISPLAY SCREEN EQUIPMENT

People working with display screen equipment can be exposed to the risk of visual fatigue, postural fatigue and work-related upper limb disorders. To prevent or control exposure to these risks, employers must undertake a workstation risk analysis in respect of identified 'users'. Self-employed 'operators' (as defined) must make a similar assessment. A risk analysis or assessment must take into account the requirements of the schedule to the regulations.

STRESS AT WORK

Recent civil claims involving stress-induced injury have highlighted the need for employers, insurance companies and the legal profession, in particular, to be more aware of the potential for stress among employees and strategies for preventing or reducing same.

What is stress?

'Stress' means different things to different people. A range of terms is mentioned when people discuss stress – pressure, difficulties, anxiety, coping, psychosomatic disorders, overload, conflict, to mention a few.

Stress has been defined in a number of ways since Hans Selye, the forefather of stress research in the 1930s, brought the subject to discussion in his book *The Stress of Life*. Selye defined stress as 'the common response to attack'. He referred to the 'flight or fight syndrome', the situation where an individual may decide either to fight something which may be unwanted or unpleasant in his life or, conversely, to run away from same.

Generally, a stressful circumstance is one with which an individual is unable to cope successfully, or believes he cannot cope successfully, and which results in unwanted physical, mental or emotional responses. It implies some form of demand on the individual, it can be perceived as a threat, it can produce the classic 'flight or fight' response, it may create some form of physiological imbalance and it can certainly affect individual performance.

Fundamentally, a stressor produces stress which leads to some form of stress response. However, no two people's stress response is the same. For many people, the typical stress response is insomnia. Others may suffer gastric disturbances, profuse perspiration, difficulty in breathing or frequent urination when presented with a stressful circumstance such as marital reconciliation, a change in job, change in residence or a change in work responsibilities.

Again, it should be stated that not all stress is bad for people. Everyone needs a certain amount of positive stress to cope with life situations and the demands placed on them. It is the negative stress that creates ill health, characterized by anxiety and depression.

Classification of stressors

Stressors can be classified thus:

- **physical stressors** – such as noise and extremes of temperature, lighting, ventilation and humidity;

- **chemical stressors** – such as gases, vapours, dusts and fumes;
- **biological stressors** – such as bacteria and viruses.

However, stress is most commonly associated with social or psychological stress, some form of body response to an unwanted or undesired event in people's lives or to an event which they feel unable to cope with satisfactorily. This may be of short duration, for instance where someone may be required to undertake a 30-minute presentation at a meeting, or of a more permanent nature, following, say, a death in the family.

Managerial stress

All levels of management suffer stress at some time in their working lives associated with, perhaps, their lack of career development, organizational change, the introduction of new systems and certain factors intrinsic to the job. In many cases, there may be conflicting demands on their time and energy with a family, particularly when children are young. In endeavouring to balance these factors, managers can suffer a range of stress-related symptoms. In some cases, managers may be unable to cope with the stress created and suffer stress-related ill health.

The effects of stress

The effects of stress vary from person to person. The two principal effects are anxiety and depression:

- **Anxiety.** This is defined as a state of tension, coupled with apprehension, worry, guilt, insecurity and a constant need for reassurance. It is accompanied by a range of symptoms such as psychosomatic symptoms including difficulty in breathing, gastric disturbances, profuse perspiration, rapid heartbeat, frequent need to urinate, muscle tension or high blood pressure. Insomnia is a reliable indicator of a state of anxiety.
- **Depression.** Depression has been defined as 'a mood characterized by feelings of dejection and gloom, and other permutations, such as feelings of hopelessness, futility and guilt'.

  Its milder form may be as a result of a crisis in work relationships. Severe forms of depression, however, may demonstrate biochemical disturbances and the extreme form may lead to suicide.

At organizational level, the development and implementation of a policy on stress at work accompanied by a stress management action plan is the first step in reducing the stress on employees associated with work. Such a plan should incorporate the following stages:

- senior management recognition of the need to reduce stress at work;
- recognition of the causes and symptoms of stress at all levels;
- senior management decision on the need to do something about it;
- identification of the groups who may be affected by stress at work, such as those dealing with members of the public;
- examination and evaluation by a trained person through interview or questionnaire to determine the causes of stress;
- analysis of problem areas;
- decisions on the appropriate strategies, such as time management, training, counselling of and support for individuals, revision of management policies;
- implementation of a stress management programme taking the above factors into account.

A HEALTHY LIFESTYLE

Many organizations promote the concept of a healthy lifestyle with their employees, with particular reference to healthy eating, limiting alcohol consumption and the health risks from smoking. There are many benefits not only to employees, but to employers, in such an approach, such as improved fitness of the workforce, reduced sickness absence and an improved working environment. Most organizations have policies on smoking at work and many organizations have specific policies dealing with alcohol abuse and drug abuse.

OCCUPATIONAL HEALTH-RELATED LEGISLATION

While there is a general duty on employers under the HSWA to protect the health of their employees, other legislation deals with the more specific aspects of health protection. The requirements of this legislation are outlined below.

Health and Safety (First Aid) Regulations 1981

In these regulations, 'first aid' is defined as meaning:

- in cases where a person will need help from a medical practitioner or nurse, such treatment necessary to preserve life and minimize the consequences of injury and illness until such help is obtained; and
- treatment of minor injuries which would otherwise receive no treatment or which do not need treatment by a medical practitioner.

There are three general duties under the regulations, namely:

- the duty of the employer to provide first aid arrangements;
- the duty of the employer to inform his employees of these arrangements; and
- the duty of the self-employed person to provide first aid equipment.

These duties are expanded further in the ACOP and guidance notes accompanying the regulations.

Employers must:

- make adequate and appropriate arrangements for first aid in the workplace, based on:
  - (a) the number of employees;
  - (b) the nature of the undertaking;
  - (c) the size of the establishment and distribution of employees; and
  - (d) the location of the establishment and of the employees' places of work;
- provide an adequate number of 'suitable persons' able to provide first aid, who must be adequately trained and hold an appropriate first aid qualification approved by the HSE; in certain cases, for instance where high-risk activities are involved, additional training may be necessary;
- ensure adequate first aid cover at all times when people are at work; and
- where it is not necessary to appoint first-aiders, eg in low-risk undertakings, designate 'appointed persons' who can take charge of situations, arranging to call a doctor and/or ambulance in the event of serious injury or illness.

First aid rooms

The ACOP provides that an employer should generally provide a suitably equipped and staffed first aid room only where 400 or more employees are at work. However, in the case of:

- establishments with special hazards;
- construction sites with more than 250 persons at work; and
- when access to casualty centres, or emergency facilities, is difficult, for example owing to distance or inadequacy of transport facilities,

a first aid room should be provided.

First aid kits

In the case of employees working away from base, such as representatives, specialist advisers, drivers and auditors, an employer must make adequate and appropriate first aid facilities available and ensure these facilities are in order. In the case of employees working alone or in small groups, where the work involves travelling long distances, or where employees may be using potentially dangerous equipment or machinery, travelling first aid kits must be provided and maintained by the employer.

Guidance on first aid

The regulations require certain information to be kept in every first aid box, commonly in the form of a card. This information, 'Basic advice on first aid at work', is also available in the HSE advice leaflet INDG 347.

Manual Handling Operations Regulations 1992

These regulations implemented the European 'Heavy Loads' Directive, and lay down requirements for a wide range of manual handling operations at work, not just merely lifting of loads.

Manual handling risk assessments

Every employer shall, so far as is reasonably practicable, avoid the need for his employees to undertake any manual handling operations at work which involve a risk of their being injured.

Where it is not reasonably practicable to avoid the need for employees to undertake manual handling operations at work which involve a risk of their being injured, he must:

- make a suitable and sufficient assessment of all such manual handling operations to be undertaken by them, having regard to the factors which are specified in the schedule;
- take appropriate steps to reduce the risk of injury to those employees arising out of their undertaking such manual handling operations to the lowest level reasonably practicable; and
- take appropriate steps to provide any of those employees who are undertaking such manual handling operations with general indications and, where it is reasonably practicable to do so, precise information on:
  - the weight of each load; and
  - the heaviest side of any load whose centre of gravity is not positioned centrally.

Any assessment shall be reviewed by the employer who made it if:

- there is reason to suspect it is no longer valid; or
- there has been a significant change in the manual handling operations to which it relates.

If changes to an assessment are required, as a result of any such review, the relevant employer shall make them.

Employees shall, while at work, make full and proper use of any system of work provided for their use by their employer in compliance with the above duties.

Noise at Work Regulations 1989

These regulations impose specific requirements on employers with a view to protecting the hearing of employees, and introduced the concepts of 'daily personal noise exposure' and 'action levels' with respect to such exposure:

- **Daily personal noise exposure** means the level of daily personal noise exposure of an employee ascertained in accordance with Part 1 of the schedule to the regulations, but taking no account of any ear protector used.
- **The first action level** means a daily personal noise exposure of 85 dBA.
- **The peak action level** means a level of peak sound pressure of 200 pascals.
- **The second action level** means a daily personal noise exposure of 90 dBA.

Employers must:

- when any of their employees is likely to be exposed to the first action level or above or to the peak action level or above, ensure that a competent person makes a noise assessment that is adequate for the purposes of:
  (a) identifying which employees are so exposed;
  (b) providing them with information about the noise to which those employees may be exposed that will facilitate compliance with Regulation 7 (reducing exposure to noise), Regulation 8 (ear protection), Regulation 9 (ear protection zones) and Regulation 11 (provision of information to employees).
  The noise assessment shall be reviewed when:
  (a) there is reason to suspect the assessment is no longer valid; or
  (b) there has been a significant change in the work to which the assessment relates,
  and where, as a result of the review, changes in the assessment are required, these changes shall be made;

- ensure that an adequate record of the assessment, and any review of it that is carried out, is kept until a further noise assessment is made;
- reduce the risk of damage to the hearing of their employees due to exposure to noise to the lowest level reasonably practicable;
- when any of their employees is likely to be exposed to the second action level or above or to the peak action level or above, reduce, so far as is reasonably practicable (other than by the provision of ear protectors), the exposure to noise of that employee;
- ensure, so far as is practicable, that when any of their employees is likely to be exposed to the first action level or above in circumstances where the daily personal noise exposure of that employee is likely to be less than 90 dBA, that employee is provided, at his own request, with suitable and sufficient personal ear protectors;
- when any of their employees is likely to be exposed to the second action level or above or to the peak action level or above, ensure, so far as is practicable, that this employee is provided with suitable ear protectors which, when properly worn, can reasonably be expected to keep the risk of damage to the employee's hearing to below that arising from exposure to the second action level or, as the case may be, to the peak action level;
- in respect of any premises under their control, ensure, so far as is reasonably practicable, that:
  (a) each ear protection zone is demarcated and identified by means of a sign that includes text indicating: (i) that it is an ear protection zone; and (ii) the need for their employees to wear personal ear protectors while in any such zone;
  (b) none of their employees enters any such zone unless that employee is wearing personal ear protectors;
  Note: **Ear protection zone** means any part of the premises referred to above where any employee is likely to be exposed to the second action level or above or to the peak action level or above.
- ensure, so far as is practicable, that anything provided by them:
  (a) to or for the benefit of an employee complies with their duties under these regulations (other than ear protectors provided) and is fully and properly used;
  (b) complies with their duties under these regulations and is maintained in an efficient state, in efficient working order and in good repair;
- provide appropriate information, instruction and training for employees on the risk arising from noise exposure and the steps that employees can take to minimize the risk.

Employees shall, so far as is practicable, use personal ear protectors fully and properly when they are provided by their employer and any other protective measures provided by their employer. If employees discover any defect in the protective equipment or other measures, they shall report it to their employer straight away.

Health and Safety (Display Screen Equipment) Regulations 1992

These regulations apply only in the case of defined 'users' and 'operators' of display screen equipment:

- **Operator** means a self-employed person who habitually uses display screen equipment as a significant part of his normal work.
- **User** means an employee who habitually uses display screen equipment as a significant part of his normal work.
- **Workstation** means an assembly comprised of:
    (a) display screen equipment (whether provided with software determining the interface between the equipment and its operator or user, a keyboard and any other input device);
    (b) any optional accessories to the display screen equipment;
    (c) any disk drive, telephone, modem, printer, document holder, work chair, work surface or other item peripheral to the display screen equipment;
    (d) the immediate environment around the display screen equipment.

Under the regulations, employers must:

- perform a suitable and sufficient analysis of those workstations for the purpose of assessing health and safety risks to which those people are exposed in consequence of such use, reducing the risks to the lowest extent reasonably practicable;
- ensure that any workstation which may be used for the purposes of their undertaking meets the requirements laid down in the schedule;
- so plan the activities of users at work in their undertaking that their daily work on display screen equipment is periodically interrupted by such breaks or changes of activity as will reduce their workload at that equipment;
- ensure that each user is provided at his request with an appropriate eye and eyesight test, any such test to be carried out by a competent person; further eye and eyesight tests must be provided at regular intervals and where a user experiences visual difficulties caused by work on display screen equipment;
- ensure that each user is provided with special corrective appliances appropriate for the work being done by the user concerned where:

(a)   normal corrective appliances cannot be used; and

(b)   the result of an eye and eyesight test which the user has been given in accordance with this regulation shows such provision to be necessary;

- ensure users are provided with adequate health and safety training;
- ensure operators and users are provided with adequate health and safety information respecting the use of display screen equipment.

Control of Asbestos at Work Regulations 2002

These comprehensive regulations lay down a strict regime for dealing with the health risks associated with the various forms of asbestos to which employees may be exposed whilst at work. Employers and other 'duty holders' must:

- manage asbestos in non-domestic premises;
- identify any types of asbestos present;
- assess the potential exposure of employees;
- prepare written plans of work before commencing work with asbestos;
- notify the HSE before work with asbestos commences;
- provide information, instruction and training to employees liable to be exposed to asbestos;
- install a range of preventive and protective measures aimed at preventing exposure, including exhaust ventilation systems, which must be adequately maintained and tested regularly;
- maintain the premises in a clean state;
- designate specific asbestos areas and respirator zones;
- monitor the exposure of employees to asbestos;
- maintain health records of exposed employees and provide medical surveillance for such persons;
- provide and maintain adequate and separate facilities for washing, changing clothes, and storage of personal clothing, personal protective clothing and respiratory protective equipment; and
- ensure raw asbestos and waste containing asbestos is safely stored, received and distributed within the workplace.

In order to enable him to manage the risk from asbestos in non-domestic premises, the employer or other duty holder shall ensure that a suitable and sufficient assessment is carried out as to whether asbestos is or is liable to be present in the premises.

Employees shall make full and proper use of any control measure, other thing or facility provided pursuant to these regulations.

KEY POINTS

- People at work can be exposed to a wide range of hazards of a physical, chemical, biological or work-related nature.
- Occupational health is defined as a branch of preventive medicine concerned with the relationship of work to health and the effects of work on the worker.
- Certain diseases and conditions may be 'reportable' and /or 'prescribed'.
- The pneumoconioses are a broad range of diseases associated with the inhalation of dust of various kinds.
- Dermatitis is the most common occupational disease.
- Many carcinogen-induced diseases have a latent period of over 40 years.
- Certain diseases, the zoonoses, are transmissible from animals to humans.
- Work-related upper limb disorders due to repetitive strain injury include tenosynovitis and carpal tunnel syndrome.
- Occupational health practice involves a range of procedures including placing people in suitable work, counselling on health-related issues and supervision of vulnerable groups.
- The principal aims of first aid treatment are restoration of breathing, control of bleeding and prevention of collapse.
- Manual handling injuries are the principal cause of lost time from work.
- Overexposure to noise at work can cause various forms of hearing damage.
- The principal risks associated with display screen equipment are visual fatigue, postural fatigue and repetitive strain injury.
- Stress at work can arise from a wide range of occupational situations.
- Occupational hygiene is concerned with the identification, measurement, evaluation and control of airborne contaminants and physical phenomena, such as noise and radiation, which could otherwise have adverse effects on the health of people at work.
- Occupational health-related legislation is fundamentally concerned with either preventing or controlling the exposure of employees to a range of health risks arising from exposure to, for example, noise, asbestos and the handling of excessive loads.

9

Personal protective equipment

INTRODUCTION

The provision and use of personal protective equipment (PPE) is the classic 'safe person' strategy. Provided it is worn or used correctly all the time that the person is exposed to a hazard, it should give a reasonable level of protection. However, this is not always the case and there are serious limitations in the use of PPE as the sole measure in protecting people.

CLASSIFICATION OF PERSONAL PROTECTIVE EQUIPMENT

The range of PPE available to persons at work is extensive. PPE includes equipment used and worn by persons at work to protect them from both general and specific risks.

PPE can be classified thus:

- **head protection** – safety helmets, various forms of riding helmet, industrial scalp protectors (bump caps), caps and hairnets;
- **eye protection** – safety spectacles, safety goggles, eye shields;
- **face protection** – face shields (visors) which can be held in the hand, attached to a safety helmet or strapped to the head;
- **respiratory protection** – general-purpose dust respirators, positive pressure powered dust respirators, helmet-contained positive pressure respirators, gas

respirators, emergency escape respirators, air-line breathing apparatus, self-contained breathing apparatus;

- **ear protection** – ear defenders, ear muffs, ear plugs, ear valves, acoustic wool;
- **skin protection** – barrier creams and sprays;
- **body protection** – one-piece and two-piece overalls, donkey jackets, rubber and PVC-coated aprons, chain-mail aprons, vapour suits, splash-resistant suits, warehouse coats, body warmers, thermal and weather protection overclothing, oilskin overclothing, high-visibility clothing, personal buoyancy equipment, such as life jackets;
- **hand and arm protection** – general-purpose fibre gloves, PVC-coated fabric gauntlets and gloves, leather gloves and sleeves, wrist protectors, chain-mail hand and arm protectors;
- **leg and foot protection** – safety boots and shoes, wellington boots, clogs, foundry boots, anti-static footwear, together with gaiters and anklets.

PERSONAL PROTECTIVE EQUIPMENT AT WORK REGULATIONS 1992

These regulations:

- amend certain regulations made under the HSWA which deal with personal protective equipment (PPE), so that they fully implement the European directive in circumstances where they apply;
- cover all aspects of the **provision, maintenance and use** of PPE at work in the circumstances; and
- revoke and replace almost all pre-HSWA and some post-HSWA legislation which deals with PPE.

Specific requirements of current regulations dealing with PPE, namely the Control of Lead at Work Regulations 1998, the Ionising Radiations Regulations 1999, the Control of Asbestos at Work Regulations 2002, the COSHH Regulations 2002, the Noise at Work Regulations 1989 and the Construction (Head Protection) Regulations 1989, take precedence over the more general requirements of the Personal Protective Equipment at Work Regulations.

Personal protective equipment (PPE) means all equipment (including clothing affording protection against the weather) which is intended to be worn or held by a person at work and which protects him against one or more risks to his health and safety, and any addition or accessory designed to meet that objective.

Under the regulations, employers must:

- ensure that 'suitable' PPE is provided to their employees who may be exposed to a risk to their health and safety while at work except where and to the extent that such risk has been adequately controlled by other means which are equally or more effective;

  Note: PPE shall not be suitable unless:

  (a) it is appropriate for the risk or risks involved and the conditions at the place where exposure to the risk may occur, and the period for which it is worn;

  (b) it takes account of ergonomic requirements and the state of health of the person or persons who may wear it, and the characteristics of the workstation of each such person;

  (c) it is capable of fitting the wearer correctly, if necessary after adjustments within the range for which it is designed;

  (d) so far as is practicable it is effective to prevent or adequately control the risk or risks involved without increasing overall risk.

- where it is necessary to ensure that PPE is hygienic and otherwise free of risk to health, ensure that PPE provided is provided to a person for use only by him;

- ensure that, where the presence of more than one risk to health or safety makes it necessary for their employee to wear or use simultaneously more than one item of PPE, such equipment is compatible and continues to be effective against the risk or risks in question;

- before choosing any personal protective equipment which they are required to provide, make an assessment to determine whether the PPE they intend to provide is suitable;

- ensure that any PPE provided is maintained in an efficient state, in efficient working order, in good repair and in hygienic condition;

- ensure that appropriate accommodation is provided for PPE provided when it is not being used;

- provide employees with such information, instruction and training as is adequate and appropriate to enable them to know:

  (a) the risk or risks which the PPE will avoid or limit;

  (b) the purpose for which and the manner in which the PPE is to be used; and

  (c) any action to be taken by the employee to ensure that the PPE remains in an efficient state, in efficient working order, in good repair and in hygienic condition,

  and shall ensure that such information is kept available to employees;

- where appropriate, and at suitable intervals, organize demonstrations in the wearing of PPE;

- take all reasonable steps to ensure that it is properly used.

Employees who have been provided with PPE shall:

- make full and proper use of the PPE;
- take all reasonable steps to ensure it is returned to the accommodation provided for it after use; and
- forthwith report to their employer any loss of or obvious defect in that PPE.

Guidance on the regulations

Detailed HSE guidance is provided on the requirements of the regulations.

KEY POINTS

- The provision and use of PPE is the classic 'safe person' strategy.
- There are serious limitations in relying on the use of PPE as the sole means of protecting people at work.
- Under the Personal Protective Equipment at Work Regulations, PPE must be 'suitable'.
- Employers are required to undertake PPE risk assessments prior to selecting PPE.
- Employers must ensure PPE is maintained in an efficient state, in efficient working order, in good repair and in hygienic condition.
- Employees must make full and proper use of any PPE provided.

10

Human factors

INTRODUCTION

Human factors is an area of health and safety concerned with the role of the organization, the jobs that people do and behavioural factors, such as attitude, motivation and perception. It is also covers particular areas of importance such as ergonomics, the potential for human error, the systems for communication within organizations, developing and promoting the right safety culture and the significance of training in ensuring a safe and healthy workforce.

PEOPLE AT WORK

The HSE guidance notes *Human Error and Influencing Behaviour* (HS(G)48) and *Successful Health and Safety Management* (HS(G)65) place considerable emphasis on the need for organizations to consider the way people work, the systems of work they operate and the potential for human error, so frequently a contributory cause of accidents.

Human factors

HS(G)48 defines 'human factors' as covering a range of issues including:

- the perceptual, physical and mental capabilities of people and the interaction of individuals with their job and working environments;
- the influence of equipment and system design on human performance; and
- those organizational characteristics which influence safety-related behaviour.

These are directly affected by:

- the system for communication within the organization; and
- training systems and procedures in operation,

all of which are directed at preventing human error.

THE PERCEPTUAL, PHYSICAL AND MENTAL CAPABILITIES OF PEOPLE

This area of human factors examines how behavioural factors such as attitude, perception and motivation can affect human performance. The physical and mental capabilities of people also need consideration.

Attitude

Attitudes are an important feature of human behaviour. People have attitudes on a wide range of matters which, in some cases, may change as a result of certain situations, such as a road accident. One person may hold the view that 'An accident is an act of God', that is, something over which he has no control. Conversely, another person may hold the attitude that all accidents are preventable provided people behave in a particular way, for instance by following the safety procedures laid down.

'Attitude' can be defined as 'a predetermined set of responses built up as a result of experience of similar situations'. Attitude is associated with a person's self-image, that is, how that person likes to present himself to the outside world as, for instance, tough-minded, generous or considerate. Groups have a significant influence on attitudes.

Motivation

A motivator is something which provides the drive to modify or mould behaviour or to change behaviour. It may take the form of a cash incentive (a reduction in price) to purchase a particular product or the inference that, by acting in a particular manner, it may eventually be to that person's advantage.

Motivating people to behave safely has been achieved through better joint consultation between employers and employees in planning the organization of work, the use of committees to define health and safety objectives, the quality of leadership at all levels, improved communication on safety, and improved attitudes to the subject.

Planned motivation

Planned motivation is a method by which the attitudes, and thereby the performance of people, can be improved. Planned motivation schemes are seen as an industrial catalyst, a tool to maximize performance, and have been used to improve performance in many areas of commercial activity – sales, marketing, maintenance, etc.

Safety incentive schemes are a form of planned motivation, the main objective being that of improving motivation by: 1) identifying targets which can be rewarded if reached; and 2) making the rewards meaningful and desirable to the people concerned.

A scheme linked with safety inspections has been found to produce the best results, providing the results of inspections are made known to all employees and the criteria for inspection are understood by all concerned.

Perception

Perception is the process of taking in information. Visual perception is the principal means of receiving information, whereas the senses of hearing, touch, taste and smell are less significant in the perception process. However, no two people necessarily perceive risk in the same way. Factors such as the skills available to the person, his attitude, degree of training received and ability to process information are all significant. Any safety strategy must be dedicated to increasing people's perception of risk.

The mental and physical capabilities of people

Under the MHSWR an employer must, when entrusting tasks to his employees, take into account their capabilities as regards health and safety. In this case, he must consider both the mental and physical capabilities of employees.

Matching the person to the job will ensure that he is not overloaded and that he makes the most effective contribution to the enterprise. This entails:

- **Physical match.** In addition to assessing physical capacity for a range of tasks, such as manual handling operations, driving a fork-lift truck or laying bricks, this includes the design of the whole workplace to achieve the best performance from employees.

- **Mental match.** This takes into account the person's information and decision-making requirements, his perception of tasks and his confidence in undertaking the tasks.

HUMAN ERROR

Why do people make mistakes? Mismatches between job requirements and a person's mental capabilities commonly provide the potential for human error. In particular, limitations in human capacity to perceive, attend to, remember, process and act on information are all relevant in the context of human error.

The HSE guidance note *Human Error and Influencing Behaviour* outlines a number of factors which can contribute to human error, a significant cause of accidents in the workplace. These include:

- **Inadequate information.** People do not make errors merely because they are careless or inattentive. Often they have understandable (albeit incorrect) reasons for acting in the way they did. One common reason is ignorance of the production processes in which they are involved and the potential consequences of the actions.
- **Lack of understanding.** This often arises as a result of failure to communicate accurately and fully the stages of a process that an item has been through. As a result, people make presumptions that certain actions have been taken when this is not the case.
- **Inadequate design.** Designers of plant, processes or systems of work must always take into account human fallibility and never presume that those who operate or maintain plant or systems have a full and continuous appreciation of their essential features. Indeed, a failure to consider such matters is, itself, an aspect of human error.

  Where it cannot be eliminated, error must be made evident or difficult. Compliance with safety precautions must be made easy. Adequate information on hazards must be provided. Systems should be 'fail safe', that is, they should not produce unsafe modes of operation.
- **Lapses of attention.** In some cases, an individual's intentions and objectives are correct and the proper course of action is selected, but a slip occurs in its performance. This may be due to competing demands for attention, which is limited. Paradoxically, highly skilled performers, because they depend upon the finely tuned allocation of their attention, to avoid having to think carefully about every minor detail, may be more likely to make a slip.

- **Mistaken actions.** This is the classic situation of doing the wrong thing under the impression that it is correct. For example, the individual knows what needs to be done, but selects an inappropriate method to achieve it.
- **Misperceptions.** Misperceptions tend to occur when a person's limited capacity to give attention to competing information under stress produces 'tunnel vision', or when a preconceived diagnosis blocks out sources of inconsistent information. There is a strong tendency to assume that an established pattern holds good so long as most of the indications are to that effect, even if there is an unexpected indication to the contrary.
- **Mistaken priorities.** An organization's objectives, particularly the relative priorities of different goals, may not be clearly conveyed to, or understood by, individuals. A crucial area of potential conflict is between safety and other objectives, such as output or the saving of cost or time. Misperceptions may then be partly intentional as certain events are ignored in the pursuit of competing objectives. When senior management's goals are not clear, individuals at any level in the organization may superimpose their own.
- **Wilfulness.** Wilfully disregarding safety requirements and rules is rarely a primary cause of accidents. Sometimes, however, there is a fine dividing line between mistaken priorities and wilfulness. Managers may need to be alert to the influences that, in combination, persuade employees to take short cuts through the safety rules and procedures because, mistakenly, the perceived benefits, such as increased production, outweigh the risks, and because of the fact that they have got away with it in the past.

Classification of human error

Human error can take a number of forms:

- **Mistakes.** Here an individual may be aware of a particular problem but develops an unsuitable plan for dealing with same. As a result, he follows a particular path, intentionally but erroneously, producing solutions which are incorrect and which could have disastrous outcomes. This commonly applies in the operation and maintenance of work equipment and in activities involving assembly work. The failure to correct individual mistakes at an early stage through the provision of information, instruction, training and supervision can have serious consequences.
- **Violations.** Violation implies the deliberate taking of an action which contravenes a rule or instruction promoted throughout the organization such a formally designated safe system of work. The intentional removal of a guard or safety device to a machine in order to increase output is a classic example. In some cases, employees have been known to carry out acts of sabotage on machinery to make it inoperable.

Violations involve many complex issues with respect to discipline within an organization, morale, an organization's culture, communications and conformity with prescribed standards.

- **Unintentional error.** This form of error may arise when a person fails to perform a task correctly, such as operating a control or reading a display. Such errors are classified as 'slips' or 'lapses', commonly associated with 'careless working' or 'lack of attention to the task'.

- **Skill-based errors.** This type of error frequently occurs among the more highly skilled employees, such as fork-lift truck drivers, electricians, and keyboard and machine operators, and arises during the execution of a well-learnt and practised routine task. It is common for this particular group to adopt the attitude that their inherent skills will automatically protect them from hazards. The resulting overconfidence can lead to machinery-related accidents in particular.

- **Rule-based errors.** Rules and operating instructions may be established for, as an example, the operation of certain classes of machinery in a particular sequence. The majority of people follow the operating instructions. However, some people may see these operating instructions as an imposition and, over a period of time, develop their own 'short cuts' for machine operation. This may result in incorrect operation and the potential for accidents.

- **Knowledge-based errors.** Known as 'errors of general intention', this form of error may arise when a choice decision has to be made between two or three plans of action. While the individual may know the system of operation for a particular task, his 'mental model' of the system may differ from the approved way of undertaking the task, or be incorrect, and result in unsafe actions. This form of error is difficult to predict.

Human error and risk assessment

In carrying out risk assessments of work activities in particular, the potential for human error must be considered. Any safe system of work, operating procedure or processing operation arising from a risk assessment must ensure that supervisors, in particular, are aware of the potential for human error. The training of operators must draw these points to their attention.

THE INFLUENCE OF EQUIPMENT AND SYSTEM DESIGN ON HUMAN PERFORMANCE

The design of work equipment and working systems is an important factor influencing compliance with health and safety practices. The design of the task and the organization of the working environment should be based on techniques such as task analysis and job safety analysis leading to the development of safe systems of work. These techniques provide the information for evaluating the suitability of tools and equipment, procedures, work patterns and the operator's physical and social surroundings.

Major considerations in the design of tasks

In the design of tasks, a number of factors need consideration including:

- identification and comprehensive analysis of the critical tasks expected of individuals and the appraisal of likely errors;
- evaluation of the required operator decision-making and the optimum balance between human and automatic contributions to safety actions;
- application of ergonomic principles to the design of human–machine interfaces, including displays of plant and process information, control devices and panel layouts;
- design and presentation of procedures and operating instructions;
- organization and control of the working environment, including the extent of workspaces, access for maintenance work, and the effects of environmental stressors, such as noise, incorrect temperature, lighting, ventilation and humidity, together with the presence or otherwise of airborne contaminants;
- provision of correct tools and equipment;
- scheduling of work patterns, including shift organization, control of fatigue and stress, and the arrangements for emergency operations and situations; and
- effective communications, both immediate and over periods of time.

ORGANIZATIONAL CHARACTERISTICS WHICH INFLUENCE SAFETY-RELATED BEHAVIOUR

Organizations incorporate a chain of command from the most senior people downwards to employees. Fundamentally, orders pass down the system and information passes back up the system. There are many factors which influence the way people behave at work, particularly with regard to, for example, the operation of safe procedures, the use of personal protective equipment, safe driving on site and the correct use of hazardous substances.

A number of organizational characteristics influence safety-related behaviour, including:

- the promotion of a positive safety climate in which health and safety is seen by both management and employees as being fundamental to the organization's day-to-day operations, that is, the creation of a positive safety culture;
- the need to ensure that policies and systems which are devised for the control of risk from the organization's activities take proper account of human capabilities and fallibilities;
- commitment to the achievement of progressively higher standards which are demonstrated at the top of the organization and cascaded through successive levels of same;
- demonstration by senior management of their active involvement, thereby galvanizing managers throughout the organization into action; and
- leadership where an environment is created which encourages safe behaviour.

COMMUNICATION

Communication is defined as the transfer of information, ideas, feelings, knowledge and emotions between one individual or group of individuals and another. The basic function of communication is to convey meanings.

Communication on health and safety issues

Communication of the right kind has an important part to play in health and safety as a participative process. The following methods of communicating are important:

- **Safety posters.** Safety propaganda is the process of getting a range of messages across to people and may take a number of forms, in particular the use of safety posters. Safety posters are used to reinforce messages to employees on, for example, the use of eye protection, correct manual handling techniques and procedures in the event of an emergency. To maintain impact, they should be changed on a regular basis, perhaps as part of a monthly safety theme.
- **Safety videos.** There are many excellent videos available to reinforce messages and provide information on a range of topics. To have the maximum impact, videos should be used as part of a scheduled training activity and not shown in isolation.
- **Information, instruction and training.** The duties on employers to inform, instruct and train employees runs as a thread through all health and safety legislation.

  The giving of information implies the imparting of factual knowledge by one person to another, for example a supervisor to an employee. Under the MHSWR, any information provided by an employer to an employee must be 'comprehensible and relevant'.

'Instruction', on the other hand, involves actually telling people what they must do and not do. It may incorporate an element of supervision to ensure the instructions are followed correctly.

'Training' is defined by the Department of Work and Pensions as 'the systematic development of attitude, knowledge and skill patterns required by an individual to perform adequately a given task or job'. Training is an ongoing process throughout a person's career.

HEALTH AND SAFETY TRAINING

Section 2 of the HSWA places a duty on employers 'to provide such information, instruction, training and supervision as is necessary to ensure, so far as is reasonably practicable, the health and safety at work of his employees'. This duty is extended in subordinate legislation, such as the COSHH Regulations and, in particular, Regulation 11 (2) of the MHSWR.

Training is defined as 'the systematic development of attitude, knowledge and skill patterns required by the individual to perform adequately a given task or job. It is often integrated with further education.'

The term 'systematic' immediately distinguishes this form of development from the traditional approach consisting most often of the trainee 'sitting by Nellie' and acquiring haphazardly what he could through listening and observation. Systematic training, in effect, makes full utilization of skills available in training all grades of personnel.

Health and safety training, as with other areas of training, should take place in a number of clearly defined stages:

- **Identification of training needs.** A training need is said to exist when the optimum solution to an organization's problem is through some form of training. For training to be effective, it must be integrated to some extent with the selection and placement policies of the organization. Selection procedures must, for instance, ensure that the trainees are capable of learning what is to be taught.

  Training needs should be assessed to cover:
  (a) **induction training** for new recruits;
  (b) **orientation training** of existing employees, for instance on promotion, on change of job, on their exposure to new or increased risks, on appointment as competent persons, on the introduction of new plant, equipment and technology, and prior to the introduction of safe systems of work; and
  (c) **refresher training** directed at maintaining competence.

- **Development of training plan and programme.** Training programmes must be coordinated with the current personnel needs of the organization. The first step in the development of a training programme is that of defining the training objectives. Such objectives or aims may best be designed by job specification in the case of new training, or by detailed task analysis and job safety analysis in respect of existing jobs.
- **Implementation of the training plan and programme.** Decisions must be made as to the extent of both active and passive learning systems to be incorporated in the programme. Examples of active learning systems are group discussion, role play, syndicate exercises, programmed learning and field exercises, eg safety inspections and audits. Active learning methods reinforce what has already been taught on a passive basis.
- **Evaluation of the results.** There are two questions that need to be asked at this stage: 1) Have the training objectives been met? 2) If they have been met, could they have been met more effectively?

A further objective of health and safety training is to bring about long-term changes in attitude on the part of trainees, which must be linked with job performance. Any decision, therefore, as to whether training objectives have been met cannot be taken immediately the trainee returns to work or after only a short period of time. It may be several months or even years before a valid evaluation can be made after continuous assessment of the trainee.

The answer to the second question can only be achieved through feedback from personnel monitoring the performance of trainees, and from the trainees themselves. This feedback can usefully be employed in setting objectives for further training, in the revision of training content and in the analysis of training needs for all groups within the organization.

ERGONOMICS

Ergonomics is defined in a number of ways:

- the scientific study of work;
- human factors engineering;
- the scientific study of the interrelationships between people and their work;
- fitting the task to the individual;
- the study of the relationship between humans, the equipment with which they work and the physical environment in which this 'human–machine system' operates.

Ergonomics is concerned with the design and specification of working environments in which people, by virtue of their physical and mental limitations, receive maximum consideration. The careful design of tasks, equipment and workstations to suit the physical and mental needs of the operator can reduce operator error, accidents and ill health.

The interface between ergonomics and health and safety

The application of ergonomic principles in accident and ill-health prevention takes a number of factors into account:

- the human system, in terms of physical and mental capabilities of people;
- environmental stressors, such as extremes of temperature, lighting, ventilation and humidity, noise and vibration;
- the human–machine interface, namely the passing of information from the machine to the operator through the various display elements associated with the machine;
- task characteristics;
- task demands;
- instructions and written procedures;
- the stress aspects of certain tasks; and
- socio-technical factors, namely factors embracing the relationships between members of groups and their interface with working systems.

THE TOTAL WORKING SYSTEM

The various features of this interface between human characteristics, the working environment, the tasks they undertake and the human–machine interface can be summarized as the total working system, as shown in the box.

Design ergonomics

This area of ergonomic study is involved with the specification and design of a range of features in the human–machine interface, in particular controls and displays. Controls include the various forms of manual controls applied to machinery, vehicles and other forms of work equipment. Displays, on the other hand, provide information to the operator and take the form of digital and analogue displays, clocks, gauges and various forms of visual display.

The total working system

Human characteristics:
Body dimensions
Strength
Physical and mental limitations
Stamina
Learning
Perception
Reaction
Human–machine interface:
Displays
Controls
Communications
Automation

Environmental factors:
Temperature
Humidity
Lighting
Ventilation
Noise
Vibration
Total working system:
Fatigue
Work rate
Posture
Productivity
Accidents
Safety aspects
Occupational ill health

Important aspects of the human–machine interface include:

- **Work area and workstation layout.** The layout of working areas and workstations should allow free movement and safe access and egress together with unhindered visual and oral communication between operators. Congested, badly planned and badly organized layouts result in operator fatigue, operator isolation, stress and an increased potential for human error leading to accidents.
- **Vision.** The operator should be able to set and use controls and read displays with ease. This reduces fatigue and accidents arising from faulty or incorrect perception.
- **Posture.** The more abnormal the working posture, such as bent stances or having continually to reach upwards, the greater the potential for fatigue and long-term injury. Work processes should be designed to permit a comfortable working posture which reduces excessive job movements. The siting of controls and the organization of working systems, such as inspection, assembly or other repetitive tasks, should consider the potential for fatigue.
- **Comfort.** The relative comfort of the operator when undertaking tasks, such as operating machinery or driving a fork-lift truck, is essential for his mental and physical well-being. Attention must be paid to environmental factors, such as temperature, ventilation and lighting, which directly affect comfort.

- **Interface design.** Good design of the human–machine interface is essential in order to prevent human error leading to accidents. A number of factors must be considered with regard to controls and displays.
- **Separation.** Physical controls, such as wheels, handles and braking devices, should be completely separate from visual displays. The safest system is achieved where there is no relationship between controls and displays.
- **Order of use.** Controls and displays should be set in the order in which they are used, such as left to right for starting a process and the reverse order for shutting down.
- **Comfort.** If complete separation cannot be achieved, control and display elements should be mixed to produce a system which can be operated with ease.
- **Priority of use.** The controls most frequently used should be located in prominent positions. In the case of emergency controls, such as emergency stop buttons, these should be sited in a position which is most easily seen and reached by the operator.
- **Function.** It is common with large consoles to processes for the controls to be divided and located according to function. A well-trained operator benefits from this arrangement and the potential for human error is greatly reduced.
- **Fatigue.** Fatigue arising from badly located controls can be a contributory factor in human error. Controls should be sited to suit the convenience of the operator and, in designing the best layout for controls, the hand movements and body position of the operator should be observed with a view to designing out excessive hand and body movements.

ANTHROPOMETRIC STUDIES

Anthropometry is an area of ergonomic study dealing with the measurement of body dimensions, the orderly treatment of resulting data and the application of these data in the design of workplace layouts and equipment. It is concerned with designing, in particular, machinery controls and workstation layouts to fit the physical dimensions and limitations of people.

THE RIGHT SAFETY CULTURE

Developing and promoting the right safety culture within an organization involves changing people's attitudes, commitment at all levels and the promotion of health and safety as an important feature of the management system. Both the HSE and the CBI have provided guidance on this matter.

In his submission to the Piper Alpha Enquiry in1989, the HSE's Director General outlined the main principles involved in the establishment of a safety culture thus:

- the acceptance of responsibility at and from the top, exercised through a clear chain of command, seen to be actual and felt throughout the organization;
- a conviction that high standards are achievable through proper management;
- setting and monitoring of relevant targets/objectives, based upon satisfactory information systems;
- systematic identification and assessment of hazards and the devising and exercise of preventive systems which are subject to audit and review; in such approaches, particular attention is given to the investigation of error;
- immediate rectification of deficiencies; and
- promotion and reward of enthusiasm and good results.

(JR Rimington (1989) *The Onshore Safety Regime, HSE Director General's Submission to the Piper Alpha Inquiry*, December)

The CBI's publication *Developing a Safety Culture* (1991) is based on a study undertaken. Several features can be identified from the study which are essential to a sound safety culture. A company wishing to improve its performance will need to judge its existing practices against them:

- Leadership and commitment from the top which is genuine and visible. This is the most important feature.
- Acceptance that it is a long-term strategy which requires sustained effort and interest.
- A policy statement of high expectations and conveying a sense of optimism about what is possible supported by adequate codes of practice and safety standards.
- Health and safety should be treated as other corporate aims, and properly resourced.
- It must be a line management responsibility.
- 'Ownership' of health and safety must permeate at all levels of the workforce. This requires employee involvement, training and communication.
- Realistic and achievable targets should be set and performance measured against them.
- Incidents should be thoroughly investigated.
- Consistency of behaviour against agreed standards should be achieved by auditing, and good safety behaviour should be a condition of employment.
- Deficiencies revealed by an investigation or audit should be remedied promptly.
- Management must receive adequate and up-to-date information to be able to assess performance.

THE ROLE OF THE SUPERVISOR

Supervisors have an important role in promoting the right safety culture within their area of control. But what are the most important features of an effective supervisor? These can be summarized thus:

- introduction;
- instruction;
- demonstration;
- practice;
- monitoring;
- reporting; and
- correcting and encouraging.

All the above factors should be considered in supervisor training, particularly their responsibilities for ensuring sound levels of health and safety performance in their area of control.

ATYPICAL WORKERS

These are employees who are not in normal daytime employment, together with shift workers, part-time employees and people who work at night.

The effects on health of atypical working

Around 30 per cent of employees in the UK work some form of shift pattern and 25 per cent of employees undertake night shifts. Research indicates that:

- 60–80 per cent of all shift workers experience long-standing sleep problems;
- shift workers are 5 to 15 times more likely to experience mood disorders as a result of poor-quality sleep;
- drug and alcohol abuse are much higher among shift workers;
- 80 per cent of all shift workers complain of chronic fatigue;
- approximately 75 per cent of shift workers feel isolated from family and friends;
- digestive disorders are four to five times more likely to occur in shift workers; and
- from a safety viewpoint, more serious errors and accidents, resulting from human error, occur during shift-work operations.

Atypical work and stress

The psychological factors which affect a person's ability to make the adjustments required by various work schedules are:

- **Age.** Young people adapt more easily to changing shift patterns due to the need for sleep being less than that of an older person.
- **Sleep needs.** Some people need less sleep than others and can adjust to shift work more easily on this basis. Sleep and sleep patterns are, however, a complex psychological phenomenon. Sleep takes place in a series of four stages and, because of daytime disturbances, many shift workers do not experience the 'beneficial delta' or deep-sleep stage, so important in terms of physical restoration.
- **Sex.** Women can experience complex sleep problems in adapting to shift work, particularly in their reproductive cycles.
- **'Day persons' and 'night persons'.** Some people are naturally alert in the morning and have more difficulty in adjusting to shift changes. Other people perform more efficiently at night. Much of this variation is associated with arousal levels which vary from person to person.
- **The type of work.** Generally, people experience less stress when undertaking work which requires physical activity, such as assembly work, than work which is inactive. This is due to the fact that sleep-deprived persons are likely to lose concentration, particularly if undertaking work involving some form of monitoring, such as inspection work.
- **Desynchronization of body rhythms.** Long-term problems arise when people rotate schedules at a rate more quickly than that to which the body can adjust. Body rhythms get out of synchrony with the external environment and internal processes normally synchronized, such as the digestive system, begin to drift apart. This drifting happens because internal processes adjust at different rates. The gradual desynchronization leads to long-standing tiredness, a feeling of being generally 'run down', depression, which is of course a classic manifestation of stress, and lack of energy.

The health and safety implications

In many organizations accident rates are substantially higher for shift-work and night-work operations. Many people would write this fact down to reduced supervision levels, a lack of training of shift workers in safe working practices or to the view that shift workers 'couldn't care less'. Very rarely do senior management endeavour to ascertain the reasons for these high accident rates, however.

Sleep deprivation results in chronic fatigue in 60–80 per cent of shift workers. Fatigue is frequently associated with impaired memory, judgement, reaction time and concentration. It is not uncommon for shift workers to doze off on the job and even be found asleep. 'Falling asleep at the wheel', especially between the hours of 1 am and 4 am, is a common problem with HGV drivers.

A number of strategies are available aimed at minimizing the desynchronization of body rhythms and other health problems associated with shift working. The principal objective is to stabilize body rhythms and to provide consistent time cues to the body.

Firstly, there is a need to recognize that employees need training to appreciate the potentially stressful effects of shift working and to recognize that there is no perfect solution to this problem. However, they do have some control as to how they adjust their lives to the working arrangements and the change in lifestyle that this implies.

Secondly, shift workers need to plan their sleeping, family and social contact schedules in such a way that the stress of this adjustment is minimized. Most health problems arise as a result of changing daily schedules at a rate quicker than that at which the body can adjust. This can result in desynchronization, with reduced efficiency generally due to sleep deprivation.

In particular, employees need to be advised of the effects of shift work and of the need to adjust lifestyle, taking the above points into account particularly with respect to sleep deprivation, diet, the use of alcohol and drugs, and maintaining contact with family and friends.

Managing the stress of shift work

A number of remedies are available to organizations. These include:

- consultation prior to the introduction of shift work;
- recognition by management that shift work can be stressful for certain groups of employees and of the need to assist in their adjustment to this type of work;
- regular health surveillance for shift workers to identify any health deterioration or change at an early stage;
- training of shift workers to recognize the potentially stressful effects and the changes in lifestyle that may be needed to reduce these stressful effects; and
- better communication between management and shift workers aimed at reducing the feeling of isolation frequently encountered among this group of employees.

LONE WORKING

A 'lone worker' or 'solitary worker' is defined an employee who works alone and out of contact with other persons. Typical examples of lone workers are police officers, security guards, housing officers, rent collectors, people working for estate agents who show prospective purchasers around empty houses and, in fact, anyone who meets total strangers away from base as part of their work, such as sales representatives, people involved in 'cold canvassing' and those who provide a range of services and repair work on other people's premises.

Lone working arrangements

The duty on employers to protect lone workers from hazards is well established under the HSWA and the MHSWR. Prior to introducing lone working procedures, the following factors should be considered:

- careful selection of operators who are fit, competent and reliable;
- the need to undertake a suitable and sufficient risk assessment of the particular lone working activity, which must be kept under review, together with regular monitoring of individual performance;
- operators must be provided with sufficient information, instruction and training so that they are quite clear as to all the significant foreseeable risks that may arise and the measures they must take to ensure their own safety and the safety of other persons, including withdrawal from a particular situation where the operator feels threatened for a variety of reasons;
- a formally established safe system of work, which incorporates detailed emergency procedures, must always be operated;
- the need to provide certain lone workers, such as those meeting new clients at locations away from base, with a range of personal protective devices, such as deterrent facial sprays;
- suitable and sufficient communication must be maintained, such as a radio- or telephone-based 'buddy' system, central control or electronic monitoring incorporating non-body movement/panic alarm and radio/satellite location appropriate to the environment in which operators may be working; and
- there must be adequate recognition of the more serious consequences for lone workers of fatigue and stress whilst travelling or undertaking their particular duties.

VULNERABLE GROUPS AT WORK

Employers have specific and extended duties with respect to certain persons at work by virtue of their age, physical and/or mental condition, state of health, lack of experience and skills, immaturity, work methods and work situations, who may be more at risk than the average employee. Included in this group are young persons, elderly persons, new or expectant mothers, disabled persons, people working away from base, temporary employees and those who deal with clients and members of the public.

Risk assessment

Under the MHSWR employers must consider risks specific to some of the above groups when undertaking risk assessment and in the establishment of management systems directed at preventing or controlling exposure to risk.

The following specific aspects must be considered in risk assessments:

- **Young persons:**
  - their physical and psychological capacity;
  - risk of harmful exposure to agents;
  - risk of harmful exposure to radiation;
  - risk of exposure to risk of accidents owing to their insufficient attention to safety or lack of experience or training; and
  - risk to health from extreme cold or heat, noise or vibration.
- **Employees working away from base.** The risks arising from the host employer's undertaking.
- **New or expectant mothers.** Work which could involve risk, by reason of her condition, to the health and safety of a new or expectant mother, or to that of her baby, from any processes or working conditions, or physical, biological or chemical agents.
- **Disabled and elderly employees.** While there is no reference in health and safety law to disabled and elderly employees, the general duty on employers to take into account capabilities as regards health and safety when entrusting tasks to their employees is significant. This may entail assessment of physical or mental capability of these persons.
- **Employees dealing with members of the public.** Any employee whose job entails dealing with or meeting members of the public is exposed to the risk of violence which may be of a physical or mental nature. Means for protecting such employees must be considered in a risk assessment and installed.

Information, instruction, training and supervision

The information, instruction, training and supervision requirements may be greater for members of vulnerable groups compared with those of other employees. This factor should be taken into account in the identification of health and safety training needs and in the assessment of supervision requirements.

Health surveillance

In certain cases, such as with young persons, new or expectant mothers and disabled persons, there may be a need for some form of health surveillance for ensuring that exposure to risks has not caused deterioration in health.

KEY POINTS

- The human factors area of health and safety is primarily concerned with the interface between the organization, the tasks that people undertake and personal factors, such as attitudes and motivation.
- All people are different in terms of skills, knowledge, experience, intelligence, interests, background, education, age and aptitude.
- The perceptual, physical and mental capabilities of people are associated with factors such as mental and physical match to the task, perception, motivation and attitude, together with physical and physiological limitations.
- Human error associated with, for example, mistakes and violations is a significant contributory factor in accidents.
- The design of equipment and work systems should take into account a range of factors such as procedure and operating instructions, analysis of critical tasks and the application of ergonomic principles in the design of the human–machine interface.
- Organizational culture and characteristics have a significant influence on safety-related behaviour.
- Communication, and the barriers to same, must be considered when devising strategies to improve health and safety performance.
- Health and safety training must be provided in a range of situations involving employees.
- The application of ergonomic principles in accident prevention is essential in eliminating the potential for human error.
- Design ergonomics is concerned with the design and specification of controls and displays to eliminate operator fatigue and the potential for human error-based accidents.
- Organizations must strive towards achieving a satisfactory safety culture.
- Supervisors have probably the most important role in promoting the right safety culture in their areas of control.
- Special attention must be paid by employers to atypical workers, lone workers and the more vulnerable groups.

11

Hazardous substances

INTRODUCTION

People at work can be exposed to a wide range of substances, some of which may be hazardous to their health. Other substances may have properties which make them dangerous in other respects. For instance, these substances may be explosive or flammable.

CLASSIFICATION OF HAZARDOUS SUBSTANCES

Hazardous substances are classified according to Schedule 1 of the Chemicals (Hazard Information and Packaging for Supply) (CHIP) Regulations. They make take the form of 'preparations' or 'substances':

- A **preparation** means a mixture or solution of two or more substances.
- A **substance**, on the other hand, means a chemical element or its compounds in the natural state or obtained by any production process, including any additive necessary to preserve the stability of the product and any impurity deriving from the process used, but excluding any solvent which may be separated without affecting the stability of the substance or changing its composition.

Categories of danger

In Schedule 1, hazardous substances are allocated a 'category of danger' based on their physical properties, as shown in Table 11.1.

SAFETY DATA FOR HAZARDOUS SUBSTANCES

Under the CHIP Regulations suppliers of substances and preparations are required to provide safety data incorporating the following headings:

- identification of the substance or preparation;
- composition or information on ingredients;
- hazard identification;
- first aid measures;
- fire-fighting measures;
- accidental release measures;
- handling and storage;
- exposure controls/personal protection;
- physical and chemical properties;
- stability and reactivity;
- toxicological information;
- ecological information;
- disposal considerations;
- transport information;
- regulatory information;
- other information.

The ACOP to the regulations provides further information on this matter.

THE PHYSICAL STATE OF HAZARDOUS SUBSTANCES

The physical state or form of a hazardous substance is significant in its potential for harm.

Substances can take many forms, thus:

- **Solids.** This is probably the least dangerous form of a substance and, in certain cases, heat or some other process may have to be applied before it reaches a dangerous state. Typical examples are waxes and combustible substances. However, certain solids can cause injury in their natural state, such as asbestos, silica, lead and cullet (broken glass).

Table 11.1   *Categories of danger under the CHIP Regulations*

Category of Danger	Property (see Note 1)	Symbol Letter
Physico-chemical properties:		
Explosive	Solid, liquid, pasty or gelatinous substances and preparations which may react exothermically without atmospheric oxygen, thereby quickly evolving gases, and which under defined test conditions detonate, quickly deflagrate or upon heating explode when partially confined.	E
Oxidizing	Substances and preparations which give rise to an exothermic reaction in contact with other substances, particularly flammable substances.	O
Extremely flammable	Liquid substances and preparations having an extremely low flash point and a low boiling point and gaseous substances and preparations which are flammable in contact with air at ambient temperature and pressure.	F+
Highly flammable	The following substances and preparations, namely: (a) substances and preparations which may become hot and finally catch fire in contact with air at ambient temperature without any application of energy; (b) solid substances and preparations which may readily catch fire after brief contact with a source of ignition and which continue to burn or to be consumed after removal of the source of ignition; (c) liquid substances and preparations having a very low flash point; (d) substances and preparations which, in contact with water or damp air, evolve highly flammable gases in dangerous quantities (see Note 2).	F
Flammable	Liquid substances and preparations having a low flash point.	None
Health effects:		
Very toxic	Substances and preparations which in very low quantities can cause death or acute or chronic damage to health when inhaled, swallowed or absorbed via the skin.	T+
Toxic	Substances and preparations which in low quantities can cause death or acute or chronic damage to health when inhaled, swallowed or absorbed via the skin.	T
Harmful	Substances and preparations which may cause death or acute or chronic damage to health when inhaled, swallowed or absorbed via the skin.	Xn
Corrosive	Substances and preparations which may, on contact with living tissues, destroy them.	C
Irritant	Non-corrosive substances and preparations which, through immediate, prolonged or repeated contact with the skin or mucous membrane, may cause inflammation.	Xi
Sensitizing	Substances and preparations which, if they are inhaled or if they	

Table 11.1 *Continued*

Schedule 1 Category of Danger	Property	Symbol Letter
	penetrate the skin, are capable of eliciting a reaction by hypersensitization such that, on further exposure to the substance or preparation, characteristic adverse effects are produced.	
Sensitizing by inhalation		Xn
Sensitizing by skin contact		Xi
Carcinogenic (see Note 3)	Substances and preparations which, if they are inhaled or ingested or if they penetrate the skin, may induce cancer or increase its incidence.	
Category 1		T
Category 2		T
Category 3		Xn
Mutagenic (see Note 3)	Substances and preparations which, if they are inhaled or ingested or if they penetrate the skin, may induce heritable genetic defects or increase their incidence.	
Category 1		T
Category 2		T
Category 3		Xn
Toxic for reproduction (see Note 3)	Substances and preparations which, if they are inhaled or ingested or if they penetrate the skin, may produce or increase the incidence of non-heritable adverse effects in the progeny and/or an impairment of male or female reproductive functions or capacity.	
Category 1		T
Category 2		T
Category 3		Xn
Dangerous for the environment (see Note 4)	Substances which, were they to enter into the environment, would or might present an immediate or delayed danger for one or more components of the environment.	N

Notes:
1. As further described in the approved classification and labelling guide.
2. Preparations packed in aerosol dispensers shall be classified as flammable in accordance with the additional criteria set out in Part II of this schedule.
3. The categories are specified in the approved classification and labelling guide.
4. (a) In certain cases specified in the approved supply list and in the approved classification and labelling guide, substances classified as dangerous for the environment do not require to be labelled with the symbol for this category of danger.
(b) This category of danger does not apply to preparations.

- **Liquids.** Many hazardous substances are dangerous in their liquid form, such as acids, alkalis, solvents, fuels, insecticides and detergents.
- **Gases.** A gas is a formless fluid, commonly produced by a chemical process, which fills the space into which it is liberated. Some gases, such as acetylene, are flammable and others may by highly toxic, such as carbon monoxide.
- **Dusts.** Dusts are solid airborne particles commonly produced in operations such as grinding, cutting, sanding and milling. Those dust particles in the respirable range, namely 0.5 to 7 microns, are particularly dangerous.
- **Smoke.** During combustion, smoke is produced. Smoke is the product of incomplete combustion and includes soot, ash, grit and gritty particles emitted in smoke.
- **Vapours.** A vapour is the gaseous form of a material normally encountered in liquid or solid form at normal temperature and pressure. Some liquids may produce a vapour on heating or release vapour on contact with air, as when a bottle of liquid is opened, as with solvents such as trichloroethylene.
- **Fogs.** A fog is, fundamentally, a vapour but the airborne liquid droplets are much larger in particle size.
- **Mists.** This is a finely dispersed liquid suspended in air, commonly created by processes such as electroplating, spraying, pickling and foaming. Acid mists are particularly dangerous.
- **Fumes.** Fumes are solid, commonly metallic, particles which form an oxide on contact with air. Fumes are created in processes involving the heating of metals, such as welding, smelting and soldering. Lead fumes are particularly dangerous, causing lead poisoning in many cases.

PRINCIPLES OF TOXICOLOGY

Toxicology is defined as the quantitative study of the body's responses to toxic substances. In many cases, toxic substances attack or affect specific target organs and/or target systems.

Target organs and target systems

Certain substances entering the body are deposited in specific organs or body systems. The most common target organ is the liver. Typical examples of substances and the organs or systems involved are shown in Table 11.2.

Table 11.2 *Target organs and systems*

Substance	Target organ/system
Mercury and derivatives	Central nervous system
Asbestos and dusts	Respiratory system and lungs in particular
Lead and other heavy metals	Circulatory system and the blood
Solvents	Liver
Beta-naphthylamine	Bladder

The body's responses to toxic substances

The toxicity of a substance represents the ability of that substance to produce damage once it reaches a susceptible site in or on the body. The body's responses may be:

- **Acute.** This is a rapidly produced effect following a single exposure to an offending substance. A sub-acute effect implies a reduced form of acute effect.
- **Chronic.** 'Chronic' implies the result of prolonged exposure, sometimes over many years, or through repeated exposures of long duration to low concentrations of a substance. In some cases, however, one single prolonged exposure can produce chronic effects.
- **General.** This is an effect on the whole body, such as paralysis, arising from exposure.
- **Local.** Here a body effect is generally confined to the point of contact, such as the skin, liver, eyes, nose and throat.
- **Systemic.** In this case a particular body system, such as the respiratory system or central nervous system, is affected.

Routes of entry

Substances enter the body through a number of routes, the most common route being that of inhalation. These routes of entry or forms of absorption into the body are dealt with below:

- **Inhalation.** This is the principal route of entry of substances into the body, where substances take the form of a dust, gas, mist, fume, fog or vapour. The effect may be acute, as with gassing incidents, or chronic, where employees may be exposed to, for example, lead compounds over many years.
- **Pervasion.** Pervasion implies passing through the skin into the underlying tissue layers without necessarily damaging the skin layer. This percutaneous effect varies

according to race, age, diet, sex and skin colour. Pervasion is commonly associated with non-infective dermatitis, the causes of which can be attributed to:

- **primary irritants**, namely substances, such as acids and alkalis, which cause dermatitis at the site of contact if permitted to act on the skin in sufficient concentration and for sufficient time;
- **secondary cutaneous sensitizers**, which do not necessarily cause skin changes but produce a specific sensitization of the skin. The result is that further contact with the offending agent, even in very small quantities, will produce a skin response. Typical secondary cutaneous sensitizers are certain wood dusts, nickel and some rubber additives. Where a person has become sensitized the only way to prevent further exposure is through segregation of that person from the substance.

- **Ingestion.** Substances may enter the gastro-intestinal system through food contaminated with a wide range of chemical compounds. The need for high levels of personal hygiene, particularly before consuming food, is vital wherever employees are exposed to a range of substances.
- **Injection, implantation and inoculation.** Again, substances may enter the body through the skin, perhaps as a result of injury.

Threshold limits

A standard concept in the prevention and control of occupational diseases is that of 'threshold limits' of dose or exposure, that is, a dose which most people can tolerate without short-term or long-term damage to their health. On this basis, for many commonly used chemicals, it is possible to establish a link or connection between the actual dose received and the body's response, such as coughing, lacrymation and tightness of the chest and throat. This characteristic is known as a 'dose–response relationship'.

Much will depend upon the state of the offending agent as to the nature of the body's response. For example, with the majority of dusts, there is a directly proportional response to the dose received over a period of time, that is, the greater the dose, the greater the body response. In the case of other substances, there is a period of nil response by the body as the level of dose increases. However, at a certain 'threshold' of dose, the body will respond with some form of response, such as coughing. This is known as the 'threshold limit' and forms the basis for threshold limit values (TLVs).

OCCUPATIONAL EXPOSURE LIMITS

HSE guidance note EH40, *Occupational Exposure Limits*, gives details of occupational exposure limits (OELs) which should be used for the purposes of determining the adequacy of control of exposure by inhalation to substances hazardous to health. These limits form part of the duties under the COSHH Regulations.

OELs are listed in guidance note EH40 as either maximum exposure limits (MELs) or occupational exposure standards (OESs):

- **Maximum exposure limits.** An MEL is the maximum concentration of an airborne substance, averaged over a reference period, to which employees may be exposed by inhalation under any circumstances, and is specified, together with the appropriate reference period, in Schedule 1 of the COSHH Regulations.
- **Occupational exposure standards.** An OES is the concentration of an airborne substance, averaged over a reference period, at which, according to current knowledge, there is no evidence that it is likely to be injurious to employees if they are exposed by inhalation, day after day, to that concentration and which is specified in a list approved by the HSC.

   OESs are approved by the HSC following consideration of available scientific data by the Working Group on the Assessment of Toxic Chemicals (WATCH).

Reference periods for OELs

In the case of the majority of substances listed in guidance note EH40, two specific reference periods, a long-term exposure limit (LTEL) and short-term exposure limit (STEL), are quoted. The limits may further be stated in either, or both, mg/m^3 and ppm.

- **Long-term exposure limit.** An LTEL is concerned with the total intake over long periods and is therefore appropriate for protecting against the effects of long-term exposure.
- **Short-term exposure limit.** This limit is aimed primarily at avoiding the acute effects, or at least reducing the risk of their occurrence. Specific STELs are listed for those substances for which there is evidence of a risk of acute effects occurring as a result of brief exposures. In cases where no STEL is listed, the HSE recommend that a figure three times the LTEL averaged over a 15-minute reference period be used as a guideline for controlling exposure to short-term excursions.

'Skin' annotation

Certain substances listed in guidance note EH40 carry the 'Skin' annotation (Sk). This implies that the route of entry is through the skin and may be significant when carrying out health risk assessments under the COSHH Regulations.

CONTROL OF SUBSTANCES HAZARDOUS TO HEALTH (COSHH) REGULATIONS 2002

The COSSH Regulations apply to every form of workplace and every type of work activity involving the use of substances which may be hazardous to health to people at work. The regulations are supported by a number of HSC approved codes of practice, including:

- 'Control of substances hazardous to health';
- 'Control of carcinogenic substances'; and
- 'Control of biological agents'.

The following definitions are important:

- **Approved Supply List** has the meaning assigned to it in Regulation 4 of the Chemicals (Hazard Information and Packaging for Supply) (CHIP) Regulations 1994.
- **Biological agent** means any micro-organism, cell, culture or human endoparasite, including any which have been genetically modified, which may cause any infection, allergy, toxicity or otherwise create a hazard to human health.
- **Carcinogen** means:
  - (a) any substance or preparation which if classified in accordance with the classification provided for by Regulation 5 of the CHIP Regulations 1994 would be in the category of danger carcinogenic (category 1) or carcinogenic (category 2) whether or not the substance or preparation would be required to be classified under those regulations; or
  - (b) any substance or preparation: (i) listed in Schedule 1; or (ii) arising from a process specified in Schedule 1 which is a substance hazardous to health.
- **Maximum exposure limit** for a substance hazardous to health means the maximum exposure limit approved by the HSC for that substance in relation to the specified reference period when calculated by a method approved by the HSC.
- **Micro-organism** means a microbiological entity, cellular or non-cellular, which is capable of replication or of transferring genetic material.
- **Occupational exposure standard** for a substance hazardous to health means the standard approved by the HSC for that substance in relation to a reference period when calculated by a method approved by the HSC.
- **Preparation** means a mixture or solution of two or more substances.
- **Respirable dust** means airborne material which is capable of penetrating the gas exchange region of the lung.

- **Substance** means any natural or artificial substance, whether in solid or liquid form or in the form of a gas or vapour (including micro-organisms).
- **Substance hazardous to health** means any substance (including any preparation) which is:
  - (a) a substance which is listed for supply in Part I of the Approved Supply List as dangerous for supply within the meaning of the CHIP Regulations 1994 and for which an indication of danger specified for the substance in Part V of that list is very toxic, toxic, harmful, corrosive or irritant;
  - (b) a substance for which the HSC has approved a maximum exposure limit or an occupational exposure standard;
  - (c) a biological agent;
  - (d) dust of any kind, except dust which is a substance within paragraph (a) or (b) above, when present at a concentration in air equal to or greater than: (i) 10 mg/m^3, as a time-weighted average over an eight-hour period, of total inhalable dust; or (ii) 4 mg/m^3, as a time-weighted average over an eight-hour period, of respirable dust; or
  - (e) a substance, not being a substance mentioned in sub-paragraphs (a) to (d) above, which creates a hazard to the health of any person which is comparable with the hazards created by substances mentioned in those sub-paragraphs.
- **Total inhalable dust** means airborne material which is capable of entering the nose and mouth during breathing and is thereby available for deposition in the respiratory tract.

Under the COSHH Regulations, an employer must:

- not carry on any work which is liable to expose any employees to any substance hazardous to health unless he has made a suitable and sufficient assessment of the risks created by that work to the health of those employees and of the steps that need to be taken to meet the requirements of these regulations;
- ensure that the exposure of his employees to substances hazardous to health is either prevented or, where this is not reasonably practicable, adequately controlled;
- so far as is reasonably practicable, secure the prevention or adequate control of exposure, except in the case of a carcinogen or biological agent, by measures other than the provision of personal protective equipment;
- take specific measures where there may be a risk of exposure to a carcinogen;
- where the above measures do not prevent, or provide adequate control of, exposure, then, in addition to taking those measures, provide those employees with suitable personal protective equipment such as will adequately control their exposure to those substances;

- ensure any personal protective equipment provided complies with any provision in the Personal Protective Equipment (EC Directive) Regulations 1992 which is applicable to that item of personal protective equipment;
- where respiratory protective equipment is provided, ensure it is suitable for the purpose;
- in the event of the failure of a control measure which might result in the escape of carcinogens into the workplace, ensure that specific measures are taken;
- take reasonable steps to ensure all protective measures and controls are properly used or applied as the case may be;
- ensure any control measure to meet the requirements of Regulation 7 is maintained in efficient state, in efficient working order and in good repair and, in the case of personal protective equipment, in a clean condition;
- keep a suitable record of the examinations and tests carried out and of any repairs carried out as a result of those examinations and tests, and ensure that record or a suitable summary thereof shall be kept available for at least five years from the date on which it was made;
- ensure that the exposure of employees to substances hazardous to health is monitored in accordance with a suitable procedure, keep a suitable record of any monitoring carried out and ensure that record or a suitable summary thereof shall be kept available;
- ensure that employees who could be exposed are under suitable health surveillance and, in certain cases, medical surveillance; and
- provide employees with suitable and sufficient information, instruction and training.

Employees must make full and proper use of any control measure and, where relevant, take all reasonable steps to ensure it is returned after use to any accommodation provided for it. Any defect in any control measure must be reported to the employer forthwith.

HEALTH RISK ASSESSMENTS

A typical health risk assessment document is shown in Figure 11.1.

HEALTH RISK ASSESSMENT

CONTROL OF SUBSTANCES HAZARDOUS TO HEALTH REGULATIONS

This Health Risk Assessment should be undertaken taking into account the supplier's safety data information provided in accordance with the Chemicals (Hazard Information and Packaging for Supply) Regulations

Assessment No

Location   Process/activity/use

SUBSTANCE INFORMATION

Name of substance   Chemical composition

Supplier

RISK INFORMATION

Risk classification   Stated occupational exposure limits

TOXIC/CORROSIVE/HARMFUL/IRRITANT   MEL/OES

                                            LTEL   STEL

Routes of entry   Effects

                                            Acute/chronic/local/general/systemic

Exposure situations

Effects of exposure

Estimate of potential exposure   Frequency of use

Quantities used   Duration of use

STORAGE REQUIREMENTS

1. Small-scale storage

2. Large-scale (bulk) storage

AIR MONITORING REQUIREMENTS AND STANDARDS

Figure 11.1   *Health risk assessment under the COSHH Regulations*

FIRST AID REQUIREMENTS

HEALTH SURVEILLANCE REQUIREMENTS

ROUTINE DISPOSAL REQUIREMENTS

Procedure in the event of spillage:

1. Small-scale spillage

2. Large-scale spillage

INFORMATION, INSTRUCTION AND TRAINING REQUIREMENTS AND ARRANGEMENTS

SUPERVISION REQUIREMENTS

GENERAL CONCLUSIONS AS TO RISK   High/medium/low risk

RISK ASSESSMENT SUMMARY
General comments as to extent of health risk

ACTION

1. Immediate action

2. Short-term action (7 days)

3. Medium-term action (3 months)

4. Long-term action (12 months)

Date of reassessment

Assessor   Date

Figure 11.1 *Continued*

KEY POINTS

- Hazardous substances are classified in accordance with Schedule 1 of the CHIP Regulations.
- Suppliers of substances and preparations must provide safety data incorporating specific headings indicated in the CHIP Regulations.
- The physical state of a substance is significant in its potential for harm.
- Routes of entry of substances to the body are principally by inhalation, pervasion and ingestion.
- The term 'substance hazardous to health' is extensively defined in the COSHH Regulations.
- Under the COSHH Regulations employers are required to undertake health risk assessments in respect of substances hazardous to health.

Index